Hello! 365 Father's Day Recipes

(Father's Day Recipes - Volume 1)

Best Father's Day Cookbook Ever For Beginners

Mr. Hooper

Mr. Holiday

Content

CHAPTER 3: FATHERS DAY SIDE DISH RECIPES

CHAPTER 4: FATHERS DAY DINNER RECIPES 115

CHAPTER 5: FATHERS DAY DESSERT RECIPES......................................154

Introduction

***

Cooking Anything You Want Is My Holiday Tradition

Hi all,

Welcome to MrandMsCooking.com – a website created by a community of cooking enthusiasts with the goal of providing books for novice cooks featuring the best recipes, at the most affordable prices, and valuable gifts.

Before we go to the recipes in the book "Hello! 365 Father's Day Recipes", I have an interesting story to share with you.

When I was still a kid, Christmas would mean having takeout usually Chinese, because they were the only ones open during the holidays. Getting takeout was always special. When I was 12 or 13 years old I entered foster care. Parents would usually pay a visit during the holidays, but my mom was not allowed to see me as ordered by the court, so there are no visits for me.

So, holidays for me is a lonely time as a grownup and I am mostly down. However, when I became a private chef about 6 years ago, I worked every Christmas and Thanksgiving cooking food for other people. These experiences of meeting many people is the reason why I fell in love with food. It's really a special feeling to cook anything and see the people get together.

I have never met my father and my mother is a substance abuser. But it was with food that my mother and I got along pretty well. There were times that my mother would arrive home very late and would have baguette and cheese. I was 7 years then and would go to the kitchen and cut some toast, then put cheese on it, and give it to my mother with a cup of her favorite warm tea, those times are great memories for me. That is how my mother and I got connected and I can still recall her face during those precious moments. She is so grateful and full of love for me because of what I have done for her. My mother was usually annoyed with me, maybe because she was sick, and I understood it wasn't necessarily me. Nevertheless, even though she was sick, food was still needed to survive.

As a chef these days especially during the holidays, I prepare food for everybody and make it exactly the way they want. I want to know what they feel like eating today and I will cook it for them. Sounds difficult, but it's nothing more compared to Thanksgiving where you have to prepare 9 million sides. It's just the same, you just need to do some tweaking. For example, this Thanksgiving, I prepared my own pizzas at home. I used 3 different types of dough and different toppings like sauce and Brussels sprouts, everyone got what they wanted. And that is my holiday tradition.

We have never seen such a deep connection like that between food and feelings. There is nothing like that in the whole universe. You might ask a loved one what he or she feels for lunch or dinner. You cannot see the connection, but food and feelings are intertwined. Having an awesome meal with your loved ones, makes you love them more and love that great food as well. I feel more loved after preparing and cooking food for someone. It has that kind of strong connection because we share a special moment of survival, which is me feeding them. It's very fascinating to think about that we want to be with our loved ones and eat great food together. That is the greatest essence of a tradition and food will always be a part of it. My love for food will always be my passion and it's the perfect gift that I give to you.

From my unending love for cooking in Holiday, I'm creating this book and hoping to share my passion with all of you. With my many experiences ofhaving failuresed so many times, I have created this book andit is my hopefully it to helps you through my book. This Holiday Recipes Series covers these subjects:

- Christmas Recipes
- Thanksgiving Recipes
- Easter Recipes
- ...

I really appreciate that you have selected "Hello! 365 Father's Day Recipes" and for reading to the end. I anticipate that this book shall give you the source of strength during the times that you are really exhausted, as well as be your best friend in the comforts of your own home. Please also give me some love by sharing your own exciting cooking time in the comments segment below.

List of Abbreviations

CᵒᵒKing LIST OF ABBREVIATIONS	
tbsp(s).	tablespoon(s)
tsp(s).	teaspoon(s)
c.	cup(s)
oz.	ounce(s)
lb(s).	pound(s)

Chapter 1: Fathers Day Appetizer Recipes

***

1. Almond Cheese Spread

"This recipe brings to you a good way to use up so many remaining types of cheeses."
Serving: 2 servings. | Prep: 10m | Ready in: 10m

Ingredients

- 1/2 cup shredded sharp white cheddar cheese
- 2 tbsps. mayonnaise
- 1/8 tsp. onion powder
- Dash pepper
- Dash Louisiana-style hot sauce
- 1 green onion, chopped
- 1 tbsp. sliced almonds
- Celery ribs or assorted crackers

Direction

- Mix the first 5 ingredients together in a small bowl, then stir in almonds and green onion. Place on a cover and chill for a minimum of 4 hours. Serve together with crackers or celery.

Nutrition Information

- Calories: 185 calories
- Total Carbohydrate: 3 g
- Cholesterol: 35 mg
- Total Fat: 16 g
- Fiber: 1 g
- Protein: 8 g

- Sodium: 297 mg

2. Almond Curry Spread

"This recipe shows that chutney and curry go really well with each other."
Serving: 8-10 servings. | Prep: 10m | Ready in: 10m

Ingredients

- 2 packages (8 oz. each) cream cheese, softened
- 1/2 cup chopped green onions
- 1/3 cup chopped sweet red pepper
- 1 tbsp. curry powder
- 2 tsps. Worcestershire sauce
- 2 tsps. Dijon mustard
- 1 tsp. ground nutmeg
- 1 jar (9 oz.) chutney
- 1/2 cup slivered almonds, toasted
- Assorted fruit, vegetables or crackers

Direction

- Whisk cream cheese in a mixing bowl until smooth. Put in nutmeg, mustard, Worcestershire sauce, curry powder, red pepper, and onions until well combined. Spoon mixture onto a serving platter. Place chutney on top; scatter almonds on top. Serve this dip alongside crackers, vegetables, or fruit.

Nutrition Information

- Calories: 158 calories
- Total Carbohydrate: 13 g
- Cholesterol: 25 mg
- Total Fat: 11 g
- Fiber: 2 g
- Protein: 3 g
- Sodium: 110 mg

3. Apricot-glazed Bacon Spirals

"Great for brunch buffets or as an appetizer."
Serving: 15 servings. | Prep: 10m | Ready in: 25m

Ingredients

- 1 tbsp. butter
- 1/2 cup finely chopped onion
- 3 tbsps. apricot preserves
- 1 tube (8 oz.) refrigerated crescent rolls
- 1 package (2.1 oz.) ready-to-serve fully cooked bacon

Direction

- Preheat the oven to 375°. Heat butter on medium heat in a small skillet. Add onion. Stir and cook until tender for 3-5 minutes. Lower heat to low. Put preserves. Stir and cook until melted.
- Unroll crescent dough to 1 long rectangle. Roll to a 15x9-in. rectangle. Seal perforations and seams. Crosswise, cut to 15 1-in. strips. Put a bacon piece on top of each. Roll up, beginning with a short side, like a jelly-roll style. To seal pinch the seam. Put onto ungreased baking sheet with the cut side down.
- On each spiral, spoon apricot mixture. Bake until golden brown or for 12-15 minutes. Stand for 5 minutes. Serve. Refrigerate leftovers.

Nutrition Information

- Calories: 97 calories
- Total Carbohydrate: 9 g
- Cholesterol: 2 mg
- Total Fat: 5 g
- Fiber: 0 g
- Protein: 3 g
- Sodium: 185 mg

4. Artichoke Spinach Dip In A Bread Bowl

""It's easy to clean up and you can bake the dip with the bread shell. People are surprised that it's so healthy!""
Serving: 4 cups. | Prep: 25m | Ready in: 45m

Ingredients

- 3 jars (7-1/2 oz. each) marinated quartered artichoke hearts, drained and chopped
- 1 cup grated Parmesan cheese
- 3/4 cup mayonnaise
- 3 green onions, sliced
- 1 can (4 oz.) chopped green chilies, drained
- 1 package (10 oz.) frozen chopped spinach, thawed and squeezed dry
- 1 cup shredded Swiss cheese
- 1 round loaf (1 lb.) rye or pumpernickel bread

Direction

- Mix the first 7 ingredients together in a big bowl. Slice a thin part off the top of the bread. Hollow the bottom half, creating a shell that's 1/2 inches. Cut the bread you took out into 1 inch cubes.
- Put the cubes on a baking sheet without grease. Broil it for 2-3 minutes or until golden. Keep it 6 inches away from the heat. Stir it once.
- Put bread shell on the ungreased baking sheet. Place the dip in the bread sheet. Bake it for 20-25 minutes at 350 degrees Fahrenheit without a cover or until completely heated through. Serve with the bread cubes.

Nutrition Information

- Calories: 263 calories
- Total Carbohydrate: 18 g
- Cholesterol: 15 mg
- Total Fat: 19 g
- Fiber: 3 g
- Protein: 7 g
- Sodium: 520 mg

5. Bacon Tomato Spread

"This creamy and rich spread is really a big hit at any gatherings."
Serving: about 1-3/4 cups. | Prep: 15m | Ready in: 15m

Ingredients

- 1 package (8 oz.) cream cheese, softened
- 2 tsps. prepared mustard
- 1/2 tsp. celery seed
- 1 medium tomato, peeled, seeded and finely chopped
- 1/4 cup chopped green pepper
- 8 bacon strips, diced
- Crackers or raw vegetables

Direction

- Beat together celery seed, mustard and cream cheese in a bowl until mixed. Stir in green pepper and tomato, then cover and chill for a minimum of an hour. Cook bacon in a skillet until crispy, then transfer to paper towels to drain. Get rid of drippings, then stir in spread with bacon right before serving. Serve together with crackers.

Nutrition Information

- Calories: 132 calories
- Total Carbohydrate: 1 g
- Cholesterol: 26 mg
- Total Fat: 13 g
- Fiber: 0 g
- Protein: 2 g
- Sodium: 152 mg

6. Balsamic-glazed Fig & Pork Tenderloin

"Ran out of ideas to use figs? Try drying them out and follow this recipe for a wonderful smoky treat!"
Serving: 12 kabobs. | Prep: 35m | Ready in: 45m

Ingredients

- 2 pork tenderloins (about 3/4 lb. each), trimmed and silver skin removed
- 1 tbsp. smoked paprika
- 1 tsp. salt
- 1 tsp. pepper
- 1 tsp. onion powder
- 1/2 tsp. garlic powder
- 1/2 tsp. white pepper
- 1/4 tsp. cayenne pepper
- 1/4 cup balsamic vinegar
- 3 tbsps. honey
- 1 tbsp. Dijon mustard
- 2 tsps. olive oil
- 12 dried figs, halved
- 12 cherry tomatoes
- 1/2 cup crumbled blue cheese
- 4 fresh basil leaves, thinly sliced

Direction

- Cube the pork to 1-inch sizes. Mix all of the next 7 ingredients then rub it on the cubed pork. Cover the coated pork and keep it in the fridge until it's time for grilling. While the pork is marinating, mix the mustard, vinegar, oil and honey to make the glaze. Put the glaze mixture aside.
- Insert the fig halves and marinated cubed pork onto wooden skewers soaked in water. Put the pork-and-fig skewers on an oiled grill rack placed directly over medium-high heat. Grill then cover. Let it grill for 8 to 10 minutes until an inserted thermometer on the meat indicates 145°F; turn the skewers from time to time. Use the prepared glaze mixture to baste the cooked parts of the skewers often halfway through the grilling process.

- Allow the grilled skewers to rest for 5 minutes then insert a tomato onto each of the skewers. Place the skewers on a serving platter and top it off with a little bit of basil and blue cheese.

Nutrition Information

- Calories: 139 calories
- Total Carbohydrate: 13 g
- Cholesterol: 35 mg
- Total Fat: 4 g
- Fiber: 1 g
- Protein: 13 g
- Sodium: 306 mg

7. Barbecued Meatballs

"These meatballs never fail to get compliments."
Serving: 8 | Prep: 15m | Ready in: 1h20m

Ingredients

- 2 lbs. ground beef
- 1 1/2 cups fresh bread crumbs
- 1/4 cup chopped onion
- 1/2 cup milk
- 1 1/2 tsps. salt
- 2 eggs
- 1 (18 oz.) bottle barbecue sauce

Direction

- Start preheating the oven to 375°F (190°C).
- Combine the eggs, salt, milk, onion, bread and beef in large bowl. Form into little 1-in. meatballs. Put meatballs into a baking dish, about 9x13 inches.
- Bake for 25-30 mins at 375°F (190°C). Add barbecue sauce over meatballs. Bake for 35 mins longer.

Nutrition Information

- Calories: 554 calories;
- Total Carbohydrate: 38.7 g
- Cholesterol: 144 mg
- Total Fat: 32.9 g

- Protein: 23.7 g
- Sodium: 1390 mg

8. Bases Loaded Nachos

"These crispy bites are absolutely a big hit to munch with your friends."
Serving: 8 servings. | Prep: 30m | Ready in: 30m

Ingredients

- 1 cup refried beans, warmed
- 3 cups tortilla chips
- 1 cup shredded lettuce
- 1 cup (4 oz.) finely shredded cheddar cheese
- 1 large tomato, chopped
- 1 can (3.8 oz.) sliced ripe olives, drained
- 1/4 cup sour cream

Direction

- Spread about 1 tsp. of refried beans over each tortilla chip, then arrange on a serving platter. Sprinkle olives, tomato, cheese and lettuce over, then put a dollop of sour cream on top.

Nutrition Information

- Calories: 163 calories
- Total Carbohydrate: 14 g
- Cholesterol: 24 mg
- Total Fat: 9 g
- Fiber: 3 g
- Protein: 6 g
- Sodium: 344 mg

9. Brat & Bacon Appetizer Pizza

"Brats and bacon on Pizza with apricot preserves and honey mustard are tasty."
Serving: 24 servings. | Prep: 15m | Ready in: 25m

Ingredients

- 1 tube (11 oz.) refrigerated thin pizza crust

- 4 maple-flavored bacon strips, chopped
- 1/4 cup finely chopped onion
- 3 fully cooked beer bratwurst links, finely chopped
- 1/3 cup apricot preserves
- 2 tsps. honey mustard
- 2 cups shredded white or yellow cheddar cheese

Direction

- Preheat oven to 400 degrees. In a greased 15x10x1-inch baking pan, unroll and press the dough at the bottom and half inch up sides. Bake until edges are lightly browned or for 8 to 10 minutes.
- Meanwhile, over medium heat, cook onion and bacon until bacon is crisp in a big skillet, stirring occasionally. Use a slotted spoon to take it out from the skillet and drain in paper towels. Dispose the drippings.
- To the same pan, add bratwurst. For 2 to 3 minutes, cook and stir until browned.
- Mix mustard and preserves in a small bowl and spread over crust. Put cheese, bacon mixture and bratwurst on top. Bake until the cheese is melted or for 8 to 10 minutes.

Nutrition Information

- Calories: 124 calories
- Total Carbohydrate: 10 g
- Cholesterol: 16 mg
- Total Fat: 7 g
- Fiber: 0 g
- Protein: 5 g
- Sodium: 229 mg

10. Braunschweiger Snowball

"This creamy spread is a natural for holiday entertaining with the addition of green and red peppers on top that is irresistible."
Serving: 1 ball (5 cups). | Prep: 20m | Ready in: 20m

Ingredients

- 1 lb. braunschweiger
- 1 package (8 oz.) cream cheese, softened
- 1/2 cup chili sauce
- 1 tbsp. chopped onion
- 1 tsp. Worcestershire sauce
- 1 tsp. prepared horseradish, optional
- TOPPING:
- 3 oz. cream cheese, softened
- 1/4 cup mayonnaise
- 2 tbsps. finely chopped sweet red pepper and/or green pepper
- Assorted crackers

Direction

- Mix the first 6 ingredients in a big bowl then beat until combined. Put on a big plastic wrap sheet and form into a big ball with the plastic wrap. Turn to a serving plate and chill.
- For topping, beat mayonnaise and cream cheese in a small bowl until smooth. Take plastic wrap off the braunschweiger ball and spread with topping. Sprinkle over with chopped pepper and serve together with crackers.

Nutrition Information

- Calories: 159 calories
- Total Carbohydrate: 3 g
- Cholesterol: 54 mg
- Total Fat: 15 g
- Fiber: 0 g
- Protein: 4 g
- Sodium: 410 mg

11. Breaded Chicken Wings

"The coating for these tender wings is made with onion,
garlic, and basil. They're very tasty."
Serving: 6-8 servings. | Prep: 15m | Ready in: 45m

Ingredients

- 2/3 cup dry bread crumbs
- 1 tsp. onion powder
- 1 tsp. dried basil
- 1/2 tsp. garlic salt
- 1/2 tsp. paprika
- 1 large egg
- 1 tbsp. water
- 10 whole chicken wings

Direction

- Mix paprika, garlic salt, basil, onion powder, and bread crumbs together in a big resealable plastic bag. Stir together water and egg in a small bowl. Slice chicken wings into 3 portions; dispose of the wingtips. In the egg, dip the wings, and then put in the bag and shake to coat. Put in an oil-coated 15x10x1-inch baking pan. Bake at 425° until the juices run clear, about 30-35 minutes, flipping 1 time.

Nutrition Information

- Calories: 170 calories
- Total Carbohydrate: 7 g
- Cholesterol: 62 mg
- Total Fat: 9 g
- Fiber: 0 g
- Protein: 13 g
- Sodium: 234 mg

12. Caramel-toffee Apple Dip

"Everyone loves this dish with a beautiful circle of apples.
Great for autumn events."
Serving: 4-1/4 cups. | Prep: 15m | Ready in: 15m

Ingredients

- 1 carton (12 oz.) whipped cream cheese
- 1-1/4 cups caramel apple dip
- 1 package (8 oz.) milk chocolate English toffee bits
- Apple wedges

Direction

- In a serving dish, slather cream cheese and put a layer of apple dip; scatter toffee bits on top. Serve dish with apple wedges.

Nutrition Information

- Calories: 233 calories
- Total Carbohydrate: 22 g
- Cholesterol: 37 mg
- Total Fat: 15 g
- Fiber: 0 g
- Protein: 2 g
- Sodium: 198 mg

13. Chicken Wings With Spicy Apricot Sauce

"Flavorful sweet-and-sour sauce for a delicious appetizer."
Serving: 6 dozen. | Prep: 15m | Ready in: 25m

Ingredients

- 3 dozen whole chicken wings
- 1-1/2 cups cornstarch
- 1 tbsp. baking powder
- 1-1/2 tsps. salt
- 1/2 tsp. pepper
- 1/2 tsp. sugar
- 3 eggs, beaten
- Oil for deep-fat frying
- SAUCE:

- 1 cup (3 oz.) dried apricots
- 1-1/4 cups water
- 2 tbsps. sugar
- 2 tbsps. cider vinegar
- 2 tbsps. honey
- 1/8 to 1/4 tsp. cayenne pepper

Direction

- Cut chicken wings into 3 parts; remove the wing tip part. In a large resealable plastic bag or shallow bowl, combine sugar, pepper, salt, baking powder, and cornstarch. First, dip the chicken pieces in eggs, then generously coat with the cornstarch mixture.
- Heat oil to 350° in a deep-fat fryer or an electric skillet. Fry the chicken wings, a few at a time, until juices run clear, for about 9 minutes. Drain on paper towels and keep warm.
- In the meantime, combine water and apricots in a large saucepan; bring to a boil. Lower the heat; simmer, covered, until the apricots are softened.
- Transfer to a food processor or blender. Add cayenne, honey, vinegar, and sugar; process until smooth on high. Cool slightly. Enjoy with the chicken wings.

14. Chili-lime Roasted Chickpeas

"Please the crowd with this light snack."
Serving: 2 cups. | Prep: 10m | Ready in: 50m

Ingredients

- 2 cans (15 oz. each) chickpeas, rinsed, drained and patted dry
- 2 tbsps. extra virgin olive oil
- 1 tbsp. chili powder
- 2 tsps. ground cumin
- 1 tsp. grated lime zest
- 1 tbsp. lime juice
- 3/4 tsp. sea salt

Direction

- Set the oven to 400 degrees to preheat. Use foil to line a 15-inch x10-inch x1-inch baking sheet. Spread foil with one single layer of chickpeas, getting rid of any loose skins. Bake for 40 to 45 minutes while stirring after each 15 minutes, until extremely crunchy.
- In the meantime, whisk leftover ingredients together. Take chickpeas out of the oven and allow to cool about 5 minutes. Drizzle oil mixture over top and shake pan to coat. Allow to cool through and transfer to an airtight container for storage.

Nutrition Information

- Calories: 178 calories
- Total Carbohydrate: 23 g
- Cholesterol: 0 mg
- Total Fat: 8 g
- Fiber: 6 g
- Protein: 6 g
- Sodium: 463 mg

15. Corn Salsa

"This salsa is very special and unique as made of fresh ingredients such as fresh herbs, garlic, peppers and tomatoes."
Serving: 4 cups. | Prep: 10m | Ready in: 10m

Ingredients

- 1 can (15-1/4 oz.) whole kernel corn, drained
- 1/2 cup chopped green pepper
- 1/2 cup chopped sweet red pepper
- 1/2 cup chopped red onion
- 1 medium tomato, chopped
- 1/4 cup sliced ripe olives
- 2 tbsps. chopped pickled jalapeno peppers
- 1 tsp. juice from pickled jalapenos
- 2 tbsps. vinegar
- 2 tbsps. cider or red wine vinegar
- 1/2 tsp. garlic salt
- 1/2 tsp. pepper

Direction

- In a big bowl, mix all ingredients together, then cover and refrigerate for a couple of hours.

Nutrition Information

- Calories: 29 calories
- Total Carbohydrate: 5 g
- Cholesterol: 0 mg
- Total Fat: 1 g
- Fiber: 1 g
- Protein: 1 g
- Sodium: 154 mg

16. Crab-egg Cracker Spread

"It goes very greatly with crackers, chips or veggies for a little kick."
Serving: 2-1/2 cups. | Prep: 15m | Ready in: 15m

Ingredients

- 1/3 cup mayonnaise
- 1/3 cup chili sauce
- 1 tbsp. prepared horseradish
- 1 garlic clove, minced
- 1/2 tsp. prepared mustard
- 1/4 to 1/2 tsp. hot pepper sauce
- 1/2 tsp. salt
- 2 cans (6 oz. each) crabmeat, drained, flaked and cartilage removed or 1-1/2 cups flaked fresh or 1-1/2 cups frozen crabmeat
- 2 hard-boiled large eggs, finely chopped
- Assorted crackers

Direction

- Mix the first 7 ingredients together in a big bowl, then stir in eggs and crab. Place on a cover and chill for a minimum of 2 hours, then serve together with crackers.

Nutrition Information

- Calories: 112 calories
- Total Carbohydrate: 3 g

- Cholesterol: 75 mg
- Total Fat: 7 g
- Fiber: 0 g
- Protein: 8 g
- Sodium: 415 mg

17. Cranberry Cheese Spread

"If you are finding any special thing for a buffet, this creamy and sweet-tart spread is a perfect choice."
Serving: 12-14 servings. | Prep: 15m | Ready in: 15m

Ingredients

- 1 package (8 oz.) cream cheese, softened
- 1/2 cup sour cream
- 2 tbsps. honey
- 1/4 tsp. ground cinnamon
- 1 can (14 oz.) whole-berry cranberry sauce
- 1/3 cup slivered almonds, toasted
- Assorted crackers

Direction

- Beat together cinnamon, honey, sour cream and cream cheese in a small bowl until smooth. Spread on a serving plate or dish.
- Stir cranberry sauce in a small bowl until it achieves spreading consistency, then spread over the cream cheese mixture. Sprinkle almonds over top and chill, covered, about 2 to 3 hours. Serve together with crackers.

Nutrition Information

- Calories: 144 calories
- Total Carbohydrate: 16 g
- Cholesterol: 24 mg
- Total Fat: 8 g
- Fiber: 1 g
- Protein: 2 g
- Sodium: 59 mg

18. Cream Cheese/chutney Appetizer

"This is an easy and simple yet tasty appetizer that is always a hit for any gatherings. It will certain not have any leftovers on the serving plate."
Serving: 24 appetizer servings. | Prep: 10m | Ready in: 10m

Ingredients

- 1 package (8 oz.) cream cheese, softened
- 1 jar (8 oz.) chutney or spiced peach jam
- 1/4 cup finely sliced green onions
- Snack crackers of choice

Direction

- Press into a greased mold with softened cream cheese to get wanted shape. (Spray mold with cooking spray and use plastic wrap to line for easy removal, if needed.) Unmold on cold plate. Drizzle chutney over mold then sprinkle with onions. Use crackers to ring the plate (buttery crackers are recommended). Serve promptly.

Nutrition Information

- Calories: 48 calories
- Total Carbohydrate: 4 g
- Cholesterol: 10 mg
- Total Fat: 3 g
- Fiber: 0 g
- Protein: 1 g
- Sodium: 30 mg

19. Creamy Herbed Cheese Spread

"This delicious herb spread is really awesome to serve with fresh vegetables or along with crackers."
Serving: about 1-1/2 cups. | Prep: 10m | Ready in: 10m

Ingredients

- 1-1/2 cups (12 oz.) 4% cottage cheese
- 3 oz. cream cheese, softened
- 1 tbsp. minced chives
- 1 tbsp. minced fresh parsley
- 1-1/2 tsps. minced fresh thyme or 1/2 tsp. dried thyme
- 3/4 tsp. minced fresh basil or 1/4 tsp. dried basil
- 3/4 tsp. minced fresh savory or 1/4 tsp. dried savory
- 1/8 to 1/4 tsp. salt
- Assorted crackers

Direction

- In a blender, add cream cheese and cottage cheese, then cover and process until smooth. Turn cheese mixture into a small bowl, then fold in savory, salt, basil, thyme, parsley and chives. Cover and chill about 2 hours then serve together with crackers.

Nutrition Information

- Calories: 53 calories
- Total Carbohydrate: 1 g
- Cholesterol: 14 mg
- Total Fat: 4 g
- Fiber: 0 g
- Protein: 4 g
- Sodium: 140 mg

20. Creamy Smoked Salmon Spread

"The combination of salmon and herb gives this spread a special taste."
Serving: 1-1/2 cups. | Prep: 10m | Ready in: 10m

Ingredients

- 1/2 lb. smoked salmon fillet
- 1 package (6-1/2 oz.) garlic-herb spreadable cheese
- 1/4 cup minced fresh parsley
- Miniature bagels, split and toasted

Direction

- Flake salmon into small chunks. Mix together salmon, parsley, and spreadable cheese in a small bowl. Put on bagels to serve.

Nutrition Information

- Calories: 98 calories
- Total Carbohydrate: 1 g
- Cholesterol: 26 mg
- Total Fat: 9 g
- Fiber: 0 g
- Protein: 5 g
- Sodium: 262 mg

21. Creamy Thyme Spread

"This is a delicious cracker spread made with garlic and thyme that is simple and special to stir up to serve at a party."
Serving: about 1 cup. | Prep: 10m | Ready in: 10m

Ingredients

- 1 package (8 oz.) cream cheese, softened
- 1 tbsp. minced fresh thyme or 1 tsp. dried thyme
- 1 tbsp. minced fresh parsley or 1 tsp. dried parsley flakes
- 1/2 tsp. minced garlic
- Assorted crackers

Direction

- Mix well together garlic, parsley, thyme and cream cheese in a bowl, then cover and chill until serving. Serve along with crackers.

Nutrition Information

- Calories: 100 calories
- Total Carbohydrate: 1 g
- Cholesterol: 31 mg
- Total Fat: 10 g
- Fiber: 0 g
- Protein: 2 g
- Sodium: 84 mg

22. Cucumber Shrimp Spread

"Serve this savory spread on rye bread, but it tastes better with bagel chips or crackers"
Serving: about 1 cup. | Prep: 10m | Ready in: 10m

Ingredients

- 3 oz. cream cheese, softened
- 2 tbsps. mayonnaise
- 1 tbsp. ketchup
- 1/2 to 3/4 tsp. ground mustard
- 1/8 tsp. garlic powder
- 1 can (4 oz.) tiny shrimp, rinsed and drained
- 1/4 cup chopped seeded peeled cucumber
- 1 tsp. finely chopped onion
- Assorted crackers

Direction

- Beat garlic powder, mustard, ketchup, mayonnaise, and cream cheese in a small bowl until smooth. Mix in the onion, cucumber, and shrimp. Refrigerate with a cover until serving. Enjoy with crackers.

Nutrition Information

- Calories: 44 calories
- Total Carbohydrate: 2 g
- Cholesterol: 38 mg
- Total Fat: 2 g
- Fiber: 0 g
- Protein: 4 g
- Sodium: 265 mg

23. Easy Olive Snacks

""Yummy and chewy appetizers that olive lovers will enjoy.""
Serving: about 4 dozen. | Prep: 10m | Ready in: 15m

Ingredients

- 1 cup shredded part-skim mozzarella cheese

- 1 cup shredded cheddar cheese
- 1 can (4-1/4 oz.) chopped ripe olives, drained
- 1/2 cup mayonnaise
- 1/3 cup chopped green onions
- Triscuit crackers

Direction

- Mix the first five ingredients in a large bowl. Put on crackers and spread. Transfer to a baking sheet that is ungreased. Bake for 7 minutes at 375 degrees. Serve right away.

Nutrition Information

- Calories: 102 calories
- Total Carbohydrate: 1 g
- Cholesterol: 14 mg
- Total Fat: 9 g
- Fiber: 0 g
- Protein: 3 g
- Sodium: 179 mg

24. Easy Roasted Red Pepper Hummus

"A hummus made from tahini. This can be made a day in advance."
Serving: 2

Ingredients

- 2 cloves garlic, minced
- 1 (15 oz.) can garbanzo beans, drained
- 1/3 cup tahini
- 1/3 cup lemon juice
- 1/2 cup roasted red peppers
- 1/4 tsp. dried basil

Direction

- Process the lemon juice, tahini, garbanzo beans and garlic in an electric food processor until the mixture becomes smooth. Stir in basil and roasted peppers then blend until the peppers are chopped finely. Sprinkle pepper and salt to season, then move it into a small bowl, cover,

and let it chill in the fridge until it's time to serve.

Nutrition Information

- Calories: 445 calories;
- Total Carbohydrate: 44.1 g
- Cholesterol: 0 mg
- Total Fat: 26.9 g
- Protein: 15.9 g
- Sodium: 908 mg

25. Festive Baked Brie

"This dish is really a showpiece at a holiday meal with the smooth and rich Brie cheese accented with caramelized onions."
Serving: 6-8 servings. | Prep: 20m | Ready in: 30m

Ingredients

- 1 large onion, halved and thinly sliced
- 2 tbsps. butter
- 2 tbsps. olive oil
- 1/2 cup oil-packed sun-dried tomatoes, drained and chopped
- 1/4 cup minced fresh parsley
- 2 tbsps. minced fresh basil
- Dash pepper
- 1 round (8 oz.) Brie cheese
- Assorted crackers

Direction

- Cook onion with oil and butter in a big skillet on medium heat until turns golden brown while stirring often, about 15 to 20 minutes, then set aside.
- Mix pepper, basil, parsley and tomatoes in a small bowl. Remove the rind from top of the Brie, then put it in an ungreased ovenproof serving dish. Place onion mixture and tomato mixture on top.
- Bake at 400° without a cover, until cheese is softened, about 10 to 12 minutes, then serve warm along with crackers.

Nutrition Information

- Calories: 172 calories
- Total Carbohydrate: 4 g
- Cholesterol: 36 mg
- Total Fat: 15 g
- Fiber: 1 g
- Protein: 7 g
- Sodium: 227 mg

26. Finger-lickin'-good Shrimp

"A wonderful bacon-wrapped shrimp appetizer that is restaurant-quality, you'll feel like you are on a vacation. Anyone will surely love it!"
Serving: 6 servings. | Prep: 30m | Ready in: 40m

Ingredients

- 12 uncooked jumbo shrimp, peeled and deveined
- 1/4 cup Italian salad dressing
- 1/4 cup orange juice
- 6 bacon strips, cut in half
- 1 oz. pepper Jack or cheddar cheese, julienned

Direction

- In each shrimp, cut a small slit at the back. Mix orange juice and salad dressing together in a big Ziplock plastic bag then put in the shrimps. Seal the Ziplock bag and turn to coat the shrimps. Keep in the fridge for 30 minutes.
- While the marinated shrimps are chilling in the fridge, fry the bacons in a big frying pan on medium heat until the bacons are cooked but not crispy. Put the fried bacons on paper towels to drain excess oil.
- Drain the marinated shrimps and throw marinade. Push a piece of cheese into the slit of every shrimp. Wrap each shrimp with fried bacon and secure with toothpicks.
- Use cooking oil to wet a paper towel. Use tongs to lightly rub an oiled paper towel on the grill rack. Put a drip pan in the grill and prepare for indirect heat.

- Put the marinated shrimps on the grill on indirect medium heat then cover, place the shrimps over the drip pan; or broil the shrimps in the oven 4 inches away from the heat for 3 minutes per side or until the shrimp turns pink in color.

Nutrition Information

- Calories: 110 calories
- Total Carbohydrate: 1 g
- Cholesterol: 74 mg
- Total Fat: 6 g
- Fiber: 0 g
- Protein: 12 g
- Sodium: 295 mg

27. French Onion Garlic Bread

"My husband and I came up with this recipe when we were newly married. This bread with a lot of cheese can be served as appetizer for parties too."
Serving: 12 servings. | Prep: 20m | Ready in: 55m

Ingredients

- 1 large sweet onion, thinly sliced
- 1 tbsp. olive oil
- 1/2 cup beef broth
- 4 garlic cloves, minced, divided
- 1/4 tsp. dried thyme
- 1/4 cup butter, softened
- 1 loaf (1 lb.) French bread, sliced
- 2 tbsps. grated Parmesan cheese
- 2 cups shredded Gruyere or Swiss cheese

Direction

- Sauté onion in oil in a big saucepan until tender, or for 8 to 10 minutes. Add thyme, 1 garlic clove and broth, boil them together. Lower the heat, let them simmer uncovered for 12 to 15 minutes.
- In the meantime, mix butter with the rest of garlic in a small bowl, stirring until creamy. Add the mixture on top of bread slices and spread out. Lubricate a 15x10-inch baking pan.

Put bread slices on prepared pan. Set oven at 350° and let bake until they get toasted slightly, or for 5 to 8 minutes.

- Dredge Parmesan cheese over, add Gruyere cheese and onion mixture on top. Place them 3 to 4 inch away from the heat and broil for 1 to 2 minutes or until bubbles.

Nutrition Information

- Calories: 323 calories
- Total Carbohydrate: 24 g
- Cholesterol: 52 mg
- Total Fat: 18 g
- Fiber: 1 g
- Protein: 16 g
- Sodium: 452 mg

28. Fresh Zesty Salsa

"This salsa is different from other varieties as it has the olives added inside together with some heat from the jalapeno peppers."
Serving: 8 cups. | Prep: 10m | Ready in: 10m

Ingredients

- 8 medium tomatoes, chopped
- 3/4 cup sliced green onions
- 1/3 cup finely chopped fresh cilantro
- 1/3 cup chopped onion
- 2 small jalapeno peppers, finely chopped (seeded if desired)
- 1 can (2-1/4 oz.) sliced ripe olives, drained
- 3-1/2 tsps. fresh lime juice
- 1 tbsp. cider vinegar
- 1 tbsp. canola oil
- 1 to 2 tsps. chili powder
- 1 to 2 tsps. ground cumin
- 1 tsp. garlic powder
- 1 tsp. dried oregano
- 1/4 tsp. salt

Direction

- In a big bowl, mix all ingredients then cover and chill overnight. Store for a maximum of 7 days.

Nutrition Information

- Calories: 16 calories
- Total Carbohydrate: 2 g
- Cholesterol: 0 mg
- Total Fat: 1 g
- Fiber: 0 g
- Protein: 0 g
- Sodium: 31 mg

29. Fruity Horseradish Cream Cheese

"Sweet and fruity sauce called Jezebel Sauce that goes well with chicken or pork."
Serving: 1-1/3 cups. | Prep: 10m | Ready in: 10m

Ingredients

- 1 package (8 oz.) fat-free cream cheese
- 1/3 cup apple jelly, warmed
- 1 tbsp. prepared horseradish
- 1-1/2 tsps. ground mustard
- 1/3 cup apricot spreadable fruit
- Assorted crackers

Direction

- On a serving plate, put the cream cheese. Heat the jelly in a small microwavable bowl until warmed. Mix in the mustard and horseradish until combined. Mix in spreadable fruit, then scoop it on top of the cream cheese. Serve it alongside crackers. Put the leftovers in the fridge.

Nutrition Information

- Calories: 73 calories
- Total Carbohydrate: 14 g
- Cholesterol: 2 mg

- Total Fat: 0 g
- Fiber: 0 g
- Protein: 3 g
- Sodium: 128 mg

30. Gail's Homemade Salsa

"This recipe is exactly what you found when forgot to buy a salsa from the stores for your important meal."
Serving: 7 cups. | Prep: 10m | Ready in: 10m

Ingredients

- 1 can (28 oz.) peeled tomatoes with liquid, cut up
- 1 can (28 oz.) crushed tomatoes
- 1 can (4 oz.) chopped green chilies
- 1 medium onion, chopped
- 1 tbsp. cider vinegar
- 2 tsps. salt
- 1/2 tsp. onion powder
- 1/2 tsp. garlic powder
- Tortilla chips

Direction

- Mix the first 8 ingredients in a big bowl, then cover and chill for 8 hours or overnight. Serve with tortilla chips.

Nutrition Information

- Calories: 18 calories
- Total Carbohydrate: 4 g
- Cholesterol: 0 mg
- Total Fat: 0 g
- Fiber: 1 g
- Protein: 1 g
- Sodium: 225 mg

31. German Beer Cheese Spread

"This fragrant beer cheese dip is perfect to serve with brats, pumpernickel, crackers and pretzels."
Serving: 2-1/2 cups. | Prep: 15m | Ready in: 15m

Ingredients

- 1 lb. sharp cheddar cheese, cut into 1/2-inch cubes
- 1 tbsp. Worcestershire sauce
- 1-1/2 tsps. prepared mustard
- 1 small garlic clove, minced
- 1/4 tsp. salt
- 1/8 tsp. pepper
- 2/3 cup German beer or nonalcoholic beer
- Assorted crackers or vegetables

Direction

- In a food processor, add cheese and process for 1 minute until chopped finely. Put in pepper, salt, garlic, mustard and Worcestershire sauce, then pour beer into the mixture slowly while keep on processing for 1 1/2 minutes, until the mixture is spreadable and smooth.
- Turn to gift jars or a serving bowl. Chill with a cover for up to 1 week. Serve together with crackers or vegetables.

Nutrition Information

- Calories: 95 calories
- Total Carbohydrate: 1 g
- Cholesterol: 24 mg
- Total Fat: 8 g
- Fiber: 0 g
- Protein: 6 g
- Sodium: 187 mg

32. Glazed Orange Chicken Wings

"These juicy and tender chicken wings has a base of frozen juice concentrate. My family and friends enjoys eating these wings because they are well-glaze but not too sticky."
Serving: 1-1/2 dozen. | Prep: 10m | Ready in: 40m

Ingredients

- 2 lbs. chicken wingettes and drumettes
- 1 can (6 oz.) frozen orange juice concentrate, thawed
- 2 tbsps. reduced-sodium soy sauce
- 1/2 tsp. salt
- 1/2 tsp. celery seed
- 1/2 tsp. hot pepper sauce
- 1/4 tsp. ground ginger

Direction

- Arrange chicken in an oiled 13x9-inch baking dish. Mix together the remaining ingredients; pour over chicken in the baking dish. Bake without covering for 30 to 40 minutes at 375° until chicken juices run clear, basting with glaze occasionally.

Nutrition Information

- Calories: 70 calories
- Total Carbohydrate: 4 g
- Cholesterol: 18 mg
- Total Fat: 4 g
- Fiber: 0 g
- Protein: 5 g
- Sodium: 152 mg

33. Greek Cheese Balls

"This easy, quick and tasty spread is excellent to serve with pita bread, pita chips or crackers."
Serving: 2 cheese balls (2-1/4 cups each). | Prep: 15m | Ready in: 15m

Ingredients

- 2 packages (8 oz. each) cream cheese, softened
- 2 cups (8 oz.) crumbled feta cheese
- 1 can (4-1/4 oz.) chopped ripe olives
- 1/2 cup finely chopped cucumber
- 1/2 cup chopped roasted sweet red peppers
- 1 tsp. pepper
- 2 cups finely chopped walnuts, toasted
- Assorted crackers

Direction

- Beat cream cheese in a big bowl until fluffy. Fold in pepper, red peppers, cucumber, olives and feta cheese, then make into 2 balls. Roll the balls in walnuts and use plastic wrap to wrap them tightly. Refrigerate until serving, and serve along with crackers.

Nutrition Information

- Calories: 107 calories
- Total Carbohydrate: 2 g
- Cholesterol: 17 mg
- Total Fat: 10 g
- Fiber: 1 g
- Protein: 4 g
- Sodium: 139 mg

34. Grilled Cheese & Tomato Flatbreads

"This dish can either be main dish or an appetizer."
Serving: 2 flatbreads (12 servings each). | Prep: 30m | Ready in: 35m

Ingredients

- 1 package (8 oz.) cream cheese, softened
- 2/3 cup grated Parmesan cheese, divided
- 2 tbsps. minced fresh parsley, divided
- 1 tbsp. minced chives
- 2 garlic cloves, minced
- 1/2 tsp. minced fresh thyme
- 1/4 tsp. salt
- 1/4 tsp. pepper
- 1 tube (13.8 oz.) refrigerated pizza crust
- 2 tbsps. olive oil

- 3 medium tomatoes, thinly sliced

Direction

- Place pepper, salt, thyme, garlic, chives, 1 tbsp. parsley, 1/3 cup Parmesan cheese, and cream cheese in a small bowl. Whisk together until combined.
- Unroll the pizza crust and slice into halves. Roll out each half on a slightly floured surface to form a 12x6-inch rectangle. Brush oil on each side of the rectangle. Grill over medium heat, covered, until bottoms are slightly browned, or for 1-2 minutes. Take out from the grill.
- Spread cheese mixture over grilled sides. Sprinkle the remaining Parmesan cheese over surface then place tomatoes on top. Put on the grill again. Cover and cook until cheese melts and the crust is slightly browned, or for 2-3 minutes. Rotate halfway through cooking to make sure the crust is browned evenly. Sprinkle remaining parsley on the surface.

Nutrition Information

- Calories: 99 calories
- Total Carbohydrate: 9 g
- Cholesterol: 12 mg
- Total Fat: 6 g
- Fiber: 0 g
- Protein: 3 g
- Sodium: 196 mg

35. Grilled Jerk Chicken Wings

"This dish is so amazing for any parties."
Serving: about 2 dozen. | Prep: 10m | Ready in: 30m

Ingredients

- 1/2 cup Caribbean jerk seasoning
- 2-1/2 lbs. chicken wingettes and drumettes
- 2 cups honey barbecue sauce
- 1/3 cup packed brown sugar
- 2 tsps. prepared mustard
- 1 tsp. ground ginger

Direction

- Add the jerk seasoning into a big resealable plastic bag; put in the chicken, several pieces at a time, and shake until coated. In a small-sized bowl, mix ginger, mustard, brown sugar and barbecue sauce together; put aside.
- Dampen a paper towel using cooking oil; with long-handled tongs, gently coat grill rack. Grill the chicken wings, while covered, on medium heat or broil 4 inches away from heat sauce for 12 to 16 minutes, flipping once in a while.
- Brush using the sauce mixture. Grill/broil until the juices run clear, 8 to 10 minutes more, basting and flipping a few times.

36. Guacamole Appetizer Squares

""We always eat this classic appetizer pizza.""
Serving: about 3 dozen. | Prep: 20m | Ready in: 30m

Ingredients

- 2 tubes (8 oz. each) refrigerated crescent rolls
- 1-1/2 tsps. taco seasoning
- 1 package (1 lb.) sliced bacon, diced
- 1 package (8 oz.) cream cheese, softened
- 1-1/2 cups guacamole
- 3 plum tomatoes, chopped
- 1 can (2-1/4 oz.) sliced ripe olives, drained

Direction

- Unroll and pat both of the tubes of the crescent dough into a 15x10x1-in. ungreased baking pan; seal perforations and seam, and building up the edges. Using a fork to prick dough; sprinkle taco seasoning over the dough. Bake at 375 deg until golden brown; about 10-12 minutes. Transfer to a wire rack to cool down completely.
- Add bacon in a big skillet, cook on medium heat until crisp. Place on paper towels with a slotted spoon. Whisk guacamole and cream cheese in a small bowl, until smooth.

- Spread crust with cream cheese mixture. Sprinkle bacon, olives and tomatoes. Store in refrigerator until serving. Slice into squares.

37. Haystack Supper

"This dish is so hearty."
Serving: 2 casseroles (6 servings each). | Prep: 25m |
Ready in: 25m

Ingredients

- 1-3/4 cups crushed saltines (about 40 crackers)
- 2 cups cooked rice
- 3 lbs. ground beef
- 1 large onion, chopped
- 1-1/2 cups tomato juice
- 3/4 cup water
- 3 tbsps. taco seasoning
- Seasoned salt, salt and pepper to taste
- 1/2 cup butter, cubed
- 1/2 cup all-purpose flour
- 4 cups milk
- 1 lb. process cheese (Velveeta), cubed
- 4 cups shredded lettuce
- 3 cups shredded sharp cheddar cheese
- 3 medium tomatoes, diced
- 1 jar (10 oz.) pimiento-stuffed olives
- 1 package (14-1/2 oz.) tortilla chips

Direction

- Portion the crackers between 2 unoiled baking dishes, about 13x9 inches. Add rice over top of each.
- Cook onion and beef in large skillet until the meat is no longer pink, then drain. Put in seasonings, water and tomato juice; simmer about 15 to 20 mins. Add over rice.
- Melt butter in large saucepan. Stir in the flour until they become smooth. Put in milk gradually. Boil. Cook while stirring until thickened, about 2 mins.
- Lower the heat; mix in the Velveeta cheese until it is melted. Add over the beef mixture. Place the lettuce, the cheddar cheese, the

tomatoes, and the olives on top. Enjoy with the chips. Place any leftovers in refrigerator.

Nutrition Information

- Calories: 888 calories
- Total Carbohydrate: 57 g
- Cholesterol: 164 mg
- Total Fat: 55 g
- Fiber: 3 g
- Protein: 41 g
- Sodium: 1746 mg

38. Hot Cauliflower Crab Spread

"This spread is great to feature vegetables."
Serving: 4 cups. | Prep: 5m | Ready in: 30m

Ingredients

- 1 package (16 oz.) frozen cauliflowerets, thawed
- 1 can (6 oz.) crabmeat, drained, flaked and cartilage removed or 1 cup chopped imitation crabmeat
- 1 cup mayonnaise
- 1 cup grated Parmesan cheese
- 1/2 tsp. garlic salt
- 1/2 tsp. lemon-pepper seasoning
- 1 to 2 tbsps. chopped pimientos
- Assorted crackers

Direction

- Mix together lemon-pepper, garlic salt, Parmesan cheese, mayonnaise, crab and cauliflower in a bowl, then remove to a grease-free 9-inch pie plate. Sprinkle pimientos over top.
- Bake at 350 degrees without a cover until bubbles appear and edges turn golden brown, about 25 to 30 minutes. Serve together with crackers.

Nutrition Information

- Calories: 70 calories

- Total Carbohydrate: 1 g
- Cholesterol: 9 mg
- Total Fat: 6 g
- Fiber: 0 g
- Protein: 2 g
- Sodium: 141 mg

39. Hot Wings

"These hot wings are addicting."
Serving: 15 | Prep: 5m | Ready in: 30m

Ingredients

- 4 lbs. chicken wings
- 1 tsp. garlic powder
- 1/2 tsp. ground black pepper
- 1 cup tomato-based hot pepper sauce
- 2 tbsps. vinegar-based hot pepper sauce
- 1 tsp. garlic powder
- 1/4 cup grated Parmesan cheese
- 3 tbsps. butter, melted

Direction

- Set an indoor or outdoor grill to high heat to preheat. Grease the grill lightly.
- Season the wings with ground black pepper and garlic powder. On the preheated grill, cook until they are very crispy. Flip the wings often as they're easily burned.
- While grilling the wings, combine melted butter, Parmesan cheese, both hot sauces with garlic powder in a large bowl.
- When the cooking the wings is done, in the large bowl of the hot sauce mixture, put them in and stir until they are covered.

Nutrition Information

- Calories: 317 calories;
- Total Carbohydrate: 4.9 g
- Cholesterol: 101 mg
- Total Fat: 22.2 g
- Protein: 23.4 g
- Sodium: 386 mg

40. Jalapeno Hummus

"An appetizing, spicy hummus."
Serving: 8 | Prep: 10m | Ready in: 10m

Ingredients

- 1 cup garbanzo beans
- 1/3 cup canned jalapeno pepper slices, juice reserved
- 3 tbsps. tahini
- 3 cloves garlic, minced
- 2 tbsps. lemon juice
- 1/2 tsp. ground cumin
- 1/2 tsp. curry powder
- crushed red pepper to taste

Direction

- Mix the lemon juice, garlic, tahini, jalapeno peppers and reserved juice and garbanzo beans in a food processor or blender. Put crushed red pepper, curry powder and cumin to season, then process until it becomes smooth.

Nutrition Information

- Calories: 75 calories;
- Total Carbohydrate: 9.1 g
- Cholesterol: 0 mg
- Total Fat: 3.5 g
- Protein: 2.6 g
- Sodium: 191 mg

41. Layered Ground Beef Taco Dip

"This delightful appetizer is very easy and fast to make."
Serving: 2-3 servings. | Prep: 20m | Ready in: 30m

Ingredients

- 1/4 lb. lean ground beef (90% lean)
- 1 tbsp. chopped onion
- 1/8 tsp. salt

- Dash pepper
- 3/4 cup refried beans
- 2 tbsps. chopped green chilies
- 1/4 cup taco sauce
- 1 cup shredded cheddar cheese
- 2 tbsps. sour cream
- Tortilla chips, optional

Direction

- Cook onion and beef together in a small nonstick skillet on moderate heat until beef is not pink anymore, then drain. Sprinkle pepper and salt over top, then put aside.
- Spread on the bottom of a 9-inch pie plate greased with cooking spray with refried beans. Put chilies and meat mixture on top, then drizzle taco sauce over. Sprinkle with cheese.
- Bake at 400 degrees without covering until heated through and cheese has melted, about 10 to 15 minutes. Use sour cream to decorate, then serve together with tortilla chips, if wanted.

Nutrition Information

- Calories: 282 calories
- Total Carbohydrate: 14 g
- Cholesterol: 70 mg
- Total Fat: 16 g
- Fiber: 4 g
- Protein: 19 g
- Sodium: 690 mg

42. Like 'em Hot Wings

"Well-seasoned spicy chicken wings are a simple and delightful snack."
Serving: about 2 dozen. | Prep: 10m | Ready in: 40m

Ingredients

- 2-1/2 lbs. chicken wings
- 1 bottle (2 oz.) hot pepper sauce (about 1/4 cup)
- 1 to 2 garlic cloves, minced

- 1-1/2 tsps. dried rosemary, crushed
- 1 tsp. dried thyme
- 1/4 tsp. salt
- 1/4 tsp. pepper
- Celery sticks, carrot sticks and blue cheese salad dressing, optional

Direction

- Divide the chicken wings into 3 sections; discard the wingtips. Blend the seasonings, garlic, and hot pepper sauce in a large resealable plastic bag. Put in wings; toss to cover evenly. Place into a well-greased 13x9-inch baking dish.
- Remove the cover, bake at 425 degrees until the chicken juices run clear, or for 30-40 minutes and turn every 10 minutes. If desired, serve together with blue cheese dressing, carrots, and celery.

Nutrition Information

- Calories: 43 calories
- Total Carbohydrate: 0 g
- Cholesterol: 12 mg
- Total Fat: 3 g
- Fiber: 0 g
- Protein: 4 g
- Sodium: 51 mg

43. Make-ahead Triple Cheese Spread

"This simple yet delicious cheese spread is really appealing to every palate."
Serving: 3 cups. | Prep: 10m | Ready in: 10m

Ingredients

- 2 packages (8 oz. each) cream cheese, softened
- 1/2 cup mayonnaise
- 2 tbsps. whole milk
- 1/2 tsp. salt
- 1/4 tsp. pepper
- 1/8 tsp. hot pepper sauce

- 2 cups shredded cheddar cheese
- 1/4 cup grated Parmesan cheese
- 1/4 cup minced fresh parsley
- Assorted crackers

Direction

- Beat hot pepper sauce, pepper, salt, milk, mayonnaise and cream cheese in a bowl until smooth. Fold in parsley and cheese, then cover and chill for a minimum of an hour before serving. Serve along with crackers.

Nutrition Information

- Calories: 105 calories
- Total Carbohydrate: 1 g
- Cholesterol: 23 mg
- Total Fat: 10 g
- Fiber: 0 g
- Protein: 3 g
- Sodium: 175 mg

44. Makeover Spinach Artichoke Spread

"A makeover version of the Spinach Artichoke Spread that omits almost half of the calories."
Serving: 5 cups. | Prep: 10m | Ready in: 30m

Ingredients

- 1 package (16 oz.) soft tofu, drained
- 2 cups grated Parmesan cheese
- 1 cup reduced-fat mayonnaise
- 1 can (14 oz.) water-packed artichoke hearts, rinsed, drained and chopped
- 2 packages (10 oz. each) frozen chopped spinach, thawed and squeezed dry
- 3 garlic cloves, minced

Direction

- Mix all the ingredients in a big bowl, then scoop it into an ungreased 9-inch deep-dish pie plate. Let it bake for 20 to 25 minutes at 350

degrees without a cover until heated through, then serve it warm.

Nutrition Information

- Calories: 109 calories
- Total Carbohydrate: 4 g
- Cholesterol: 11 mg
- Total Fat: 8 g
- Fiber: 1 g
- Protein: 7 g
- Sodium: 317 mg

45. Microwave Salsa

"This is a Mexican-inspired salsa with unique and tasty flavor but so easy to make."
Serving: 4 cups. | Prep: 10m | Ready in: 10m

Ingredients

- 3 medium tomatoes, chopped
- 1 green onion, sliced
- 1 to 2 garlic cloves, minced
- 3 tbsps. finely chopped green pepper
- 1 tbsp. lemon juice
- 1-1/2 tsps. minced fresh basil or 1/2 tsp. dried basil
- 1/2 tsp. chili powder
- 1/2 tsp. salt
- 1/8 tsp. pepper
- Tortilla chips

Direction

- Mix together garlic, onion and tomatoes in a microwavable bowl, then put in seasonings, lemon juice and green pepper and combine well. Microwave on high setting until heated through, about 30 to 45 seconds. Serve promptly with tortilla chips. You can keep the salsa for maximum of 3 days in the fridge.

Nutrition Information

- Calories: 7 calories
- Total Carbohydrate: 2 g

- Cholesterol: 0 mg
- Total Fat: 0 g
- Fiber: 0 g
- Protein: 0 g
- Sodium: 77 mg

46. Molded Shrimp Spread

"It will absolutely disappear in a blink of an eye."
Serving: 4-1/4 cups. | Prep: 15m | Ready in: 15m

Ingredients

- 1 can (10-3/4 oz.) condensed cream of mushroom soup, undiluted
- 1 package (8 oz.) cream cheese, cubed
- 1 envelope unflavored gelatin
- 3 tbsps. cold water
- 1 cup finely chopped celery
- 1 cup mayonnaise
- 3 tbsps. lemon juice
- 4 green onions, finely chopped
- 1/2 lb. cooked shrimp, peeled, deveined and coarsely chopped
- Lettuce leaves and additional shrimp, optional
- Assorted crackers

Direction

- Heat cream cheese and soup in a saucepan on moderate heat until cheese has melted while stirring often. Take away from the heat and put aside to cool.
- Sprinkle over water in a small microwavable bowl with gelatin, then allow to stand about a minute. Microwave on high about 40 seconds, stirring. Allow to stand until gelatin is dissolved totally, about 2 minutes. Stir into soup mixture with onions, lemon juice, mayonnaise, celery and gelatin mixture. Fold in shrimp.
- Transfer into a 5-cup ring mold greased with cooking spray, then place on a cover and chill until set, about 8 hours.

- Invert on a serving plate and fill shrimp and lettuce into center if wanted. Serve together with crackers.

Nutrition Information

- Calories: 87 calories
- Total Carbohydrate: 1 g
- Cholesterol: 20 mg
- Total Fat: 8 g
- Fiber: 0 g
- Protein: 2 g
- Sodium: 132 mg

47. Mushroom Bacon Bites

"This appetizer recipe is perfect for a big cookout."
Serving: 2 dozen. | Prep: 10m | Ready in: 20m

Ingredients

- 24 medium fresh mushrooms
- 12 bacon strips, halved
- 1 cup barbecue sauce

Direction

- Wrap 1 piece of bacon around each mushroom; use a toothpick to secure. Thread bacon-wrapped mushrooms onto soaked wooden or metal skewers. Brush evenly with barbecue sauce.
- Grill without covering for 10 to 15 minutes over indirect medium heat, turning and basting occasionally, or until mushrooms are tender and bacon is crispy.

Nutrition Information

- Calories: 226 calories
- Total Carbohydrate: 6 g
- Cholesterol: 23 mg
- Total Fat: 20 g
- Fiber: 1 g
- Protein: 5 g
- Sodium: 505 mg

48. Olive Sandwich Spread

"This cheese spread recipe is absolutely unique as well as tasty."
Serving: 12 servings. | Prep: 5m | Ready in: 5m

Ingredients

- 6 oz. cream cheese, softened
- 1/2 cup mayonnaise
- 1/2 cup chopped green olives
- 1/2 cup chopped pecans
- 1 tbsp. olive juice

Direction

- Mix all ingredients together in a small bowl, then spread on bread or crackers.

Nutrition Information

- Calories: 138 calories
- Total Carbohydrate: 2 g
- Cholesterol: 11 mg
- Total Fat: 14 g
- Fiber: 1 g
- Protein: 1 g
- Sodium: 205 mg

49. Onion-topped Cheese Spread

"This is a robust spread with the blend of caramelized onions and creamy base."
Serving: 8 servings. | Prep: 25m | Ready in: 01h15m

Ingredients

- 2-1/2 lbs. large sweet onions, coarsely chopped
- 1-1/2 tsps. sugar
- 1/2 tsp. salt
- 2 bay leaves
- 2 tbsps. olive oil
- 2 tbsps. butter
- 2 tbsps. white wine or chicken broth

- 2 packages (8 oz. each) cream cheese, softened
- Assorted crackers

Direction

- Cook bay leaves, salt, sugar and onions with butter and oil in a big skillet on medium heat until onions turn golden brown, while stirring often, for 45 to 50 minutes.
- Put in wine and stir to loosen browned bits from the pan. Cook until wine reduced halfway. Get rid of the bay leaves and allow to cool a little bit. Drizzle over cream cheese and serve together with crackers.

Nutrition Information

- Calories: 316 calories
- Total Carbohydrate: 16 g
- Cholesterol: 70 mg
- Total Fat: 26 g
- Fiber: 2 g
- Protein: 6 g
- Sodium: 341 mg

50. Party Chicken Spread

"This log is very eye-catching and very suitable for a party."
Serving: 3 cups. | Prep: 25m | Ready in: 25m

Ingredients

- 1 package (8 oz.) cream cheese, softened
- 1/4 cup mayonnaise
- 2 tbsps. lemon juice
- 1/2 tsp. salt
- 1/4 tsp. ground ginger
- 1/8 tsp. pepper
- 1/8 tsp. hot pepper sauce
- 2 cups finely chopped cooked chicken breast
- 2 hard-boiled large eggs, finely chopped
- 1/4 cup sliced green onions
- Diced pimientos and additional sliced green onions
- Assorted crackers or snack rye bread

Direction

- Beat the first 7 ingredients together in a big bowl until combined, then stir in green onions, eggs and chicken.
- Form the mixture into a log with size of 8x2-inch, then use onions and pimientos to decorate. Cover and refrigerate. Take out of the fridge about 15 minutes prior to serving. Serve log together with bread or crackers.

Nutrition Information

- Calories: 100 calories
- Total Carbohydrate: 3 g
- Cholesterol: 67 mg
- Total Fat: 5 g
- Fiber: 0 g
- Protein: 10 g
- Sodium: 223 mg

51. Party Vegetable Spread

"Chunky spread that is a delicious treat for parties or any occasion featuring finger food,"
Serving: 1-3/4 cups. | Prep: 35m | Ready in: 35m

Ingredients

- 3/4 cup shredded carrot
- 1/4 cup chopped seeded cucumber
- 1/4 cup chopped celery
- 1/4 cup chopped green pepper
- 1/4 cup finely chopped onion
- 1 package (8 oz.) fat-free cream cheese
- 2 tbsps. reduced-fat mayonnaise
- 1 tbsp. lemon juice
- 1/4 tsp. salt
- 1/8 tsp. pepper
- Snack rye bread

Direction

- Mix onion, green pepper, celery, cucumber and carrot in a small bowl. Place on paper towels for 30 minutes to drain.

- Mix pepper, salt, lemon juice, mayonnaise, and cream cheese in a large bowl. Mix in the veggies. Cover the bowl and chill for at least two hours. Serve on bread.

Nutrition Information

- Calories: 56 calories
- Total Carbohydrate: 5 g
- Cholesterol: 4 mg
- Total Fat: 2 g
- Fiber: 1 g
- Protein: 5 g
- Sodium: 303 mg

52. Pepper Steak Quesadillas

"Savory snack recipe."
Serving: 4 servings. | Prep: 10m | Ready in: 30m

Ingredients

- 1/2 lb. beef top sirloin steak
- 1/2 each medium green, sweet red and yellow pepper, julienned
- 1 tbsp. chopped red onion
- 1 garlic clove, minced
- 1 tbsp. minced fresh cilantro
- 1/4 tsp. dried rosemary, crushed
- 4 flour tortillas (6 inches)
- 6 cherry tomatoes, halved
- 1/4 cup sliced fresh mushrooms
- 1 cup shredded part-skim mozzarella cheese

Direction

- Use cooking oil to moisten a paper towel and coat the grill rack lightly using long-handled tongs. Let the steak grill on medium heat with cover or let it broil for 4 minutes per side, placed 4 inches from the heat source or until the meat achieves the preferred doneness; a thermometer should read (for well done, 170 degrees; medium, 160 degrees; medium-rare, 145 degrees). Allow it to stand for 10 minutes.

- In the meantime, sauté the onion and peppers in a big frying pan coated with cooking spray for 5 to 6 minutes or until it becomes tender. Add the garlic and let it cook for 1 minute more, then sprinkle rosemary and cilantro on top.
- Put the 2 tortillas on a cooking spray coated baking tray. Slice the steak into thin strips and put it on the tortillas. Put the pepper mixture on top of the steak using a slotted spoon, then put the cheese, mushrooms, tomatoes and leftover tortillas on top and use cooking spray to lightly spritz the top of tortillas.
- Let it bake for 5 to 10 minutes at 425 degrees or until the cheese melts and turns golden brown in color. Slice each quesadilla into 4 wedges.

Nutrition Information

- Calories: 254 calories
- Total Carbohydrate: 18 g
- Cholesterol: 39 mg
- Total Fat: 10 g
- Fiber: 1 g
- Protein: 23 g
- Sodium: 385 mg

53. Pesto Cream Cheese Spread

"This is a brilliant appetizer to serve at an Italian-theme meal that is irresistible once you've dipped in."
Serving: about 1-1/2 cups. | Prep: 15m | Ready in: 15m

Ingredients

- 1 package (8 oz.) cream cheese, softened
- 1/8 tsp. garlic powder
- 1/3 cup grated Parmesan cheese
- 3 tbsps. butter, softened
- 1/2 cup minced fresh parsley
- 1 garlic clove, minced
- 1 tsp. dried basil
- 1/2 tsp. dried marjoram
- 1/4 cup finely chopped walnuts
- 3 tbsps. olive oil
- Assorted crackers

Direction

- Use plastic wrap to line a 5 3/4"x3"x2" loaf pan. Mix garlic powder and cream cheese in a small bowl until blended and set aside. Mix together marjoram, basil, garlic, parsley, butter and Parmesan cheese in a separate small bowl until combined. Stir in walnuts then pour oil in slowly and stir well. Mix in oil slowly.
- Spread into the prepared pan with 1/4 cup of cream cheese mixture. Spread carefully 1/3 of the Parmesan mixture, then repeat layers two times. Place the remaining cream cheese mixture on top, then cover and chill for a minimum of 5 hours. Unmold and serve with crackers.

Nutrition Information

- Calories: 148 calories
- Total Carbohydrate: 1 g
- Cholesterol: 30 mg
- Total Fat: 15 g
- Fiber: 0 g
- Protein: 3 g
- Sodium: 128 mg

54. Poppin' Cheese Dip

"Showcase jalapeno pepper with this dip."
Serving: 3 cups. | Prep: 15m | Ready in: 40m

Ingredients

- 2 packages (8 oz. each) cream cheese, softened
- 2 cups shredded cheddar cheese
- 1/4 tsp. garlic salt
- 1 can (12 oz.) pickled jalapeno peppers
- 1 cup panko (Japanese) bread crumbs
- 2 tbsps. butter, melted
- Tortilla chips

Direction

- Beat garlic salt, cheddar cheese and cream cheese in a large bowl to blend and put aside. Drain and remove juice form the peppers. Cut the peppers lengthwise, open and lay it flat. If desired, discard the seeds and chop the peppers finely. Add into the cheese mixture and stir. Transfer into a 9-inch pie plate and spread.

- Combine butter and bread crumbs in a small bowl then sprinkle on top. Bake for 25-30 minutes at 350° to brown the topping lightly. Serve with tortilla chips.

Nutrition Information

- Calories: 118 calories
- Total Carbohydrate: 3 g
- Cholesterol: 33 mg
- Total Fat: 10 g
- Fiber: 0 g
- Protein: 4 g
- Sodium: 165 mg

55. Pretzel Bread Bowl With Cheese Dip

"I used pretzel mix for this bread recipe at an annual local recipe contest and everyone was amazed. Use wide range of pretzel taste for wide diversity."
Serving: 16 servings. | Prep: 30m | Ready in: 60m

Ingredients

- 1 cup finely crushed cheddar miniature pretzels
- 1 envelope ranch salad dressing mix
- 1 package (1/4 oz.) quick-rise yeast
- 2 tsps. sugar
- 1/8 tsp. baking soda
- 2 to 2-1/2 cups all-purpose flour
- 1 cup water
- 1/4 cup 2% milk
- 2 tbsps. butter
- 1 cup shredded pepper jack cheese
- 1 tsp. yellow cornmeal
- EGG WASH:
- 1 large egg white
- 1 tbsp. water
- Kosher salt, optional

- DIP:
- 2 cups (16 oz.) sour cream
- 1 cup shredded pepper jack cheese
- 1 envelope ranch salad dressing mix
- Chopped seeded jalapeno peppers and additional shredded pepper jack cheese, optional
- Assorted fresh vegetables

Direction

- Combine 1 cup of flour, baking soda, sugar, yeast, dressing mix and pretzels together. Pour butter, milk and water into a small saucepan and heat to 120° to 130°. Add the dry ingredients, whisk on low speed until moistened. Add cheese, whisk for 3 minutes on medium speed. Mix in enough flour left to get a stiff dough.
- Take the dough to a floured surface; knead for about 6 to 8 minutes until the dough gets elastic and smooth. Use plastic wrap to cover and let sit for 10 minutes.
- Use cooking spray to coat a baking tray, dredge cornmeal over. Form a round loaf; put it on the greased pan. Cover and let rest for about 60 minutes in a warm place until it rises double in size.
- Beat egg white with water, brush this on top of loaf. If preferred, dredge some salt over. Set oven at 375° and start preheating. Bake for 30 to 35 minutes, until it turns golden brown and has a hollow sound when tapped. Let cool for 5 minutes in pan then take to a wire rack to cool totally.
- To make dip: combine the dressing mix, jack cheese, pepper and sour cream. Chill in fridge until serving.
- When serving, remove 1/4 off the bread's top. Empty the bottom; keep a 1/2-inch thick shell. Divide taken out bread into cubes. Add dip to the bowl. If preferred, add more cheese and pepper on top. Serve dip with vegetables and bread cubes.

56. Quick Salsa

"This is a zesty and colorful salsa that pairs well with chips or other dishes."
Serving: 4-1/2 cups. | Prep: 15m | Ready in: 15m

Ingredients

- 6 Anaheim peppers, roasted and peeled
- 4 large tomatoes, chopped
- 3 green onions, sliced
- 2 tbsps. minced fresh cilantro
- 1/2 to 1 jalapeno pepper, seeded and minced
- 1 garlic clove, minced
- 1/3 cup red wine vinegar
- 1/3 cup olive oil
- 1/2 tsp. pepper
- 1 tsp. salt, optional

Direction

- Mix together garlic, jalapeno, cilantro, onions, tomatoes and chilies in a big bowl. Mix pepper, oil, vinegar and salt, if wanted, in a separate bowl then stir into the vegetable mixture. Cover and refrigerate for a minimum of 2 hours.

Nutrition Information

- Calories: 27 calories
- Total Carbohydrate: 2 g
- Cholesterol: 0 mg
- Total Fat: 2 g
- Fiber: 0 g
- Protein: 1 g
- Sodium: 3 mg

57. Roasted Garlic & Tomato Spread

"This spread has a great creamy texture with funny bold flavor."
Serving: 1-1/2 cups. | Prep: 15m | Ready in: 45m

Ingredients

- 2 whole garlic bulbs
- 3 tsps. olive oil, divided
- 3 plum tomatoes, quartered
- 1 carton (8 oz.) spreadable chive and onion cream cheese
- 1/4 tsp. Italian seasoning
- 1/4 tsp. salt
- Crackers or snack breads

Direction

- Take off papery outer skin from garlic; avoid peeling or separating cloves. Cut off the tops of garlic bulbs, then use 1/2 tsp. of oil to brush each bulb. Use heavy-duty foil to wrap each bulb. Put in a 9-inch square baking pan lined with foil with tomatoes and garlic, then brush leftover oil on tomatoes.
- Bake at 425 degrees until garlic is soft, about 30 to 35 minutes. Allow to cool about 10 to 15 minutes, then squeeze garlic into a small bowl. Drain any liquid from tomatoes, then chop them and put into garlic. Stir in salt, Italian seasoning and cream cheese, then serve with your preferred snack breads or crackers.

Nutrition Information

- Calories: 89 calories
- Total Carbohydrate: 4 g
- Cholesterol: 18 mg
- Total Fat: 7 g
- Fiber: 0 g
- Protein: 1 g
- Sodium: 133 mg

58. Salmon Dip With Cream Cheese

"Here's a wonderful hors d'oeuvre that is incredible for any event. The mix of salmon, cream cheddar and flavors gives it marvelous flavor."
Serving: 1-1/2 cups. | Prep: 10m | Ready in: 10m

Ingredients

- 2 packages (3 oz. each) cream cheese, softened
- 3 tbsps. mayonnaise
- 1 tbsp. lemon juice
- 1/2 tsp. salt
- 1/2 tsp. curry powder
- 1/4 tsp. dried basil
- 1/8 tsp. pepper
- 1 can (7-1/2 oz.) salmon, drained, bones and skin removed
- 2 green onions, thinly sliced
- Crackers

Direction

- Mix lemon juice, mayonnaise and cream cheese together in a bowl. Add pepper, basil, curry powder and salt; blend well. Mix in the onions and salmon gently. Cover and refrigerate for a minimum of 1 hour. Enjoy with crackers.

Nutrition Information

- Calories: 78 calories
- Total Carbohydrate: 1 g
- Cholesterol: 17 mg
- Total Fat: 7 g
- Fiber: 0 g
- Protein: 4 g
- Sodium: 234 mg

59. Salmon Party Spread

"Our guests love Alaskan salmon. We often serve it with smoky spread and crackers."
Serving: 2 cups. | Prep: 10m | Ready in: 10m

Ingredients

- 1 package (8 oz.) cream cheese, softened
- 1 can (7-1/2 oz.) pink salmon, drained, flaked and cartilage removed
- 3 tbsps. chopped fresh parsley
- 2 tbsps. finely chopped green pepper
- 2 tbsps. finely chopped sweet red pepper
- 2 tsp. lemon juice
- 1 tsp. prepared horseradish
- 1/2 tsp. liquid smoke, optional
- Finely chopped pecans or additional parsley
- Crackers

Direction

- Mix the first 8 ingredients together in a bowl, toss until thoroughly combined. Put a cover on and refrigerate for 2 hours to 1 day. Remove into serving a bowl if you want, sprinkle parsley or pecans over. Enjoy with crackers.

Nutrition Information

- Calories: 71 calories
- Total Carbohydrate: 1 g
- Cholesterol: 21 mg
- Total Fat: 6 g
- Fiber: 0 g
- Protein: 4 g
- Sodium: 115 mg

60. Scallop Kabobs For 2

""Lower in fat and good for the heart – these are things that I look for in recipes. This one fits those descriptions to a tee. Serve with a salad of mixed fruits and a light confectionery after the meal.""
Serving: 2 servings. | Prep: 30m | Ready in: 40m

Ingredients

- 4-1/2 tsps. lemon juice
- 4-1/2 tsps. reduced-sodium soy sauce
- 1 tbsp. canola oil
- Dash garlic powder
- Dash pepper
- 3/4 lb. sea scallops
- 2 small green peppers, cut into 1-1/2-inch pieces
- 1 cup cherry tomatoes

Direction

- Combine the first five ingredients in a small bowl. Take 2 tbsps. of the mixture and drizzle over the scallops in a large re-sealable plastic bag. Seal the bag and move it around to coat the scallops, then refrigerate for 20 minutes. Keep the remaining marinade in a covered container in the fridge until ready for grilling. While scallops are marinating, boil 3 cups of water in a large saucepan. Add the peppers, put the lid on the saucepan, and let boil for 2 minutes. Drain and immerse peppers in ice water to stop the cooking process. Drain and pat the peppers dry. Take scallops out, discarding its marinade. Cue the scallops alternately with tomatoes and peppers on four metal or water-soaked wooden skewers. Oil the grill rack and arrange the skewers on it, cover the grill and cook over medium heat, or broil 4 in. from the heat, until the scallop flesh is opaque and firm to the touch, about 3-5 minutes per side. Baste with reserved marinade from time to time.

Nutrition Information

- Calories: 235 calories
- Total Carbohydrate: 12 g
- Cholesterol: 56 mg
- Total Fat: 7 g
- Fiber: 2 g
- Protein: 30 g
- Sodium: 616 mg

61. Sesame Chicken With Creamy Satay Sauce

"Asian style chicken skewers marinated in a sesame salad dressing."
Serving: 4 servings. | Prep: 20m | Ready in: 30m

Ingredients

- 3/4 cup Asian toasted sesame salad dressing
- 1 lb. boneless skinless chicken breast halves, cut into 1-inch strips
- 1/2 cup reduced-fat cream cheese
- 1/4 cup coconut milk
- 3 tbsps. creamy peanut butter
- 2 tbsps. lime juice
- 1 tbsp. reduced-sodium soy sauce
- 1/2 tsp. crushed red pepper flakes
- 1 tbsp. minced fresh cilantro

Direction

- Pour salad dressing into a large re-sealable plastic bag with the chicken. Seal the bag, turn multiple times to coat, and refrigerate for 4 hours or overnight. Drain chicken, discarding its marinade. Thread chicken onto metal or water-soaked wooden skewers. Use long-handled tongs to dab an oil-moistened paper towel onto the grates. Grill the skewers, covered, over medium heat, or broil 4 in. from the heat, for 10-15 minutes or until chicken is not pink anymore, turning once. In a small bowl, combine the coconut milk, peanut butter, cream cheese, soy sauce, lime juice, and pepper flakes. Top with cilantro. Serve chicken with the sauce.

Nutrition Information

- Calories: 356 calories
- Total Carbohydrate: 10 g
- Cholesterol: 83 mg
- Total Fat: 22 g
- Fiber: 1 g
- Protein: 30 g
- Sodium: 692 mg

62. Shrimp Corn Cakes With Soy Mayo

""These savory corn cakes go well with hot sauce.""
Serving: 2 dozen (2/3 cup sauce). | Prep: 30m | Ready in: 35m

Ingredients

- 1/2 cup mayonnaise
- 1 tbsp. reduced-sodium soy sauce
- 1 tbsp. ketchup
- 2 tsps. Dijon mustard
- 1/2 tsp. garlic powder
- 1/2 tsp. hot pepper sauce, optional
- 1/8 tsp. pepper
- SHRIMP CORN CAKES:
- 1/2 cup chopped onion (about 1 small)
- 1 tbsp. oil plus additional for frying, divided
- 2 garlic cloves, minced
- 1/2 lb. uncooked peeled and deveined shrimp, finely chopped
- 3/4 cup all-purpose flour
- 1/4 cup cornmeal
- 1 tbsp. cornstarch
- 1 tsp. baking powder
- 1/4 tsp. salt
- 1/4 tsp. pepper
- 1 cup cream-style corn
- 1 cup whole kernel corn
- 1 large egg, lightly beaten

Direction

- Mix together the first seven ingredients in a small bowl. Chill with a cover till serving.
- Cook while stirring onion in a large skillet with 1 tbsp. of oil over medium-high heat till tender. Put in garlic; cook for 1 more minute. Put in shrimp; cook while stirring till shrimp becoming pink. Take away from the heat.
- Combine pepper, salt, baking powder, cornstarch, cornmeal and flour together in a large bowl. In a small bowl, combine the shrimp mixture, egg and corn; mix into dry ingredients just till well moistened.
- Heat 1/4 in. of oil in an electric skillet to 375°. Drop the corn mixture in oil by rounded tablespoonfuls, working in batches; fry till golden brown, 1 1/2 minutes per side. Drain on paper towels. Serve with sauce.

Nutrition Information

- Calories: 109 calories
- Total Carbohydrate: 8 g
- Cholesterol: 22 mg
- Total Fat: 7 g
- Fiber: 1 g
- Protein: 3 g
- Sodium: 183 mg

63. Smoked Mozzarella Mushroom Pizza

"This recipe can be served as an entrée."
Serving: 24 servings. | Prep: 25m | Ready in: 40m

Ingredients

- 2 tbsps. butter, divided
- 2 tbsps. olive oil, divided
- 2/3 cup sliced red onion
- 1/2 lb. sliced baby portobello mushrooms
- 1 garlic clove, minced
- 2 tsps. minced fresh rosemary or 1/2 tsp. dried rosemary, crushed
- 1 tube (13.8 oz.) refrigerated pizza crust
- 1-1/2 cups shredded smoked mozzarella cheese
- 2 oz. sliced prosciutto or deli ham, finely chopped

Direction

- Preheat oven to 400 degrees. Over medium-high heat, heat 1 tbsp. of oil and 1 tbsp. of butter in a big skillet. Put in the onion. Cook and stir until softened, about 2 to 3 minutes. Turn the heat down to medium low. Let it cook, stirring occasionally, until golden brown, about 8 to 10 minutes. Take it out of the pan.
- Over medium-high heat, heat the oil and remaining butter in the same skillet. Put in the mushrooms then cook and stir until tender, about 2 to 3 minutes. Put in rosemary and garlic. Cook until liquid is evaporated, about 1 to 2 minutes more.
- On the bottom of a greased 15x10x1 inches baking pan, unroll and press the dough. Press several dimples into the dough using your fingertips. Sprinkle using 1/2 cup of cheese and put prosciutto, mushroom mixture and onion on top. Use the remaining cheese to sprinkle. Bake it until cheese has melted and the pizza is golden brown, about 15 to 18 minutes.

64. Southwestern Taco Bean Dip

"Blend the ingredients well for a large plateful of this crowd-pleasuring dip."
Serving: 12-14 servings. | Prep: 15m | Ready in: 15m

Ingredients

- 1 can (16 oz.) refried beans
- 1/4 cup picante sauce
- 1-1/2 cups prepared guacamole
- 1/2 cup sour cream
- 1/2 cup mayonnaise
- 4-1/2 tsps. taco seasoning
- 1 cup shredded cheddar cheese
- 1 can (2-1/4 oz.) sliced ripe olives, drained
- Chopped green onion, shredded lettuce and chopped tomatoes
- Tortilla chips

Direction

- Combine picante sauce and beans in a small bowl. Transfer into a serving platter and spread. Spread the mixture with guacamole.
- Combine taco seasoning, mayonnaise and sour cream in a separate small bowl then top off the guacamole, spread. Sprinkle with tomatoes, lettuce, onions, olives and cheese. Store in the fridge till serve. Serve with tortilla chips.

Nutrition Information

- Calories: 192 calories
- Total Carbohydrate: 10 g
- Cholesterol: 20 mg
- Total Fat: 15 g
- Fiber: 4 g
- Protein: 5 g
- Sodium: 465 mg

65. Steak & Blue Cheese Bruschetta With Onion & Roasted Tomato Jam

"The flavors of this appetizer featuring balsamic vinegar, blue cheese, jam, and caramelized onion will surely please your taste buds."
Serving: 16 appetizers. | Prep: 45m | Ready in: 55m

Ingredients

- 5 tbsps. olive oil, divided
- 1 large sweet onion, halved and thinly sliced
- 1 cup grape tomatoes, halved
- 1/2 tsp. kosher salt, divided
- 1/4 tsp. freshly ground pepper, divided
- 6 oz. cream cheese, softened
- 3 oz. crumbled blue cheese
- 3 garlic cloves, minced
- 16 slices French bread baguette (1/2 inch thick)
- 2 beef ribeye steaks (3/4 inch thick and 8 oz. each)
- 1-1/2 tsps. Montreal steak seasoning
- 2 tbsps. balsamic vinegar

Direction

- Preheat the oven to 400 degrees F. On medium-high heat, heat 2 tbsp. oil in a big pan; add onion. Sauté onion until soft. Turn heat to medium-low and continue cooking for 25-30 minutes until golden; stir from time to time.
- Mix 1/8 tsp pepper, a tbsp. oil, and quarter tsp. salt and spread in a pan measuring 15-in x 10-in x 1-in. Roast for 10 -15 minutes until the mixture is soft. Mix tomatoes into the onion and mash softly. Combine leftover pepper and salt, cream cheese, garlic, and blue cheese in a bowl.
- Slather oil over the slices of bread. On medium heat, grill bread for 1-2 minutes per side while covered until slightly toasted. On medium heat, grill meat while covered until it reaches the preferred doneness (an inserted thermometer in the steak should register 145° Fahrenheit for medium-well, 140 degrees F for medium done, and 135° Fahrenheit for medium rare).
- Slather cheese mixture over the toasts; add onion mixture and steak on top. Lightly pour vinegar; serve.

Nutrition Information

- Calories: 185 calories
- Total Carbohydrate: 7 g
- Cholesterol: 32 mg
- Total Fat: 14 g
- Fiber: 0 g
- Protein: 8 g
- Sodium: 292 mg

66.Stuffed Gouda Spread

"This make-ahead appetizer is a good way to use cheese and absolutely ideal for those who don't have time in the kitchen."
Serving: 1-1/3 cups. | Prep: 20m | Ready in: 20m

Ingredients

- 1 package (7 oz.) Gouda cheese
- 1/4 cup beer or nonalcoholic beer
- 2 tbsps. butter, cubed
- 1 tsp. Dijon mustard
- 1-1/2 tsps. snipped fresh dill or 1/2 tsp. dill weed
- Crackers or pretzels

Direction

- On the cheese round, slice off the top of the waxed shell carefully, then spoon out the cheese. Set the waxed shell aside. Put cheese into a food processor. Put in mustard, butter and beer then cover and process until smooth. Mix in dill.
- Scoop into the reserved shell and chill until ready to serve. Serve along with pretzels or crackers.

Nutrition Information

- Calories: 188 calories
- Total Carbohydrate: 1 g
- Cholesterol: 58 mg
- Total Fat: 16 g
- Fiber: 0 g
- Protein: 10 g
- Sodium: 397 mg

67. Sweet & Sour Chicken Wings

"This is great to enjoy at Christmas, but you can also enjoy it all year round."
Serving: about 5-1/2 dozen. | Prep: 15m | Ready in: 55m

Ingredients

- 2 cups sugar
- 2 cups water
- 2 cups reduced-sodium soy sauce
- 1 cup unsweetened pineapple juice
- 1/2 cup canola oil
- 2 tsps. garlic powder
- 2 tsps. ground ginger
- 8 lbs. frozen chicken wingettes and drumettes, thawed

Direction

- Combine the first 7 ingredients together in a big bowl. Split the soy sauce mixture and chicken wings between 2 big resealable plastic bags; close the bag and flip to coat. Chill for 8 hours to overnight.
- Turn the oven to 350° to preheat. Strain the chicken, disposing of the marinade. Put in 2 oil-coated 15x10x1-inch baking pans. Cover and bake until the juices run clear, about 40-45 minutes.

Nutrition Information

- Calories: 124 calories
- Total Carbohydrate: 1 g
- Cholesterol: 40 mg
- Total Fat: 9 g
- Fiber: 0 g
- Protein: 10 g
- Sodium: 75 mg

68. Sweet 'n' Spicy Wings

"These are hot, spicy, and super delicious chicken wings."
Serving: about 4 dozen. | Prep: 20m | Ready in: 30m

Ingredients

- 5 lbs. chicken wings
- 1/2 cup butter, cubed
- 1/2 cup Louisiana-style hot sauce
- 1/4 cup balsamic vinegar
- 1/4 cup soy sauce
- 3 tbsps. brown sugar
- 3 tbsps. honey
- 2 tbsps. plus 1 tsp. celery seed, divided
- 2 tbsps. lemon juice
- 2/3 cup all-purpose flour
- 1 tsp. each salt, paprika and cayenne pepper
- 1/2 tsp. garlic powder
- Oil for deep-fat frying

Direction

- Cut wings into 3 parts; remove the wing tip parts. Boil lemon juice, 2 tbsps. celery seed, honey, brown sugar, soy sauce, vinegar, hot sauce, and butter in a large saucepan. Reduce the heat; uncover and simmer until reduced by half.
- In the meantime, combine the remaining celery seed, garlic powder, cayenne, paprika, salt, and flour in a large resealable plastic bag. Put in the wings a few at a time, and shake to coat well.
- Heat oil to 375° in a deep-fat fryer or an electric skillet. Fry the wings until no longer pink, a few at a time, about 3-4 minutes on each side. Drain on paper towels. Put in a large bowl, then add the sauce and toss to cover.

Nutrition Information

- Calories: 129 calories
- Total Carbohydrate: 4 g
- Cholesterol: 20 mg
- Total Fat: 10 g
- Fiber: 0 g

- Protein: 5 g
- Sodium: 156 mg

69. Sweet-and-sour Meatballs Appetizer

"People who have tried these meatballs always ask me for the recipe."
Serving: 3-4 dozen. | Prep: 15m | Ready in: 35m

Ingredients

- 2 cups soft bread crumbs
- 1/2 cup milk
- 1/2 cup lean ground beef
- 1/2 lb. Jones No Sugar Pork Sausage Roll sausage
- 1 can (8 oz.) whole water chestnuts, finely chopped and drained
- 1 tbsp. soy sauce
- 1/2 tsp. garlic powder
- 1/4 tsp. onion salt
- Prepared sweet-and-sour sauce, optional

Direction

- In a small bowl, combine milk and bread crumbs; put aside. In the meantime, combine sausage, ground beef with onion salt, garlic powder, soy sauce, and water chestnuts. Put beef mixture into the bread crumb mixture and mix until well combined. Shape mixture into meatballs of 1 1/2 inches in diameter. Arrange meatballs on an oiled rack in a shallow baking pan.
- Bake for 20 minutes at 350° until a thermometer registers 160°; drain well. If desired, serve meatballs with sweet-and-sour sauce.

70. Three-cheese Nachos

"These nachos are super yummy and super easy."
Serving: 10-12 servings. | Prep: 15m | Ready in: 25m

Ingredients

- 1 package (8 oz.) plus 3 oz. cream cheese, softened
- 1 can (4 oz.) chopped green chilies
- 3 tbsps. chopped onion
- 2 garlic cloves, minced
- 1 tbsp. canned chopped jalapeno pepper
- 1-1/2 tsps. ground cumin
- 1-1/2 tsps. chili powder
- 2 cups cubed cooked chicken
- 2 cups shredded Monterey Jack cheese, divided
- 1 package (14 oz.) pita bread (6 inches)
- 1 cup shredded cheddar cheese
- Salsa, optional

Direction

- Beat chili powder, cumin, jalapeno, garlic, onion, chilies and cream cheese in a large bowl until they become smooth. Stir in one cup of the Monterey Jack cheese and chicken.
- Split per pita into 2 circles. Spread each circle with a quarter cup of the chicken mixture; arrange on unoiled baking sheets.
- Bake for 5 to 10 mins at 400°. Combine remaining Monterey Jack and cheddar cheese; spread over the circles. Bake until cheese melts, about 5 more mins. Divide into wedges. If desired, enjoy with salsa.

Nutrition Information

- Calories: 339 calories
- Total Carbohydrate: 21 g
- Cholesterol: 77 mg
- Total Fat: 20 g
- Fiber: 1 g
- Protein: 19 g
- Sodium: 478 mg

71. Tomato-walnut Pesto Spread

"This popular spread is really festive for Christmas with the blend of white, green and red layers."
Serving: 2-1/3 cups. | Prep: 15m | Ready in: 15m

Ingredients

- 3 tbsps. chopped oil-packed sun-dried tomatoes, patted dry
- 1 package (8 oz.) cream cheese, softened
- 1/2 cup grated Parmesan cheese
- 1/4 cup sour cream
- 2 tbsps. butter, softened
- 1/2 cup finely chopped walnuts
- 1/2 cup prepared pesto
- Assorted crackers

Direction

- Use plastic wrap to line a 4-cup mold and use cooking spray to coat mold well. Put in the bottom of mold with tomatoes and set mold aside.
- Beat butter, sour cream and cream cheese in a big bowl until combined. Mix pesto and walnuts together in a separate bowl, then spread over tomatoes in the prepared mold with cheese mixture. Place walnut mixture on top.
- Gather edges of plastic wrap together over pesto and gently press down to seal. Chill until firm, for a minimum of 4 hours. Open plastic wrap and invert mold onto a serving plate. Serve along with crackers.

Nutrition Information

- Calories: 129 calories
- Total Carbohydrate: 2 g
- Cholesterol: 24 mg
- Total Fat: 12 g
- Fiber: 0 g
- Protein: 4 g
- Sodium: 137 mg

72. Triple Cheese Spread

"This cheesy and creamy spread has a pretty crunch as well as color coming from the addition of carrots."
Serving: 1-3/4 cups. | Prep: 10m | Ready in: 10m

Ingredients

- 1 cup (8 oz.) fat-free cottage cheese
- 1/2 cup shredded reduced-fat Swiss cheese
- 1/4 cup grated Parmesan cheese
- 2 tbsps. fat-free milk
- 1/2 tsp. dill weed
- 1/8 tsp. pepper
- 1/4 cup shredded carrots
- 1/4 cup unsalted sunflower kernels, optional

Direction

- Mix together pepper, dill, milk and cheeses in a blender, then process until smooth. Turn to a small bowl, then stir in carrots. Cover and refrigerate. Stir in sunflower kernels right before serving, if wanted.

Nutrition Information

- Calories: 41 calories
- Total Carbohydrate: 1 g
- Cholesterol: 6 mg
- Total Fat: 2 g
- Fiber: 0 g
- Protein: 5 g
- Sodium: 0 mg

73. Turkey Sandwiches With Red Pepper Hummus

"You can use other cheeses, meats and breads."
Serving: 4 servings. | Prep: 20m | Ready in: 25m

Ingredients

- 1/3 cup mayonnaise
- 1 tbsp. lime juice

- 1 can (15 oz.) garbanzo beans or chickpeas, rinsed and drained
- 1/4 cup chopped roasted sweet red peppers, drained
- 2 garlic cloves, peeled
- 1/2 tsp. chili powder
- 1/4 tsp. ground cumin
- 2 tbsps. butter, softened
- 8 slices rye bread
- 4 slices Muenster cheese
- 8 thin slices cooked turkey
- 1 small red onion, sliced
- 2 medium tomatoes, sliced

Direction

- Hummus: In blender, process initial 7 ingredients till smooth, covered. Put in small bowl; cover. Refrigerate for an hour.
- Spread butter on a side of every bread slice. Spread hummus on opposite side. Put 4 slices on griddle, buttered side down. Layer with leftover bread, hummus side down, tomatoes, onion, turkey and cheese. Toast till cheese melts and bread browns lightly or for 2-3 minutes per side.

74. Veggie Nachos

"This vegetarian Mexican recipe is delicious."
Serving: 6 | Prep: 10m | Ready in: 20m

Ingredients

- 1 (12 oz.) bag round tortilla chips
- 1 1/3 tbsps. vegetable oil
- 1/3 cup chopped green bell pepper
- 1/3 cup chopped red bell pepper
- 1/3 cup chopped green onions
- 1 cup chopped tomato
- 1/2 cup frozen corn
- 1 pinch chili powder
- 1 pinch onion powder
- 1 pinch garlic salt
- 8 oz. nacho cheese, or to taste
- 2 jalapeno peppers, chopped

Direction

- On a big serving dish, put tortilla chips.
- In a frying pan, heat oil over medium heat. Put in bell peppers and cook for 1 minute. Put in onions and cook for another 2 minutes. Put in corn and tomato, cook for 2 minutes and use garlic salt, onion powder, and chili powder to season. Take away from the heat.
- In a microwave-safe bowl, put nacho cheese and put in the microwave to heat, about 2 minutes. Gently add the cheese to tortilla chips. Pour over the cheese with vegetables. Put jalapenos on top.

Nutrition Information

- Calories: 390 calories;
- Total Carbohydrate: 47.2 g
- Cholesterol: 3 mg
- Total Fat: 20.8 g
- Protein: 6.1 g
- Sodium: 624 mg

Chapter 2: Fathers Day Salad Recipes

***

75. 10-minute Taco Salad

""We made this dish every weekend whenever we have a guest in our house. It's so delicious! My family loves it!""
Serving: 8 servings. | Prep: 10m | Ready in: 10m

Ingredients

- 2 cans (16 oz. each) chili beans, undrained
- 1 package (10-1/2 oz.) corn chips
- 2 cups shredded cheddar cheese

- 4 cups chopped lettuce
- 2 small tomatoes, chopped
- 1 small onion, chopped
- 1 can (2-1/4 oz.) sliced ripe olives, drained
- 1-1/4 cups salsa
- 1/2 cup sour cream

Direction

- Cook the beans in a small saucepan over medium-low heat until the mixture is heated through. In a large platter, arrange the corn chips and top them with sour cream, olives, lettuce, cheese, beans, salsa, onion, and tomatoes. Serve the salad immediately.

Nutrition Information

- Calories: 423 calories
- Total Carbohydrate: 36 g
- Cholesterol: 40 mg
- Total Fat: 25 g
- Fiber: 7 g
- Protein: 13 g
- Sodium: 727 mg

76. Asian Sugar Snap Peas And Cabbage

"This very easy salad with cabbage, peas for the Chinese New Year buffet."
Serving: 8 servings. | Prep: 15m | Ready in: 20m

Ingredients

- 1 lb. fresh sugar snap peas, trimmed
- 1/4 cup hoisin sauce
- 1/4 cup reduced-sodium soy sauce
- 2 tbsps. agave nectar
- 1 tbsp. lime juice
- 2 tsps. rice vinegar
- 2 tsps. Sriracha Asian hot chili sauce or 1 tsp. hot pepper sauce
- 8 Chinese or napa cabbage leaves, julienned
- 1 tbsp. sesame seeds, toasted

Direction

- Boil 6 cups of water in a big saucepan. Put in peas; keep it covered and cooked for 1 to 2 minutes. Drain and add peas into ice water right away. Drain and pat dry.
- To make dressing, mix chili sauce, vinegar, lime juice, agave nectar, soy sauce, hoisin sauce in a small-sized bowl. Mix sesame seeds, cabbage, and peas in a big serving bowl. Pour in dressing; coat by tossing.

77. Bacon Macaroni Salad

""This satisfying pasta salad is like eating a BLT in a bowl. Packed with green onion, celery, chopped tomato and crispy bacon, the amazing salad is coasted with a tangy vinegar dressing and mayonnaise. A real crowd-pleaser!""
Serving: 12 servings (3/4 cup each). | Prep: 20m | Ready in: 20m

Ingredients

- 2 cups uncooked elbow macaroni
- 1 large tomato, finely chopped
- 2 celery ribs, finely chopped
- 5 green onions, finely chopped
- 1-1/4 cups mayonnaise
- 5 tsp. white vinegar
- 1/4 tsp. salt
- 1/8 to 1/4 tsp. pepper
- 1 lb. bacon strips, cooked and crumbled

Direction

- Cook macaroni based on the package directions; strain and wash in cold water. Move to a big bowl; mix in green onion, celery and tomato. Mix in a small bowl the pepper, salt, vinegar and mayonnaise. Place on macaroni mixture and toss. Keep in the refrigerator for a minimum of 2 hours, covered. Mix in bacon just before serving.

Nutrition Information

- Calories: 290 calories
- Total Carbohydrate: 11 g

- Cholesterol: 19 mg
- Total Fat: 25 g
- Fiber: 1 g
- Protein: 6 g
- Sodium: 387 mg

78. Balsamic Green Bean Salad

"This salad is to help those who really don't line regular green beans."
Serving: 4 | Prep: 15m | Ready in: 25m

Ingredients

- 1 lb. fresh green beans, trimmed
- 2 tbsps. chopped shallots
- 2 tbsps. chopped garlic
- 1/4 cup balsamic vinegar
- 1/4 cup olive oil

Direction

- Put green beans in a big saucepan. Add enough water to cover the bean, then bring to a boil on high heat. Lower heat to moderate-low and simmer for about 10 minutes. Drain and allow to cool.
- Stir oil, balsamic vinegar, garlic and shallots together in a bowl. Drizzle over green beans. Cover and chill for a minimum of 1 hour. Serve chilled.

Nutrition Information

- Calories: 174 calories;
- Total Carbohydrate: 12.6 g
- Cholesterol: 0 mg
- Total Fat: 13.7 g
- Protein: 2.5 g
- Sodium: 12 mg

79. Balsamic Steak Salad

"Combine blue cheese and salad for a hearty meal! It is irresistible and delicious. You won't regret it!"
Serving: 4 servings. | Prep: 15m | Ready in: 30m

Ingredients

- 1/4 cup balsamic vinegar
- 1/4 cup olive oil
- 2 tsps. lemon juice
- 1 tsp. minced fresh thyme or 1/4 tsp. dried thyme
- 1/4 tsp. salt
- 1/8 tsp. coarsely ground pepper
- 1 beef flat iron steak or top sirloin steak (3/4 lb.)
- 1 package (9 oz.) ready-to-serve salad greens
- 8 cherry tomatoes, halved
- 4 radishes, sliced
- 1/2 medium ripe avocado, peeled and thinly sliced
- 1/4 cup dried cranberries
- Crumbled blue cheese and additional pepper, optional

Direction

- Prepare dressing by combining the first six ingredients together. In a plastic resealable bag, put together 1/4 cup of dressing and steak. Turn bag to coat steak. Keep in refrigerator for 8 hours or overnight. Keep the leftover dressing and refrigerate with cover until ready to use.
- Drain beef and discard marinade. On medium heat, grill with cover (or you can broil 4 inches from heat) until cooked to your desired doneness (thermometer should reach 135° for medium-rare, 160° medium) for 6 to 8 minutes a side. Set aside for 5 minutes then chop.
- To prepare for serving, distribute salad greens onto four plates. Place the steak, radishes, avocado, and tomatoes on top. Add cranberries. You can also add pepper and cheese if preferred. Serve with the remaining dressing.

Nutrition Information

- Calories: 321 calories
- Total Carbohydrate: 15 g
- Cholesterol: 55 mg
- Total Fat: 22 g
- Fiber: 4 g
- Protein: 18 g
- Sodium: 221 mg

80. Black-eyed Pea Spinach Salad

"Pecan and black peas bring more color and flavor to this classic spinach. A dish you definitely need to try!"
Serving: 16 servings (3/4 cup each). | Prep: 20m | Ready in: 20m

Ingredients

- 1/4 cup olive oil
- 1/4 cup red wine vinegar
- 4 tsps. Dijon mustard
- 1 tsp. salt
- 1 tsp. pepper
- 2 cans (15-1/2 oz. each) black-eyed peas, rinsed and drained
- 3 medium tomatoes, seeded and chopped
- 1/2 cup thinly sliced red onion
- 1 package (9 oz.) fresh spinach
- 1/2 cup chopped pecans, toasted
- 6 bacon strips, cooked and crumbled

Direction

- In a large bowl, put the first five ingredients in; whisk. Place onion, tomatoes and peas in then mix. Keep in the fridge, with cover, until ready to serve.
- In a large serving bowl, put the vegetable mixture and the spinach in; gently toss. Use bacon and pecans to sprinkle.

Nutrition Information

- Calories: 121 calories
- Total Carbohydrate: 10 g
- Cholesterol: 3 mg

- Total Fat: 7 g
- Fiber: 2 g
- Protein: 5 g
- Sodium: 356 mg

81. Blt Wedge Salad

"This simple and quick-to-fix salad is really shining with a homemade dressing that is full of flavor but requiring not so much work."
Serving: 4 servings. | Prep: 20m | Ready in: 20m

Ingredients

- 1/2 cup 2% milk
- 3 tbsps. lime juice
- 1 cup mayonnaise
- 1 shallot, finely chopped
- 1 tbsp. ranch salad dressing mix
- 1 tsp. pepper
- 1 garlic clove, minced
- 1 medium head iceberg lettuce
- 1-1/2 cups grape tomatoes, halved lengthwise
- 2/3 cup crumbled cooked bacon
- Crumbled blue cheese, optional

Direction

- Whisk together lime juice and milk in a small bowl and allow to stand for 5 minutes. Whisk together garlic, pepper, ranch dressing mix, shallot and mayonnaise until combined.
- Slice lettuce into 4 wedges, then pour dressing over and place bacon together with tomatoes on top. Sprinkle with blue cheese if wanted.

Nutrition Information

- Calories: 536 calories
- Total Carbohydrate: 15 g
- Cholesterol: 36 mg
- Total Fat: 48 g
- Fiber: 2 g
- Protein: 10 g
- Sodium: 1405 mg

82. Blue Cheese Potato Salad

"Such a flavorful and amazing potato salad.""
Serving: 5 | Prep: 30m | Ready in: 45m

Ingredients

- 4 slices bacon
- 2 lbs. red new potatoes
- 1/2 cup olive oil
- 3 tbsps. white vinegar
- 1 bunch green onions, chopped
- 1/2 tsp. salt
- 1 tsp. ground black pepper
- 1 1/2 oz. blue cheese, crumbled

Direction

- In a large, deep skillet, fry bacon over medium-high heat until browned evenly. Remove from fat, chop into small pieces and set aside.
- Salt the water in a large pot then bring water to a boil. Pour potatoes and cook for about 15 minutes until tender, but still firm. Drain off water, allow to cool and chop, do not remove the skins.
- Combine pepper, salt, green onions, vinegar, and oil together in a large bowl. Add cheese, bacon, and potatoes then gently shake to coat.

Nutrition Information

- Calories: 481 calories;
- Total Carbohydrate: 36.8 g
- Cholesterol: 22 mg
- Total Fat: 34.4 g
- Protein: 8.3 g
- Sodium: 552 mg

83. Broccoli And Apple Salad

"This salad could even satisfy the pickiest people in the world. It is a cool and creamy side dish, made with crunchy vegetable salad and yogurt dressing on top."
Serving: 6 servings. | Prep: 15m | Ready in: 15m

Ingredients

- 3 cups small fresh broccoli florets
- 3 medium apples, chopped
- 1/2 cup chopped mixed dried fruit
- 1 tbsp. chopped red onion
- 1/2 cup reduced-fat plain yogurt
- 4 bacon strips, cooked and crumbled

Direction

- Mix onion, dried fruit, apples and broccoli in a big bowl. Use yogurt to mix with the veggie mixture; coat by tossing. Dredge bacon on top. Put in the fridge until serving.

Nutrition Information

- Calories: 124 calories
- Total Carbohydrate: 22 g
- Cholesterol: 7 mg
- Total Fat: 3 g
- Fiber: 3 g
- Protein: 4 g
- Sodium: 134 mg

84. Chicken & Brussels Sprouts Salad

"This awesome meals with cranberries, nuts, veggies and protein is inspired my mom's side salads."
Serving: 6 servings. | Prep: 15m | Ready in: 30m

Ingredients

- 3 tbsps. olive oil
- 20 fresh Brussels sprouts, trimmed and halved
- 2 shallots, sliced
- 1/2 tsp. salt
- 1/2 cup balsamic vinegar

- 1 skinned rotisserie chicken, shredded
- 3 cups torn romaine
- 2/3 cup chopped roasted sweet red peppers
- 1/2 cup chopped sun-dried tomatoes (not oil-packed)
- 1/2 cup balsamic vinaigrette
- 3/4 cup pistachios, toasted
- 3/4 cup dried cranberries
- Fresh goat cheese, optional

Direction

- Heat oil in a big skillet over moderate heat. Put in shallots and Brussels sprouts, then cook and stir about 10 to 12 minutes, until softened and browned. Dredge with salt and drizzle with balsamic vinegar. Cook for 2 to 3 minutes, stirring to loosen browned bits from pan, until liquid is reduced.
- Mix together sun-dried tomatoes, red pepper, romaine and chicken, then toss together with balsamic vinaigrette and Brussels sprouts mixture. Place dried cranberries and pistachios on top then serve with goat cheese if you want.

Nutrition Information

- Calories: 500 calories
- Total Carbohydrate: 39 g
- Cholesterol: 73 mg
- Total Fat: 25 g
- Fiber: 7 g
- Protein: 30 g
- Sodium: 657 mg

85. Chicken & Chutney Salad

"This recipe is great as a salad or as a gourmet lunch wrap."
Serving: 6 servings. | Prep: 15m | Ready in: 15m

Ingredients

- 1 carton (6 oz.) plain yogurt
- 1/4 cup light coconut milk
- 1-1/2 tsps. curry powder

- 2 cups cubed cooked chicken
- 2 cups green grapes, halved
- 6 green onions, chopped
- 1/2 cup dried cranberries
- 1/3 cup mango chutney
- 1/4 cup slivered almonds, toasted

Direction

- Whisk together curry, milk and yogurt in a small bowl until smooth.
- Mix together cranberries, onions, grapes and chicken in a big bowl. Drizzle over with yogurt dressing and toss to coat well. Fold in mango chutney, then chill for a minimum of an hour.
- Sprinkle over with almonds right before serving.

Nutrition Information

- Calories: 267 calories
- Total Carbohydrate: 34 g
- Cholesterol: 45 mg
- Total Fat: 8 g
- Fiber: 2 g
- Protein: 16 g
- Sodium: 208 mg

86. Chili-rubbed Steak & Bread Salad

"The bread salad completes and adds wonderful flavors to this dish. Delish!"
Serving: 6 servings. | Prep: 35m | Ready in: 50m

Ingredients

- 2 tsps. chili powder
- 2 tsps. brown sugar
- 1/2 tsp. salt
- 1/2 tsp. pepper
- 1 beef top sirloin steak (1 inch thick and 1-1/4 lbs.)
- 2 cups cubed multigrain bread
- 2 tbsps. olive oil

- 1 cup ranch salad dressing
- 2 tbsps. finely grated horseradish
- 1 tbsp. prepared mustard
- 3 large tomatoes, cut into 1-inch pieces
- 1 medium cucumber, cut into 1-inch pieces
- 1 small red onion, halved and thinly sliced

Direction

- Combine pepper, salt, chili powder and brown sugar together and massage it onto the steak. Let it sit for 15 minutes.
- While the seasoned steak is resting on the side, coat the bread cubes with oil. Let the bread toast for 8 to 10 minutes in a big skillet over medium heat until it is crispy and browned a little bit, stir it from time to time. Mix horseradish, mustard and salad dressing together in a small bowl.
- Put the seasoned steak on a grill over medium heat and grill then cover or put the seasoned steak in a broiler and let it broil 4 inches away from the heat for 6 to 8 minutes on every side until the preferred meat doneness is achieved (a thermometer inserted on the meat should indicate 170°F for well-done, 160°F for medium and 145°F for medium-rare). Let it sit for 5 minutes.
- Mix the cucumber, tomatoes, toasted bread and onion together in a big bowl. Mix in 1/2 cup of the dressing mixture until well-coated. Cut the steak and serve it together with the salad and the remaining dressing.

Nutrition Information

- Calories: 434 calories
- Total Carbohydrate: 18 g
- Cholesterol: 45 mg
- Total Fat: 30 g
- Fiber: 3 g
- Protein: 23 g
- Sodium: 682 mg

87. Chilled Shrimp Pasta Salad

"This chilled salad is all you need to cool down on a hot summer day."
Serving: 12 servings (3/4 cup each). | Prep: 15m | Ready in: 30m

Ingredients

- 3 cups uncooked small pasta shells
- 1/2 cup sour cream
- 1/2 cup mayonnaise
- 1/4 cup horseradish sauce
- 2 tbsps. grated onion
- 1-1/2 tsps. seasoned salt
- 3/4 tsp. pepper
- 1 lb. peeled and deveined cooked small shrimp
- 1 large cucumber, seeded and chopped
- 3 celery ribs, thinly sliced
- Red lettuce leaves, optional

Direction

- Cook pasta following package directions. Drain and run under cold water.
- Mix together seasoned salt and pepper, onion, horseradish sauce, mayonnaise and sour cream in a large bowl. Stir in pasta, celery, cucumber and shrimp. Chill until serving. Serve on bed of lettuce if desired.

Nutrition Information

- Calories: 239 calories
- Total Carbohydrate: 20 g
- Cholesterol: 72 mg
- Total Fat: 12 g
- Fiber: 1 g
- Protein: 11 g
- Sodium: 344 mg

88. Creamy Red Potato Salad

""Reduced-fat mayonnaise make this dressing of nonfat yogurt richer and Dijon mustard helps it lighter in the conventional potato salad recipe.""
Serving: 8 | Ready in: 30m

Ingredients

- 3 lbs. red potatoes, scrubbed and cut into 1-inch pieces
- 1 tsp. salt
- 1 tbsp. cider vinegar
- Freshly ground pepper, to taste
- ½ cup nonfat plain yogurt
- ¼ cup reduced-fat mayonnaise
- 2 tbsps. Dijon mustard
- ⅔ cup chopped celery
- ½ cup chopped scallions
- 2 tbsps. chopped fresh parsley
- 2 tbsps. chopped fresh dill

Direction

- In a large saucepan, pour cold water over potatoes, season with salt and boil over medium heat. Cook for 7- 9 minutes until tender. Drain and remove potatoes to a large bowl. Mix with vinegar and add pepper to taste. Allow to cool.
- Combine mustard, mayonnaise, and yogurt in a small bowl, mix well. Pour into potatoes, then, add dill, parsley, scallions, and celery, mix gently until well combined. Add pepper and salt to adjust seasonings.

Nutrition Information

- Calories: 151 calories;
- Total Carbohydrate: 31 g
- Cholesterol: 2 mg
- Total Fat: 2 g
- Fiber: 3 g
- Protein: 4 g
- Sodium: 451 mg
- Sugar: 4 g
- Saturated Fat: 0 g

89. Deli-style Potato Salad

"This potato salad is very tangy, flavorful, crunchy and creamy with the addition of radishes, pickles and special Miracle Whip in the dressing."
Serving: 8 servings. | Prep: 20m | Ready in: 35m

Ingredients

- 1 lb. potatoes, peeled and cubed
- 6 hard-boiled large eggs; divided use
- 8 whole baby dill pickles, sliced
- 1 small onion, chopped
- 4 radishes, sliced
- DRESSING:
- 1 cup Miracle Whip
- 1 tbsp. 2% milk
- 1 tsp. prepared mustard
- 1/2 tsp. dill pickle juice
- 1/4 tsp. sugar
- 1/4 tsp. salt
- 1/4 tsp. pepper
- Paprika, optional

Direction

- In a big saucepan, add potatoes and water to cover, then bring to a boil. Lower heat, then cover and cook until softened about 10 to 15 minutes. Drain a set aside to cool.
- Chop 4 eggs coarsely. Mix together radishes, onion, pickles and chopped eggs in a big bowl, then put in potatoes. Mix together pepper, salt, sugar, pickle juice, mustard, milk and Miracle Whip in a small bowl, then drizzle over potato mixture and stir to blend.
- Slice leftover eggs and place over salad then sprinkle with paprika if wanted. Before serving, cover and chill about 4 hours.

Nutrition Information

- Calories: 197 calories
- Total Carbohydrate: 15 g
- Cholesterol: 150 mg
- Total Fat: 12 g

- Fiber: 1 g
- Protein: 6 g
- Sodium: 1045 mg

90. Dilly Potato & Egg Salad

"With the will to learn to cook for my husband when I was a young bride 36 years ago, I customed this recipe for potato salad from my mom's and my mother-in-law's recipes. This is my favorite!"
Serving: 12 servings (3/4 cup each). | Prep: 20m | Ready in: 40m

Ingredients

- 4 lbs. medium red potatoes (about 14), peeled and halved
- 5 hard-boiled large eggs
- 1 cup chopped dill pickles
- 1 small onion, chopped
- 1-1/2 cups mayonnaise
- 1 tsp. celery seed
- 1/2 tsp. salt
- 1/4 tsp. pepper
- Paprika

Direction

- In a large sauce pan, put in potatoes and enough water to cover the potatoes. Bring it to a boil. Lower the heat; continue cooking for 15-20 minutes without cover until it turns tender.
- Cut potatoes into 3/4-in. cubes and transfer them into a large bowl. Peel and cut 4 eggs; slice after peeling the leftover eggs. Combine the potatoes with onion, pickles and chopped eggs. Stir in salt, pepper, celery seed and mayonnaise. Gently put in potato mixture.
- Drizzle with paprika and put sliced egg on top. Put it into the refrigerator for at least 2 hours with cover until ready to serve.

Nutrition Information

- Calories: 326 calories
- Total Carbohydrate: 25 g

- Cholesterol: 80 mg
- Total Fat: 22 g
- Fiber: 3 g
- Protein: 6 g
- Sodium: 413 mg

91. Dublin Potato Salad

"This potato salad will make you never go back to the plain potato salad and it also goes well with many different dishes."
Serving: 8 servings. | Prep: 25m | Ready in: 45m

Ingredients

- 3 large white potatoes (about 1-1/2 lbs.)
- 2 tbsps. white vinegar
- 2 tsps. sugar
- 1 tsp. celery seed
- 1 tsp. mustard seed
- 3/4 tsp. salt, divided
- 2 cups finely shredded cabbage
- 12 oz. cooked or canned corned beef, cubed
- 1/4 cup chopped dill pickle
- 1/4 cup sliced green onion
- 1 cup mayonnaise
- 1/4 cup milk

Direction

- Boil the potatoes, covered, in lightly salted water until softened. Drain, peel and cut into cubes. Mix together the 1/2 tsp salt, mustard seed, celery seed, sugar and vinegar, then pour over the still-warm potatoes. Cover and refrigerate.
- Gently fold in onion, pickle, corned beef and cabbage right before serving. Mix together the remaining 1/4 tsp salt, milk and mayonnaise, then drizzle over salad. Toss gently and serve in a cabbage-lined bowl.

Nutrition Information

- Calories: 434 calories
- Total Carbohydrate: 28 g

- Cholesterol: 53 mg
- Total Fat: 31 g
- Fiber: 3 g
- Protein: 11 g
- Sodium: 927 mg

92. Easy Sirloin Caesar Salad

"Save your time by allowing the bread and steak to cook on the grill. Fill this salad with flavors of Dijon mustard, lemon juice, and salad dressing."
Serving: 6 servings. | Prep: 5m | Ready in: 20m

Ingredients

- 1 cup creamy Caesar salad dressing
- 1/4 cup Dijon mustard
- 1/4 cup lemon juice
- 1 beef top sirloin steak (3/4 inch thick and 1 lb.)
- 6 slices French bread (1 inch thick)
- 12 cups torn romaine
- 1 medium tomato, chopped

Direction

- Mix mustard, lemon juice, and salad dressing in a small bowl, and reserve 3/4 cup of the mixture. Pour the reserved mixture into a big resealable plastic bag and stir in steak. Seal the bag and flip to coat. Store it inside the refrigerator for 60 minutes, flipping the bag occasionally to marinate well. Cover the bowl with the remaining dressing mixture and store it inside the refrigerator.
- Coat sides of the bread with the remaining 1/4 cup of the reserved mixture. Wet paper towel with cooking oil and clip it into the long-handled tongs. Use the tongs to coat the grill rack. Arrange the bread into the rack and grill each side, uncovered, over medium heat for 1-2 minutes until lightly toasted. Wrap the toasted bread in a foil and set aside.
- Drain the steak and discard its marinade. Cover the steak and grill each side for 5-8 minutes over medium heat until you think

that the meat is well-done and its temperature reaches 170°F (for medium-rare, the temperature must be 145°F; for medium, the temperature must be 160°F).

- Arrange tomato and romaine on a serving platter and top it with the diagonally sliced steak. Serve it together with the toasted bread and the remaining dressing, if desired.

Nutrition Information

- Calories: 424 calories
- Total Carbohydrate: 39 g
- Cholesterol: 57 mg
- Total Fat: 18 g
- Fiber: 4 g
- Protein: 25 g
- Sodium: 836 mg

93. Faux Potato Salad

"This potato salad has olives, carrots, cauliflower and many other unexpected crunchy ingredients."
Serving: 8 servings. | Prep: 20m | Ready in: 30m

Ingredients

- 1 medium head cauliflower, broken into florets
- 1 medium carrot, chopped
- 2 hard-boiled large eggs, chopped
- 4 green onions, chopped
- 1 celery rib, chopped
- 1/4 cup pitted green olives, halved lengthwise
- 1/4 cup thinly sliced radishes
- 1/4 cup chopped dill pickle
- 1/4 cup fat-free mayonnaise
- 1 tbsp. Dijon mustard
- 1/4 tsp. salt
- 1/8 tsp. pepper

Direction

- Pour an inch of water in a large saucepan; bring to a boil. Put in cauliflower florets; cook, with cover, for about 5-8 minutes till softened.

Drain and rinse under cold water. Pat dry then put in a large bowl. Add pickle, radishes, olives, celery, green onions, eggs and carrot.

- Mix the remaining ingredients in a small bowl. Transfer into the cauliflower mixture; toss to coat. Keep in the fridge until ready to serve.

Nutrition Information

- Calories: 61 calories
- Total Carbohydrate: 7 g
- Cholesterol: 54 mg
- Total Fat: 2 g
- Fiber: 3 g
- Protein: 3 g
- Sodium: 375 mg

94. Favorite Cucumber Salad

""This fresh-tasting salad would become your new favorite dish.""
Serving: 10 servings. | Prep: 15m | Ready in: 15m

Ingredients

- 2 cups sugar
- 1 cup cider vinegar
- 1 tbsp. salt
- 1 tbsp. celery seed
- 7 cups thinly sliced peeled cucumbers (about 6 medium)
- 1 large onion, chopped
- 1 medium green pepper, chopped

Direction

- Whisk celery seed, salt, vinegar, and sugar together in a large bowl. Add pepper, onion, and cucumbers; toss to combine. Cover, chill for at least an hour, occasionally stirring.

Nutrition Information

- Calories: 183 calories
- Total Carbohydrate: 45 g
- Cholesterol: 0 mg
- Total Fat: 0 g

- Fiber: 1 g
- Protein: 1 g
- Sodium: 713 mg

95. Fiesta Corn Chip Salad

"This corn salad is really easy to make and ideal to serve alongside with any main course."
Serving: 10 servings. | Prep: 10m | Ready in: 10m

Ingredients

- 2 cans (15-1/4 oz. each) whole kernel corn, drained
- 2 cups shredded Mexican cheese blend
- 1 medium sweet red pepper, chopped
- 1 cup mayonnaise
- 1/8 tsp. salt
- 1/8 tsp. pepper
- 1 package (9-1/4 oz.) chili cheese-flavored corn chips, crushed

Direction

- Mix together pepper, salt, mayonnaise, red pepper, cheese and corn in a big bowl. Refrigerate until serving. Stir in corn chips right before serving.

Nutrition Information

- Calories: 463 calories
- Total Carbohydrate: 25 g
- Cholesterol: 28 mg
- Total Fat: 35 g
- Fiber: 3 g
- Protein: 8 g
- Sodium: 789 mg

96. Fresh Antipasto Salad

"Marinate artichokes, mushrooms, broccoli, asparagus, and cauliflower in a homemade vinaigrette made with oregano, fresh parsley, and garlic. It's so delicious!"
Serving: 16 servings (3/4 cup each). | Prep: 35m | Ready in: 40m

Ingredients

- 3 cups cut fresh asparagus (2-inch pieces)
- 3 cups quartered fresh mushrooms
- 2 cans (14 oz. each) water-packed artichoke hearts, rinsed, drained and quartered
- 1-1/2 cups chopped fresh broccoli
- 5 oz. fresh mozzarella cheese pearls
- 1 cup chopped fresh cauliflower
- 1 cup julienned sweet red pepper
- 1 cup pitted Greek olives
- 8 pepperoncini, sliced
- VINAIGRETTE:
- 2/3 cup cider vinegar
- 1/4 cup olive oil
- 1/4 cup minced fresh parsley
- 4 garlic cloves, minced
- 1 tbsp. sugar
- 2 tsps. minced fresh oregano or 3/4 tsp. dried oregano
- 1 tsp. honey
- 1/4 tsp. salt
- 1/4 tsp. pepper

Direction

- Boil 5 cups of water in a large saucepan. Stir in asparagus and cook for 2-4 minutes, uncovered, until the asparagus is crisp-tender. Drain and soak it into ice water. Drain it again and pat to dry.
- Mix artichokes, cauliflower, olives, cooked asparagus, broccoli, mushrooms, cheese, red pepper, and pepperoncini in a huge bowl.
- Combine all the vinaigrette ingredients in a small bowl. Drizzle mixture over the salad, tossing the salad until well-coated. Cover and refrigerate for 2 hours before serving.

97. Fresh Corn & Arugula Salad

"Enjoy this colorful and refreshing salad that is delicious with every bite!"
Serving: 6 servings. | Prep: 20m | Ready in: 30m

Ingredients

- BASIL VINAIGRETTE:
- 1/2 cup olive oil
- 1/4 cup balsamic vinegar
- 3 tbsps. minced fresh basil
- 1 tsp. chopped shallot
- 1 tsp. minced fresh rosemary
- 1 tsp. lemon juice
- 1/4 tsp. salt
- 1/4 tsp. pepper
- SALAD:
- 2 ears fresh corn, husked
- 1 tsp. olive oil
- 8 cups fresh arugula or baby spinach
- 4 plum tomatoes, quartered
- 1/4 cup pecan halves, toasted
- 1/4 cup shaved Parmesan cheese

Direction

- Beat vinaigrette ingredients in a small sized bowl until combined.
- Brush oil on the corn and place on medium heat, grill with cover (alternative: you can broil corn 4 inches from heat), 8 to 10 minutes until tender, crispy and browned, flipping occasionally. Allow to cool before cutting corn off cobs and transfer into a big bowl.
- Toss pecans, arugula, and tomatoes into corn. Season with half of the vinaigrette, toss until coated. Add cheese over. Serve straightaway. Place the rest of vinaigrette in the refrigerator with cover to use later.

Nutrition Information

- Calories: 171 calories
- Total Carbohydrate: 9 g
- Cholesterol: 2 mg
- Total Fat: 14 g

- Fiber: 2 g
- Protein: 4 g
- Sodium: 120 mg

98. Fresh Fruit Combo

"This fruit salad is so eye-catching with the addition of cherries and blueberries that also brings a distinctive flavor."
Serving: 14 servings. | Prep: 20m | Ready in: 20m

Ingredients

- 2 cups cubed fresh pineapple
- 2 medium oranges, peeled and chopped
- 3 kiwifruit, peeled and sliced
- 1 cup sliced fresh strawberries
- 1 cup halved seedless red grapes
- 2 medium firm bananas, sliced
- 1 large red apple, cubed
- 1 cup fresh or frozen blueberries
- 1 cup fresh or canned pitted dark sweet cherries

Direction

- Mix the first 5 ingredients together in a big bowl, then chill until serving. To serve, stir in cherries, blueberries, bananas and apple.

Nutrition Information

- Calories: 78 calories
- Total Carbohydrate: 20 g
- Cholesterol: 0 mg
- Total Fat: 0 g
- Fiber: 3 g
- Protein: 1 g
- Sodium: 3 mg

99. Fresh Tomato & Cucumber Salad

"This dish is very easy to make."
Serving: 6 servings. | Prep: 20m | Ready in: 20m

Ingredients

- 1/4 cup lemon juice
- 1/4 cup olive oil
- 1 tbsp. minced fresh basil or 1 tsp. dried basil
- 1 tbsp. white wine vinegar
- 1 garlic clove, minced
- 1 tsp. minced fresh mint or 1/4 tsp. dried mint
- 1/8 tsp. kosher salt
- 1/8 tsp. coarsely ground pepper
- 4 plum tomatoes, seeded and chopped
- 2 medium cucumbers, chopped
- 1/2 cup Greek olives, sliced
- 2 cups torn mixed salad greens
- 3/4 cup crumbled feta cheese
- 1/4 cup pine nuts, toasted

Direction

- Mix the first 8 ingredients together in a small bowl, put aside.
- In a big bowl, mix olives with tomatoes and cucumbers. Use half of the dressing to sprinkle; mix to combine. Transfer the salad greens onto a big serving dish; put the tomato mixture on top. Use the rest of the dressing, pine nuts and cheese to sprinkle.

Nutrition Information

- Calories: 209 calories
- Total Carbohydrate: 9 g
- Cholesterol: 8 mg
- Total Fat: 17 g
- Fiber: 3 g
- Protein: 6 g
- Sodium: 366 mg

100. Garden Vegetable Pasta Salad

"Start your day with this colorful and tasty garden vegetable pasta salad!"
Serving: 4 servings | Prep: 20m | Ready in: 20m

Ingredients

- 1-3/4 cups farfalle (bow-tie pasta) , uncooked
- 2 cups cut-up fresh asparagus spears (1 inch lengths)
- 1/4 cup KRAFT Classic Ranch Dressing
- 1/4 cup KRAFT Real Mayo Mayonnaise
- 1/2 cup finely chopped red onion s
- 2 cups halved cherry tomatoes
- 1/4 cup KRAFT Grated Parmesan Cheese
- 1/4 cup chopped fresh basil

Direction

- Follow packaging directions to cook pasta, don't add salt and put asparagus into boiling water for the last 3 minutes.
- While waiting, in a big bowl, combine mayo and dressing. Stir in the onions and toss in tomatoes, basil, cheese, and pasta mixture; stir lightly.
- Serve immediately or keep in the refrigerator with cover until time to serve.

Nutrition Information

- Calories: 430
- Total Carbohydrate: 52 g
- Cholesterol: 15 mg
- Total Fat: 19 g
- Fiber: 5 g
- Protein: 13 g
- Sodium: 360 mg
- Sugar: 8 g
- Saturated Fat: 4 g

101. Garden-fresh Taco Salad

"I usually like making this on summer vacation for my mom."
Serving: 4 servings. | Prep: 30m | Ready in: 30m

Ingredients

- 1 lb. ground beef
- 1 envelope taco seasoning, divided
- 1 large head lettuce, shredded
- 4 medium tomatoes, seeded and diced
- 1 medium onion, chopped
- 2 cups shredded cheddar cheese
- 1 cup Miracle Whip
- 1 tbsp. salsa
- Leaf lettuce
- Crushed tortilla chips

Direction

- Cook beef on medium heat in a big skillet until it's not pink then drain. Mix in half of taco seasoning. Take off from heat, mix in shredded lettuce, cheese, onion, and tomatoes.
- Mix the remaining taco seasoning, salsa, and miracle whip in a small bowl. Pour on salad then toss until coated.
- Line leaf lettuce on a platter or big bowl. Top with taco salad. Place tortilla chips around the edge.

Nutrition Information

- Calories: 677 calories
- Total Carbohydrate: 31 g
- Cholesterol: 150 mg
- Total Fat: 46 g
- Fiber: 4 g
- Protein: 35 g
- Sodium: 1742 mg

102. Green Bean Salad With Bacon

"This salad can be served either warm or cold and is suitable for any occasion."
Serving: 8 servings. | Prep: 10m | Ready in: 30m

Ingredients

- 1-1/2 lbs. fresh green beans, trimmed
- 4 bacon strips, chopped
- 2 medium onions, thinly sliced
- 1/4 cup cider vinegar
- 2 tbsps. sugar
- 2 tbsps. brown sugar
- 1 tsp. salt

Direction

- In a big saucepan, add beans then pour in enough water to cover. Bring to a boil, then cook without a cover until crisp-tender, about 4 to 7 minutes. Drain.
- Cook bacon in a big skillet over moderate heat until crisp while stirring sometimes. Transfer to paper towels to drain off fat with a slotted spoon. Get rid of drippings but save 2 tbsp. drippings in pan.
- Put the onions into drippings then cook and stir until softened. Stir in salt, sugar and vinegar until combined. Put in beans then toss together and heat through. Place bacon on top.

103. Grilled Corn Salad

""Satisfy your salad cravings with this delicious and easy-to-prepare recipe. Prepare this salad ahead and just store it in the fridge in an airtight container then you're good for the next couple of days! Best paired with grilled dishes but certainly tastes good in itself as well.""
Serving: 6 | Prep: 15m | Ready in: 1h10m

Ingredients

- 6 ears freshly shucked corn
- 1 green pepper, diced
- 2 Roma (plum) tomatoes, diced
- 1/4 cup diced red onion

- 1/2 bunch fresh cilantro, chopped, or more to taste
- 2 tsps. olive oil, or to taste
- salt and ground black pepper to taste

Direction

- Preheat the outdoor grill to medium heat and slightly grease the grill grate with oil.
- Put the corn onto the preheated grill and let it grill for about 10 minutes until the corn is soft and slightly charred, turn the corn from time to time; let it cool down until cool enough to the touch. Take the kernels off from the corn cob and put it in a bowl.
- Mix the grilled corn kernels together with the cilantro, diced tomato, olive oil, green pepper and onion. Put pepper and salt to taste then mix until well-combined. Put it aside for a minimum of 30 minutes and let the flavors seep through the salad right before serving.

Nutrition Information

- Calories: 103 calories;
- Total Carbohydrate: 19.7 g
- Cholesterol: 0 mg
- Total Fat: 2.8 g
- Protein: 3.4 g
- Sodium: 43 mg

104. Grilled Firecracker Potato Salad

"If you want a little kick in your salad then this yummy potato salad recipe is for you!"
Serving: 16 servings (1 cup each). | Prep: 20m | Ready in: 40m

Ingredients

- 3 lbs. small red potatoes (about 30), quartered
- 2 tbsps. olive oil
- 1 tsp. salt
- 1/2 tsp. pepper
- DRESSING:

- 1-1/2 cups mayonnaise
- 1/2 cup finely chopped onion
- 1/4 cup Dijon mustard
- 2 tbsps. sweet pickle relish
- 1/2 tsp. paprika
- 1/4 tsp. cayenne pepper
- SALAD:
- 6 hard-boiled large eggs, chopped
- 2 celery ribs, finely chopped
- Minced fresh chives, optional

Direction

- Mix the potatoes, pepper, oil and salt together and put it in a grill basket or grill wok. Place it on a grill on medium heat then cover and let it grill for 20-25 minutes until the potatoes have softened, stir the mixture occasionally. In a big bowl, put in the potatoes and let it cool down a bit.
- Combine all the dressing ingredients together in a small bowl and mix well. Mix the celery, dressing and eggs into the potatoes until well-blended. Cover the bowl and keep it in the fridge for 1-2 hours until chilled. Top it with chives if you want.

Nutrition Information

- Calories: 265 calories
- Total Carbohydrate: 16 g
- Cholesterol: 77 mg
- Total Fat: 20 g
- Fiber: 2 g
- Protein: 4 g
- Sodium: 398 mg

105. Grilled Italian Potato Salad

"Don't bore yourself with the same grilled recipe every single day or week. This potato salad is a good way to level up your grilled dish the healthy way! This salad recipe incorporates Italian flavors in it but you can absolutely incorporate any flavor you prefer."
Serving: 20 servings (3/4 cup each). | Prep: 25m | Ready in: 40m

Ingredients

- 3 lbs. fingerling potatoes
- 1 large red onion, cut into 3/4-inch slices
- 1 medium sweet red pepper, halved and seeded
- 1/4 cup olive oil
- 3/4 tsp. salt
- 1/2 tsp. pepper
- 1 lb. hard salami, cubed
- 8 oz. smoked mozzarella cheese, cut into 1/2-inch cubes
- 2 cups grape tomatoes, halved
- 1 can (14 oz.) water-packed artichoke hearts, well drained and chopped
- 2/3 cup fresh basil leaves, torn
- 1/2 cup Italian salad dressing
- 1/4 cup Greek olives, chopped

Direction

- In a 6-quart stockpot, put in the potatoes and pour in water until the potatoes are soaked. Let it boil. Lower the heat and let it cook without cover for 15-20 minutes until softened. Drain the potatoes.
- Combine the sweet pepper, potatoes, onion, pepper, oil and salt together in a big bowl and mix. Put the vegetables in a grill basket or a grill wok then put it on a grill rack. Put it on a grill on medium heat then cover and grill or put the vegetables in a broiler and let it broil 4 inches away from the heat for 15-20 minutes until soft, stir the vegetables occasionally.
- Halve the potatoes lengthwise then place in a big bowl. Chop the sweet pepper and onion roughly then put it into the potato mixture. Mix in the remaining ingredients until well-

coated. Serve the salad cold or while still warm.

106. Grilled Red Potato Salad With Blue Cheese And Bacon

"Summer is here! Turn your old-fashioned side dish into a refreshing salad. This is perfect with grilled meat."
Serving: 9 servings. | Prep: 20m | Ready in: 60m

Ingredients

- 3 lbs. small red potatoes, quartered
- 1 small red onion, thinly sliced
- 2 tbsps. olive oil
- 1 tsp. kosher salt
- 1 tsp. pepper
- 1 cup mayonnaise
- 1/4 cup minced chives
- 1/4 cup white balsamic vinegar
- 2 tsps. sugar
- 2 tsps. Dijon mustard
- 1 cup (4 oz.) crumbled blue cheese
- 6 bacon strips, cooked and crumbled

Direction

- Mix pepper, oil, salt, potatoes, and onions in a big bowl. Distribute mixture between 2 double thicknesses of heavy-duty foil (around 18 inches square). Wrap foil around mixture and tightly seal.
- On medium heat, grill the potatoes with cover, while flipping once, for 40 to 45 minutes until tender. Gently open foil, allow steam to escape. Place the potato mixture into a big bowl.
- Mix vinegar, mustard, chives, mayonnaise, and sugar in a small sized bowl then toss potatoes to coat. Add over bacon and blue cheese.

Nutrition Information

- Calories: 402 calories
- Total Carbohydrate: 28 g
- Cholesterol: 25 mg
- Total Fat: 29 g
- Fiber: 3 g
- Protein: 8 g
- Sodium: 687 mg

107. Grilled Romaine With Chive-buttermilk Dressing

"Prepare this special and yummy side dish for yourself or the family. You can try this salad with chicken as well."
Serving: 4 servings. | Prep: 15m | Ready in: 25m

Ingredients

- 2 romaine hearts, halved lengthwise
- 3 tbsps. olive oil
- 3 tbsps. buttermilk
- 3 tbsps. reduced-fat plain Greek yogurt
- 4 tsps. minced fresh chives
- 2 tsps. lemon juice
- 1/2 tsp. minced garlic
- Dash salt
- Dash pepper
- 1/4 cup shredded Parmesan cheese
- 4 bacon strips, cooked and crumbled

Direction

- Use a brush to coat the halved romaine with oil. Put the coated romaine on an open grill and let it grill for 6-8 minutes on medium-high heat until the leaves are wilted and have changed in color, turn it once to cook both sides.
- While the romaine is grilling, mix the lemon juice, buttermilk, pepper, salt, chives, garlic and yogurt together until well-combined then pour the yogurt mixture on top of the cut sides of the romaine. Finish off with bacon and cheese on top.

Nutrition Information

- Calories: 176 calories
- Total Carbohydrate: 3 g
- Cholesterol: 13 mg

- Total Fat: 15 g
- Fiber: 1 g
- Protein: 7 g
- Sodium: 299 mg

108. Grilled Romaine With Swiss

"A very quick and simple to prepare vegetable salad dish that you just won't get enough of once tasted."
Serving: 4 servings. | Prep: 10m | Ready in: 15m

Ingredients

- 2 romaine hearts, halved lengthwise
- 1 tbsp. olive oil
- 1/8 tsp. salt
- 1/8 tsp. pepper
- 1/3 cup prepared raspberry vinaigrette
- 1/2 cup shredded Swiss cheese
- 1/2 cup dried cherries
- 1/3 cup chopped walnuts

Direction

- Use a brush to coat the romaine with oil then season it with pepper and salt.
- Use tongs to lightly rub an oiled paper towel on the grill rack. Put the seasoned romaine on a grill on medium heat then cover and let it grill for 30 seconds on every side until thoroughly heated. Put the grilled romaine on a platter and pour in the vinaigrette. Top it off with walnuts, cheese and cherries.

Nutrition Information

- Calories: 299 calories
- Total Carbohydrate: 17 g
- Cholesterol: 12 mg
- Total Fat: 24 g
- Fiber: 2 g
- Protein: 7 g
- Sodium: 282 mg

109. Grilled Salmon Salad

"Try this recipe for fresh-tasting salmon salad for a cool summer meal. It's was created by the Test Kitchen staff. It's dressed lightly with tangy raspberry vinegar and has a little crunch from celery and onion."
Serving: 4 servings. | Prep: 25m | Ready in: 25m

Ingredients

- 2 salmon fillets (about 1-1/2 lbs.)
- 2 celery ribs, chopped
- 1/2 cup finely chopped red onion
- 2 tbsps. snipped fresh dill or 2 tsps. dill weed
- DRESSING:
- 1/4 cup raspberry vinegar
- 1 tbsp. olive oil
- 1-1/2 tsps. sugar
- 1/2 tsp. salt
- 1/4 tsp. pepper

Direction

- Chop the salmon fillets to 4-in. pieces widthwise. Use cooking oil to moisten a paper towel with long-handled tongs and the coat the grill rack lightly.
- Grill while covered on medium-hot heat or broil for 12 to 15 minutes, 4 inches away from heat source or until the fish easily flakes using a fork. Cover and then chill for 1 hour.
- Remove skin, bone and then flake the salmon. Put in a big bowl. Add dill, onion, and celery. Mix the dressing ingredients and then spread on top of salad. Mix gently to coat. You can serve right away or cover and chill and mix before serving.

Nutrition Information

- Calories: 317 calories
- Total Carbohydrate: 5 g
- Cholesterol: 85 mg
- Total Fat: 19 g
- Fiber: 1 g
- Protein: 29 g
- Sodium: 397 mg

110. Grilled Scallop Salad

"A green salad recipe with scallops, asparagus, bacon and walnuts served with dressing of walnut oil and balsamic vinegar."
Serving: 4 servings. | Prep: 20m | Ready in: 35m

Ingredients

- 24 asparagus spears, trimmed
- 2 tbsp. olive oil
- 1 tsp. soy sauce
- 24 sea scallops
- 2 cups sliced fresh mushrooms
- 2 cups torn red leaf lettuce
- 2 cups torn Bibb lettuce or Boston lettuce
- 1/4 cup crumbled cooked bacon
- 1 cup chopped walnuts, toasted
- 2 tbsps. grated Romano cheese
- 1/2 cup balsamic vinaigrette salad dressing

Direction

- Boil 6 cups of water in a big saucepan. Put in asparagus; cover up and let boil for 3 minutes. Drain off and put asparagus instantly into ice water. Drain off and pat dry; put aside. In a big plastic bag that is resealable, mix soy sauce and oil; put in scallops. Seal the bag and coat by flipping. Let rest for 10 minutes.
- Drain and get rid of marinade. Moisten a paper towel with cooking oil using long-handled tongs and slightly coat the grill rack. Grill scallops, without cover, on medium heat for 7-8 minutes on each side till the scallops are opaque and firm.
- On a basket or grill wok, arrange mushrooms. Grill without cover on medium heat until soft, mixing frequently, for 10 to 15 minutes.
- Arrange lettuce among 4 serving dishes. Put cheese, walnuts, bacon, mushrooms, scallops and asparagus on top. Sprinkle with dressing.

111. Grilled Sirloin Salad

"Add all the greens that you like in this salad and grill, to give more flavor and taste to this dish. Serve this steak together with grilled baguette, sun-dried tomato tapenade, and a cold beer."
Serving: 2 | Ready in: 35m

Ingredients

- 1 tbsp. reduced-sodium soy sauce
- 1 tbsp. balsamic vinegar
- 1 tsp. toasted sesame oil
- 1 tsp. brown sugar
- ½ tsp. finely chopped fresh ginger
- 1 clove garlic, peeled and smashed
- ½ tsp. coarsely ground pepper
- 8 oz. sirloin steak, trimmed of fat
- ⅛ tsp. salt
- 8 scallions, white part only
- ½ red bell pepper, seeded
- 6 cups torn salad greens, such as escarole, curly endive, radicchio and/or watercress

Direction

- Set the griller on high heat and preheat. In a big bowl, combine sugar, oil, soy sauce, garlic, ginger, and vinegar. Whisk the mixture well until the sugar is completely dissolved.
- Flavor each side of the steak with pepper and salt. In a griller, arrange the steak, bell pepper, and scallions and cook for 4 minutes. After 4 minutes, flip the vegetables and steak, and then cook for 3-4 more minutes until the steak is medium-rare and the vegetables are burned.
- Allow the steak to rest for 5 minutes before cutting it across the grain and chop it into thin slices. Chop each scallion into 1-inch slices and slice the bell pepper into big strips. Add the sliced greens into the dressing, tossing them well to coat. Distribute the mixture into 2 plates and top each with vegetables and steak.

Nutrition Information

- Calories: 251 calories;

- Total Carbohydrate: 17 g
- Cholesterol: 67 mg
- Total Fat: 8 g
- Fiber: 6 g
- Protein: 30 g
- Sodium: 517 mg
- Sugar: 8 g
- Saturated Fat: 2 g

112. Grilled Skirt Steak With Red Peppers & Onions

"Grilled vegetables and steak make a really great pair for a lovely lunch or dinner get-together! Try it now!"
Serving: 6 servings. | Prep: 01h30m | Ready in: 01h50m

Ingredients

- 1/2 cup apple juice
- 1/2 cup red wine vinegar
- 1/4 cup finely chopped onion
- 2 tbsps. rubbed sage
- 3 tsps. ground coriander
- 3 tsps. ground mustard
- 3 tsps. freshly ground pepper
- 1 tsp. salt
- 1 garlic clove, minced
- 1 cup olive oil
- 1 beef skirt steak (1-1/2 lbs.), cut into 5-in. pieces
- 2 medium red onions, cut into 1/2-inch slices
- 2 medium sweet red peppers, halved
- 12 green onions, trimmed

Direction

- Mix the first 9 ingredients together in a small bowl until well-combined then slowly add in the oil and mix well. In a big resealable plastic bag, put in 1 1/2 cups of the marinade mixture. Put in the beef then seal the bag and turn to coat the beef with the marinade. Keep it in the fridge throughout the night. Cover the remaining marinade mixture and keep it in the fridge as well.
- Mix 1/4 cup of the reserved marinade mixture and the remaining vegetables together in a big bowl. Put the peppers and red onions onto a grill over medium heat then cover and let it cook for 4 to 6 minutes on every side until the vegetables have softened. Put the green onions onto the grill and let it grill for 1 to 2 minutes on every side until the green onions have softened.
- Drain the marinated beef and throw away the marinade mixture with the bag. Put the marinated beef onto a grill over medium heat then cover; let it grill for 4 to 6 minutes on every side until the preferred meat doneness is achieved (a thermometer inserted on the meat should indicate 145°F for medium-well, 140°F for medium and 135°F for medium-rare), use the remaining reserved marinade mixture to baste the beef in the last 4 minutes of grilling. Allow the grilled beef to rest for 5 minutes.
- Slice the grilled vegetables into bite-sized pieces then place them in a big bowl. Cut the steak into thin diagonal slices perpendicular to the grain then put it into the same bowl as the grilled vegetables; mix everything together until well-combined.

Nutrition Information

- Calories: 461 calories
- Total Carbohydrate: 12 g
- Cholesterol: 67 mg
- Total Fat: 32 g
- Fiber: 3 g
- Protein: 32 g
- Sodium: 311 mg

113. Grilled Southwestern Potato Salad

"Craving for a Tex-Mex dish? Try this salad recipe and enjoy it at your next barbeque."
Serving: 6 servings. | Prep: 40m | Ready in: 60m

Ingredients

- 1-1/2 lbs. large red potatoes, quartered lengthwise
- 3 tbsps. olive oil
- 2 poblano peppers
- 2 medium ears sweet corn, husks removed
- 1/2 cup buttermilk
- 1/2 cup sour cream
- 1 tbsp. lime juice
- 1 jalapeno pepper, seeded and minced
- 1 tbsp. minced fresh cilantro
- 1-1/2 tsps. garlic salt
- 1 tsp. ground cumin
- 1/4 to 1/2 tsp. cayenne pepper
- Lime wedges

Direction

- In a big pot, put potatoes and water to cover potatoes. Boil and lower heat. Cook without cover for 5 minutes. Remove water from potatoes, add oil and toss.
- On high heat, grill with cover while occasionally flipping the poblanos for 8 to 10 minutes until skins are blackened and blistered on all sides. Put peppers straightaway into a small sized bowl, cover, and set aside for 20 minutes. Lower grill heat to medium.
- On medium heat, grill with cover while occasionally flipping the potatoes and corn for 12 to 15 minutes until lightly browned and tender. Let it slightly cool.
- Peel off the skin of poblanos and discard; take out the seeds and stems. Slice peppers into 1/2 in pieces and transfer to a big bowl. Chop corn from cobs and slice potatoes into 3/4 inch pieces. Toss into peppers.
- Beat lime juice, buttermilk, and sour cream in a small-sized bowl until combined. Whisk in cilantro, seasonings, and jalapeno. Stir into potato mixture, adding more dressing as desired to coat. Serve with lime slices and keep leftovers in the refrigerator.

Nutrition Information

- Calories: 229 calories
- Total Carbohydrate: 28 g
- Cholesterol: 14 mg
- Total Fat: 11 g
- Fiber: 3 g
- Protein: 5 g
- Sodium: 301 mg

114. Grilled Steak Salad With Tomatoes & Avocado

"With our busy schedules, I doubt if we can still cook and prepare an amazing steak for dinner. I decided to make a simple twist on our traditional steak recipe, and I came up with this delicious steak. I served it together with a salad that is mixed with lemon and cilantro. My husband loves it!"
Serving: 6 servings. | Prep: 20m | Ready in: 30m

Ingredients

- 1 beef top sirloin steak (1-1/4 inches thick and 1-1/2 lbs.)
- 1 tbsp. olive oil
- 3 tsps. Creole seasoning
- 2 large tomatoes, chopped
- 1 can (15 oz.) white kidney or cannellini beans, rinsed and drained
- 1 can (15 oz.) black beans, rinsed and drained
- 3 green onions, chopped
- 1/4 cup minced fresh cilantro
- 2 tsps. grated lemon peel
- 2 tbsps. lemon juice
- 1/4 tsp. salt
- 1 medium ripe avocado, peeled and cubed (1/2 inch)

Direction

- Coat both sides of the steak with oil. Sprinkle Creole seasoning on the steak before grilling it. Cook and grill it over medium heat for 5-8 minutes per side, covered. You can also broil the steak 4-inches away from the heat source until the meat reached its desired doneness. The following are the meat's doneness and its internal temperature: for medium-rare, 145°F; for medium, 160°F; for well-done, 170°F. Allow the meat to cool for 5 minutes.
- Mix cilantro, lemon juice, salt, tomatoes, green onions, lemon peel, and beans together in a large bowl. Add avocado and slightly combine the mixture. Cut the steak into small slices and serve it together with the bean mixture.

115.Grilled Veggie Fettuccine Salad

"Colorful and delightful meal without meat! Serve for dinner or lunch."
Serving: 6 servings. | Prep: 20m | Ready in: 40m

Ingredients

- 8 oz. uncooked fettuccine
- 1 large green pepper
- 1 large sweet red pepper
- 1 small eggplant, peeled and cut into 3/4-inch-thick slices
- 3 onion slices (3/4 inch thick)
- Cooking spray
- 1 medium tomato, chopped
- 2 tbsps. balsamic vinegar
- 1 tbsp. olive oil
- 1 garlic clove, minced
- 1 tsp. Italian seasoning
- 1 tsp. minced fresh parsley
- 1/2 tsp. salt
- 1/2 tsp. dried rosemary, crushed
- 1/2 tsp. coarsely ground pepper

Direction

- Follow packaging instructions to cook fettuccine. Slice off ends of peppers and slice lengthwise into quarters. Using cooking spray coat both sides of eggplant and onion slices.
- Prepare paper towel and moisten with cooking oil and coat grill rack lightly with long-handled tongs. On medium heat, grill with cover the vegetables for 4 to 5 minutes a side until tender and crispy. Let slightly cool before cutting into bite-size pieces.
- Drain the fettuccine and wash with cold water. Place into a big bowl and put the tomato and grilled vegetables. Beat the rest of the ingredients in a small sized bowl and toss over fettuccine mixture until coated. Keep in refrigerator until ready to serve.

Nutrition Information

- Calories: 184 calories
- Total Carbohydrate: 34 g
- Cholesterol: 0 mg
- Total Fat: 3 g
- Fiber: 4 g
- Protein: 6 g
- Sodium: 215 mg

116. Guacamole Mousse With Salsa

"I do love this colorful guacamole, capturing flavor of the Southwest because of great combination of cool creamy topped with zesty salsa."
Serving: 18-24 servings. | Prep: 30m | Ready in: 30m

Ingredients

- 3 medium ripe avocados, peeled and pitted
- 4 tsps. lemon juice
- 3/4 tsp. chili powder
- 1/4 tsp. salt
- Pinch white pepper
- 3 plum tomatoes, peeled, seeded and chopped
- 1 cup sour cream
- 1 cup heavy whipping cream
- 1/3 cup mayonnaise
- 4 tsps. finely chopped onion
- 2 envelopes unflavored gelatin

- 1/4 cup cold water
- 3 tbsps. minced fresh cilantro
- SALSA:
- 5 plum tomatoes, seeded and diced
- 2 medium sweet red peppers, diced
- 1 to 2 medium jalapeno peppers, seeded and minced
- 1/4 cup finely chopped onion
- 4 tsps. lime juice
- 4 tsps. olive oil
- 1/8 to 1/4 tsp. salt

Direction

- Cover then process avocados, lemon juice, pepper, salt and chili powder in a food processor until smooth. Put in a bowl; pour tomatoes, onion, cream, sour cream and mayonnaise.
- Sprinkle gelatin on cold water in a small saucepan; allow to stand for 1 minute. Cook on low heat, and stir until gelatin is dissolved. Pour in avocado mixture, stir. Add the mixture in a 6-cup mold greased with cooking spray; sprinkle cilantro. Cool down until set.
- At the same time, mix salsa ingredients; keep chilled. When serving, unmold mousse onto a platter; best served with salsa.

Nutrition Information

- Calories: 132 calories
- Total Carbohydrate: 4 g
- Cholesterol: 21 mg
- Total Fat: 12 g
- Fiber: 2 g
- Protein: 2 g
- Sodium: 69 mg

117. Layered Taco Salad

"Active time: 45 minutes; start to finish time: 45 minutes"
Serving: Makes 6 servings

Ingredients

- 1/4 cup fresh lime juice
- 1/2 cup chopped fresh cilantro
- 1 tsp. sugar
- 1 tbsp. chili powder
- 1/4 tsp. ground cumin
- 1/2 tsp. salt
- 1/4 tsp. black pepper
- 1/2 cup olive oil
- 1 medium onion, chopped
- 3 garlic cloves, finely chopped
- 1 to 2 fresh serrano chiles (including seeds), finely chopped
- 1 tbsp. chili powder
- 2 tsps. ground cumin
- 2 tbsps. olive oil
- 1 1/2 lb ground chuck
- 1 (8-oz) can tomato sauce
- 1/2 tsp. salt
- 1/4 tsp. black pepper
- 1 (1/2-lb) firm-ripe California avocado
- 1 head iceberg lettuce, thinly sliced (8 cups)
- 1 large tomato (1/2 lb), chopped
- 1/4 lb coarsely grated extra-sharp Cheddar (1 1/2 cups)
- 1 (15- to 19-oz) can black beans, drained and rinsed
- 1 (6-oz) can sliced pitted California black olives, drained
- Accompaniment: tortilla chips

Direction

- For the dressing: Mix chili powder, salt, lime juice, pepper, cumin, cilantro, and sugar. Add oil gradually in a stream, mix until the mixture emulsified.
- For the beef: Heat oil in a 12-inch heavy skillet over medium heat. Cook cumin, garlic, chili powder, onion, and chilies to taste for 6 minutes, stirring it for some time until the

onion is tender. Stir in beef and cook for 5 minutes, stirring and breaking up the lumps until the meat is no longer pink. Remove any excess fat from skillet.

- Pour tomato sauce, pepper, and salt into the browned beef and cook for 3 minutes, stirring it frequently until slightly thickened. Remove the mixture from heat.
- For the salad: Peel and pit the avocado and cut into halves. Slice it into 1/2-inch pieces.
- In a shallow 4-qt dish, arrange the lettuce over the bottom. Pour the beef mixture evenly on top of the lettuce. Make another layer on top by arranging avocado, beans, olives, cheese, and tomatoes. Spread the dressing all over the salad.

Nutrition Information

- Calories: 667
- Total Carbohydrate: 30 g
- Cholesterol: 100 mg
- Total Fat: 46 g
- Fiber: 12 g
- Protein: 40 g
- Sodium: 1208 mg
- Saturated Fat: 12 g

118.Loaded Potato Salad

"This salad is so rich and restaurant quality. You will need green onions, shredded cheddar, bacon, sour cream, and some more to make this."
Serving: 8 servings. | Prep: 15m | Ready in: 30m

Ingredients

- 2 lbs. red potatoes, quartered
- 1/2 lb. bacon strips, chopped
- 1/2 cup mayonnaise
- 1/4 cup creamy Caesar salad dressing
- 1/4 cup ranch salad dressing
- 3 tbsps. sour cream
- 1 tbsp. Dijon mustard
- 3 green onions, chopped
- 1/4 cup shredded cheddar cheese

- Coarsely ground pepper, optional

Direction

- In a large saucepan, put potatoes in and pour water in until cover. Boil it. Decrease the heat. Put a cover on and cook until softened or for 15-20 minutes.
- In the meantime, in a large frying pan on medium heat, cook bacon in until crunchy. Move onto paper towels, strain, save 3 spoons of drippings.
- Strain potatoes and put in a big bowl. Add the saved drippings and bacon, mix to coat. Put in the fridge until chilled.
- In a small bowl, mix mustard, sour cream, dressings, and mayonnaise. Pour over the potato mixture, mix to coat. Mix in cheese and onion. If you want, use pepper to drizzle.

Nutrition Information

- Calories: 365 calories
- Total Carbohydrate: 19 g
- Cholesterol: 24 mg
- Total Fat: 28 g
- Fiber: 2 g
- Protein: 7 g
- Sodium: 497 mg

---

119. Make-ahead Broccoli Salad

"This salad is a perfect medley of mixed dried fruit and vegetables that is so refreshing and crunchy."
Serving: 8 servings. | Prep: 15m | Ready in: 15m

Ingredients

- 2 bunches broccoli, cut into bite-size pieces (about 6 cups)
- 1/2 cup mixed dried fruit, chopped
- 1/2 cup chopped sweet onion
- 3/4 cup mayonnaise
- 1/4 cup honey
- Dash salt
- 4 bacon strips, cooked and crumbled

Direction

- Mix together onion, dried fruit and broccoli in a big bowl. Combine salt, honey and mayonnaise in a small bowl then drizzle over broccoli mixture and toss to coat well. Cover and chill for 2 hours or overnight. Place on top with bacon right before serving.

---

120. Mama's Warm German Potato Salad

"This recipe belongs to my grandmother and every family gathering of ours has this salad."
Serving: 12 servings. | Prep: 20m | Ready in: 50m

Ingredients

- 3 lbs. small red potatoes
- 1/3 cup canola oil
- 2 tbsps. champagne vinegar
- 1 tsp. kosher salt
- 1/2 tsp. coarsely ground pepper
- 1/2 English cucumber, very thinly sliced
- 2 celery ribs, thinly sliced
- 1 small onion, chopped
- 6 bacon strips, cooked and crumbled
- 1 tbsp. minced fresh parsley

Direction

- In a big saucepan, put potatoes and fill with water. Boil it. Decrease the heat, cook without a cover for 18-21 minutes until softened. Strain, let cool slightly. Take the skin off and cut thinly. Mix together pepper, salt, vinegar, and oil. Add potatoes and mix to coat. Add the rest of the ingredients, mix to coat. Eat warm.

Nutrition Information

- Calories: 163 calories
- Total Carbohydrate: 20 g
- Cholesterol: 4 mg
- Total Fat: 8 g
- Fiber: 2 g
- Protein: 4 g

- Sodium: 246 mg

121. Mexican Garden Salad

"Like a taco salad with extra tasty veggies!"
Serving: 6-8 servings. | Prep: 20m | Ready in: 40m

Ingredients

- 1 lb. ground beef
- 1 jar (16 oz.) thick and chunky salsa, divided
- 1/4 cup water
- 1 envelope taco seasoning
- 1-1/2 heads iceberg lettuce, torn
- 3 cups broccoli florets (about 1/2 lb.)
- 1 small red onion, thinly sliced into rings
- 1 medium carrot, shredded
- 1 large tomato, chopped
- 1 can (4 oz.) chopped green chilies, drained
- 1/2 to 1 cup shredded cheddar cheese
- 1 cup sour cream
- Tortilla chips, optional

Direction

- Cook beef in a big skillet on medium heat until it's not pink then drain. Add taco seasoning, water, and 1 cup of salsa; boil. Reduce heat then simmer for twenty minutes then cool.
- Layer vegetables in the order given in a 3-4-quart glass bowl. Top with cheese, beef mixture, and chilies. Mix remaining salsa and sour cream. Serve with the salad and tortilla chips if preferred.

Nutrition Information

- Calories: 241 calories
- Total Carbohydrate: 14 g
- Cholesterol: 55 mg
- Total Fat: 13 g
- Fiber: 5 g
- Protein: 15 g
- Sodium: 838 mg

122. Mexican Shrimp Salad

"A delicious and versatile shrimp recipe that you could put in tortilla wraps, in salad or on rice. Chili powder and jalapeño give this fantastic dish a good kick."
Serving: 4 servings. | Prep: 20m | Ready in: 30m

Ingredients

- 1 small onion, halved and thinly sliced
- 1/4 cup minced fresh cilantro
- 1 jalapeno pepper, seeded and chopped
- 2 tbsps. canola oil
- 2 tsps. chili powder
- 1/2 tsp. ground cumin
- 1/2 tsp. ground coriander
- 1/2 tsp. pepper
- 1/4 tsp. salt
- 1 lb. uncooked medium shrimp, peeled and deveined
- 6 cups torn leaf lettuce
- 1/2 cup fat-free ranch salad dressing

Direction

- Mix the first 9 ingredients together in a zip lock plastic bag then put in the shrimp. Seal the zip lock bag and turn to coat the shrimp. Keep in the fridge for 30 minutes.
- Insert the drained marinated shrimps onto 4 soaked wooden or metal skewers. Use tongs to lightly rub an oiled paper towel on the grill rack.
- Put the shrimp skewers on the grill over medium heat then cover or broil the shrimp 4 inches from heat for 3 to 4 minutes per side or until the shrimp turn pink in color.
- Place lettuce on a plate and put grilled shrimps on top, this recipe makes 4 plates. Serve right away with the dressing.

Nutrition Information

- Calories: 218 calories
- Total Carbohydrate: 15 g
- Cholesterol: 168 mg
- Total Fat: 9 g
- Fiber: 3 g
- Protein: 20 g
- Sodium: 716 mg

123. Minted Cucumber Salad

"This salad is a combination of tomatoes, fresh cucumbers, light vinaigrette, and herbs. It's quick to make, healthy and super tasty."
Serving: 6 servings. | Prep: 20m | Ready in: 20m

Ingredients

- 2 large cucumbers, chopped
- 2 cups seeded chopped tomatoes
- 1/2 cup chopped fresh mint
- 1/2 cup chopped fresh parsley
- 1/2 cup thinly sliced green onions
- 1/4 cup lemon juice
- 1/4 cup olive oil
- 1 tsp. salt
- 1/4 tsp. pepper

Direction

- Mix the first 5 ingredients together in a big bowl. In a small bowl, combine pepper, salt, oil, and lemon juice. Put on the cucumber mixture; mix to combine.

Nutrition Information

- Calories: 113 calories
- Total Carbohydrate: 7 g
- Cholesterol: 0 mg
- Total Fat: 9 g
- Fiber: 2 g
- Protein: 2 g
- Sodium: 403 mg

124. Minty Watermelon-cucumber Salad

"This recipe of cucumber-watermelon salad is perfect for a potluck or picnic with the refreshing summer flavor."
Serving: 16 servings (3/4 cup each). | Prep: 20m | Ready in: 20m

Ingredients

- 8 cups cubed seedless watermelon
- 2 English cucumbers, halved lengthwise and sliced
- 6 green onions, chopped
- 1/4 cup minced fresh mint
- 1/4 cup balsamic vinegar
- 1/4 cup olive oil
- 1/2 tsp. salt
- 1/2 tsp. pepper

Direction

- Mix together mint, green onions, cucumbers and watermelon in a large bowl. Combine other ingredients in a small bowl and stir well. Drizzle onto the salad and coat mixture by tossing. Ready to serve right away or you can put it into the refrigerator for up to 2 hours with cover before ready to serve.

Nutrition Information

- Calories: 60 calories
- Total Carbohydrate: 9 g
- Cholesterol: 0 mg
- Total Fat: 3 g
- Fiber: 1 g
- Protein: 1 g
- Sodium: 78 mg

125. Penne Pasta Salad

"This is tasty and colorful pasta with an interesting addition of a touch of dill plus bell peppers."
Serving: 12 | Prep: 15m | Ready in: 1h

Ingredients

- 16 oz. penne pasta
- 1 cup creamy salad dressing, e.g. Miracle Whip ™
- 1/2 cup Dijon-style prepared mustard
- 1 1/2 cups grated Parmesan cheese
- 1 tbsp. dried dill weed
- 1 red onion, julienned
- 1 yellow bell pepper, thinly sliced
- 1 orange bell pepper, julienned

Direction

- Cook pasta in a big pot of salted boiling water until al dente, then rinse in cold water and drain.
- Combine the dill, cheese, mustard and salad dressing in a big bowl.
- Put in bell peppers, red onion and pasta, then toss well together. Add salt and pepper to season, then refrigerate before serving.

Nutrition Information

- Calories: 269 calories;
- Total Carbohydrate: 35 g
- Cholesterol: 18 mg
- Total Fat: 9.8 g
- Protein: 10.2 g
- Sodium: 611 mg

126. Pineapple-glazed Fruit Medley

"This dish is an ideal plus to any meal as a side dish or dessert."
Serving: 2 servings. | Prep: 10m | Ready in: 15m

Ingredients

- 1 can (8 oz.) pineapple chunks
- 1 small banana, sliced
- 6 green grapes, halved
- 1 tbsp. sugar
- 1 tsp. cornstarch
- 1 tsp. apricot preserves
- 1/2 tsp. lemon juice

Direction

- Drain pineapple and save juice. Mix together grapes, banana and pineapple in a small bowl, then set aside.
- Mix the reserved pineapple juice, cornstarch and sugar in a small saucepan; bring the mixture to a boil. Lower heat, then cook and stir until thickened, about 2 to 3 minutes. Take away from heat, stirring in lemon juice and preserves. Allow to cool totally; put on fruit and gently toss to coat.

Nutrition Information

- Calories: 161 calories
- Total Carbohydrate: 42 g
- Cholesterol: 0 mg
- Total Fat: 0 g
- Fiber: 2 g
- Protein: 1 g
- Sodium: 3 mg

127. Pork And Balsamic Strawberry Salad

"A yummy entrée."
Serving: 4 servings. | Prep: 20m | Ready in: 35m

Ingredients

- 1 pork tenderloin (1 lb.)
- 1/2 cup Italian salad dressing
- 1-1/2 cups halved fresh strawberries
- 2 tbsps. balsamic vinegar
- 2 tsps. sugar
- 1/4 tsp. salt
- 1/4 tsp. pepper
- 2 tbsps. olive oil
- 1/4 cup chicken broth
- 1 package (5 oz.) spring mix salad greens
- 1/2 cup crumbled goat cheese

Direction

- Put pork into a shallow dish. Put salad dressing in; flip to coat. Refrigerate for a minimum of 8 hours, covered. Mix sugar, vinegar and strawberries. Cover; refrigerate.
- Preheat an oven to 425°. Drain then wipe off pork; throw away marinade. Sprinkle with pepper and salt. Heat oil in a big ovenproof skillet over medium-high heat. Put pork in; brown on all the sides.
- Bake for 15-20 minutes till thermometer reads 145°. Take off from skillet; stand for 5 minutes. Meanwhile, put broth in skillet; cook over medium heat, mixing to loosen the browned bits from the pan. Boil; lower heat. Add strawberry mixture then heat through.
- Put greens onto a serving platter; sprinkle with cheese. Cut pork; layout over greens. Put strawberry mixture on top.

Nutrition Information

- Calories: 291 calories
- Total Carbohydrate: 12 g
- Cholesterol: 81 mg
- Total Fat: 16 g
- Fiber: 3 g

- Protein: 26 g
- Sodium: 444 mg

128. Raspberry-chili Tuna On Greens

"The marinade with Thai chili sauce and raspberry preserves levels up this grilled tuna recipe. For a more complete meal, serve it with fresh fruit cups for dessert and crusty loaf bread or baked potatoes on the side. Bon appétit!"
Serving: 4 servings. | Prep: 15m | Ready in: 25m

Ingredients

- 6 tbsps. seedless raspberry preserves
- 1/4 cup balsamic vinegar
- 2 tsps. minced fresh basil or 1/2 tsp. dried basil
- 2 tsps. Thai chili sauce
- 1/2 tsp. salt
- 1/4 tsp. pepper
- 4 tuna steaks (6 oz. each)
- 1 package (10 oz.) torn romaine
- 1/2 cup shredded carrot
- 1/2 cup thinly sliced cucumber

Direction

- Mix all the initial 6 ingredients together in a small bowl. Put 1/4 cup of the marinade mixture inside a big Ziplock plastic bag. Put in the tuna then seal the Ziplock bag and turn to coat the tuna with the marinade. Keep in the fridge for 30 minutes, turn it from time to time. Cover the remaining marinade mixture and keep it in the fridge as well for the dressing.
- Drain the marinated tuna and throw away the marinade mixture. Use tongs to lightly rub an oiled paper towel on the grill rack. Put the marinated tuna on a grill on high heat then cover and grill or put the tuna in a broiler and let it broil 3-4 inches away from the heat for 3-4 minutes on every side, if you want it medium-rare, until the tuna is still a little bit pink inside.

- Mix the carrot, cucumber and romaine together in a big bowl then pour in the reserved marinade and mix until well-coated. Distribute the salad mixture onto 4 individual plates. Put the grilled tuna on top.

Nutrition Information

- Calories: 282 calories
- Total Carbohydrate: 23 g
- Cholesterol: 77 mg
- Total Fat: 2 g
- Fiber: 1 g
- Protein: 41 g
- Sodium: 390 mg

129. Ravishing Radish Salad

"This refreshing, crunchy and delicious salad made of radishes in all their glory really goes greatly with grilled main dish."
Serving: 6 servings. | Prep: 30m | Ready in: 30m

Ingredients

- 24 radishes, quartered
- 1 tsp. salt
- 1 tsp. pepper
- 6 green onions, chopped
- 1/2 cup thinly sliced fennel bulb
- 6 fresh basil leaves, thinly sliced
- 1/4 cup snipped fresh dill
- 1/4 cup olive oil
- 2 tbsps. champagne vinegar
- 2 tbsps. honey
- 2 garlic cloves, minced
- 1/2 cup chopped walnuts, toasted

Direction

- In a big bowl, add radishes, then sprinkle with pepper and salt, toss to coat well. Put in dill, basil, fennel and onions. Whisk together garlic, honey, vinegar and oil in a small bowl. Drizzle over salad and toss to coat well.

- Cover and chill for minimum of 1 hour, then sprinkle with walnuts right before serving.

Nutrition Information

- Calories: 177 calories
- Total Carbohydrate: 10 g
- Cholesterol: 0 mg
- Total Fat: 15 g
- Fiber: 2 g
- Protein: 2 g
- Sodium: 408 mg

---

130. Refreshing Grilled Chicken Salad

""This mouth-watering salad is not just flavorful, but also light and healthy. Adding olive oil, walnuts, and blueberries into this dish makes it a perfect treat for lunch.""

Serving: 4 servings. | Prep: 20m | Ready in: 30m

Ingredients

- 1/2 cup lime juice
- 2 tbsps. honey
- 4 tsps. olive oil
- 1/2 tsp. salt
- 1/2 tsp. pepper
- 4 boneless skinless chicken breast halves (4 oz. each)
- 6 cups spring mix salad greens
- 2 cups cubed seedless watermelon
- 1 cup fresh blueberries
- 1 medium sweet yellow pepper, cut into 1-inch pieces
- 1/3 cup chopped walnuts, toasted

Direction

- Mix oil, pepper, lime juice, salt, and honey in a small bowl. Reserve 1/3 cup of it and place it in a large resealable plastic bag. Add chicken into the bag and seal it, flipping the bag to coat the chicken. Store the bag inside the refrigerator for 60 minutes. Cover and reserve the remaining lime juice mixture for the dressing and place it inside the refrigerator.
- Drain the chicken and discard its marinade. Grease the grill rack with a small amount of oil. Place the chicken over the rack with medium heat and cover. Grill the chicken for 4-7 minutes per side, or you can broil it 4-inches away from the heat source until the thermometer reads 170°F.
- Mix salad greens, blueberries, yellow pepper, and watermelon in a large bowl. Pour the reserved dressing all over the salad, tossing thoroughly to coat. Distribute the salad among four serving plates. Slice the chicken and place it into the plates with salad. Top each serving with 4 tsp. of walnuts, and serve.

Nutrition Information

- Calories: 300 calories
- Total Carbohydrate: 25 g
- Cholesterol: 63 mg
- Total Fat: 12 g
- Fiber: 4 g
- Protein: 28 g
- Sodium: 257 mg

131.Roasted Salmon & White Bean Spinach Salad

"You can have a healthy meal anytime with this easy and nutritious dinner. You can prepare this for just 25 minutes."

Serving: 4 servings. | Prep: 10m | Ready in: 25m

Ingredients

- 4 salmon fillets (6 oz. each)
- 1/4 tsp. salt
- 1/4 tsp. pepper
- 1 can (15-1/2 oz.) great northern beans, rinsed and drained
- 1/2 cup prepared vinaigrette
- 1 package (11 oz.) fresh baby spinach
- 1 small red onion, cut into thin wedges

Direction

- Grease a 15x10x1-in. baking pan, and put the salmon in it. Add a dash of salt and pepper. Let it bake for 11 to 13 minutes at 40 degrees. Fork the fish to check if it flakes easily. Let it cool a bit.
- Toss beans and vinaigrette in a large bowl, and let it rest.
- Add onions and spinach with the bean mixture just before you're about to serve. Toss the ingredients, and distribute among the plates. Top each plate with salmon.

132. Roasted Sweet And Gold Potato Salad

"This potato salad has a bright texture and extra-festive flavor with the addition of black beans and Mexicorn."
Serving: 16 servings (3/4 cup each). | Prep: 45m | Ready in: 01h30m

Ingredients

- 2-1/2 lbs. Yukon Gold potatoes (about 8 medium)
- 1-1/2 lbs. sweet potatoes (about 2 large)
- 2 tbsps. olive oil
- 1 tbsp. ground cumin
- 2 tsps. chili powder
- 2 tsps. garlic powder
- 4 thick-sliced bacon strips, chopped
- 4 green onions, sliced
- 1 medium sweet red pepper, finely chopped
- 1/2 cup minced fresh cilantro
- 2 hard-boiled large eggs, chopped
- 3/4 cup mayonnaise
- 1 tbsp. chopped chipotle pepper in adobo sauce
- 2 tsps. sugar
- 1 large ripe avocado, peeled and finely chopped
- 2 tbsps. lime juice

Direction

- Peel and cube sweet potatoes and potatoes into 3/4" pieces. Transfer to a big bowl and drizzle with oil, then sprinkle with seasonings. Toss to coat. Put into 2 greased 15x10x1-in baking pans. Bake at 450° until softened while stirring from time to time, about 45 to 55 minutes. Allow to cool a little.
- Cook bacon in a small skillet on moderate heat until crisp. Transfer to paper towers with a slotted spoon to drain.
- Mix together eggs, cilantro, red pepper, onions, bacon and potatoes in a big bowl. Mix sugar, chipotle and mayonnaise, then drizzle over potato mixture and toss to coat. Toss avocado with lime juice in a small bowl, then stir into salad gently. Serve chilled or warm.

Nutrition Information

- Calories: 236 calories
- Total Carbohydrate: 24 g
- Cholesterol: 33 mg
- Total Fat: 14 g
- Fiber: 3 g
- Protein: 4 g
- Sodium: 145 mg

133. Roasted Sweet Potato Salad With Chili Lime Dressing

"This salad is very tasty, beautiful and easy to make. Everyone loves it."
Serving: 7 servings. | Prep: 30m | Ready in: 60m

Ingredients

- 2 lbs. large sweet potatoes, peeled and cubed
- 2 tbsps. olive oil
- 1 large sweet red pepper, cut into 1/2-inch pieces
- 8 green onions, chopped
- 1/2 cup minced fresh parsley
- 1/4 cup minced fresh cilantro
- DRESSING:

- 1/3 cup olive oil
- 1/4 cup lime juice
- 4 tsps. chili powder
- 3/4 tsp. salt
- 3/4 tsp. ground cumin
- 1/2 tsp. pepper
- 1/8 tsp. cayenne pepper, optional

Direction

- Mix oil with sweet potatoes in a big bowl. Grease a 15x10x1-in. baking pan and move the potatoes in. Bake at 400° until the potatoes are softened, about 30-40 minutes, tossing 2 times. Let it cool for 10 minutes. Mix sweet potatoes, cilantro, parsley, onions, and red pepper together in a big bowl.
- Combine pepper, cumin, salt, chili powder, lime juice, and oil in a small bowl, include cayenne if you want. Sprinkle on the salad, mix to coat. Eat cold or warm.

Nutrition Information

- Calories: 228 calories
- Total Carbohydrate: 24 g
- Cholesterol: 0 mg
- Total Fat: 15 g
- Fiber: 4 g
- Protein: 2 g
- Sodium: 283 mg

134. Romaine & Cherry Tomato Salad

"This salad is really tasty and yummy that can be served as an entrée or a sunny appetizer."
Serving: 8 servings. | Prep: 20m | Ready in: 20m

Ingredients

- 1 small bunch romaine, torn
- 2 cups grape tomatoes, halved
- 1 package (12 oz.) frozen peas, thawed
- 1 small red onion, thinly sliced
- 1-1/2 cups reduced-fat mayonnaise

- 1 cup shredded Parmesan cheese
- 8 bacon strips, cooked and crumbled

Direction

- Layer romaine, tomatoes, peas and onion in a 3-qt. glass bowl or trifle bowl. Drizzle mayonnaise over onion then sprinkle cheese and bacon on top. Chill until serving.

Nutrition Information

- Calories: 284 calories
- Total Carbohydrate: 14 g
- Cholesterol: 31 mg
- Total Fat: 21 g
- Fiber: 3 g
- Protein: 10 g
- Sodium: 729 mg

135. Salmon And Spud Salad

"I went to the kitchen when I wanted something healthy. I created this salmon with vegetables dish and found that smart choices are simple and satisfying."
Serving: 4 servings. | Prep: 15m | Ready in: 30m

Ingredients

- 1 lb. fingerling potatoes
- 1/2 lb. fresh green beans
- 1/2 lb. fresh asparagus
- 4 salmon fillets (6 oz. each)
- 1 tbsp. plus 1/3 cup red wine vinaigrette, divided
- 1/4 tsp. salt
- 1/4 tsp. pepper
- 4 cups fresh arugula or baby spinach
- 2 cups cherry tomatoes, halved
- 1 tbsp. minced fresh chives

Direction

- Chop the potatoes in half lengthwise. Trim and chop asparagus and green beans into 2-inch pieces. Transfer the potatoes to a 6-qt. stockpot and cover with water. Heat water to boil. Low the heat and cook without covering for about 10-15 minutes or until tender and place in the asparagus and green beans during the final 4 minutes of cooking. Drain off the water.

- In the meantime, coat the salmon with one tbsp. of vinaigrette and then season with pepper and salt. Put the fish onto the oiled grill rack with the skin side down. Grill while covered on top of medium-high heat or broil for about 6 to 8 minutes 4 in. away from the heat source or until the fish starts to easily flake with a fork.
- Mix chives, tomatoes, potato mixture, and arugula in a large bowl. Sprinkle with the rest of vinaigrette. Mix to coat and then serve with salmon.

Nutrition Information

- Calories: 480 calories
- Total Carbohydrate: 33 g
- Cholesterol: 85 mg
- Total Fat: 23 g
- Fiber: 6 g
- Protein: 34 g
- Sodium: 642 mg

136. Shrimp Mac & Cheese Salad

"The lost recipe but re-created from memory."
Serving: 16 servings. | Prep: 35m | Ready in: 45m

Ingredients

- 4 cups uncooked elbow macaroni
- 1/4 cup butter, cut up
- 1/4 cup all-purpose flour
- 1-1/2 cups half-and-half cream
- 4 oz. Gouda cheese, shredded
- 1/2 cup shredded cheddar cheese
- 1/2 cup shredded part-skim mozzarella cheese
- 2 lbs. peeled and deveined cooked medium shrimp, cut into pieces
- 1 cup chopped onion
- 1 cup chopped sweet red pepper

- 1 cup mayonnaise
- 1/2 cup chopped celery
- 1/2 cup chopped dill pickle
- 1/8 tsp. salt
- 1/8 tsp. pepper
- 8 lettuce leaves

Direction

- Following the instructions on the package, cook the macaroni; drain off water and put aside.
- At the same time, melt butter in a big sauce pan. Mix in flour till smooth; slowly put in cream. Boil; cook and stir until thickened, about 2 minutes. Take pan away from heat; mix in cheeses till melted. Put in macaroni; coat by mixing. Place in a big bowl; let it cool to room temperature.
- Mix pepper, salt, pickle, celery, mayonnaise, red pepper, onion and shrimp in different bowl. Fold in cooled macaroni mixture; keep it covered and chilled. Serve over lettuce.

Nutrition Information

- Calories: 345 calories
- Total Carbohydrate: 19 g
- Cholesterol: 124 mg
- Total Fat: 21 g
- Fiber: 1 g
- Protein: 19 g
- Sodium: 368 mg

137. Sparkling Oranges

"Created this recipe in Texas that has fresh oranges in it! Prepare in advance, so there's no nick of time fuss."
Serving: 8 servings. | Prep: 30m | Ready in: 35m

Ingredients

- 1/2 cup sugar
- 1/2 cup orange marmalade
- 1 cup white grape juice
- 1/2 cup lemon-lime soda

- 8 large oranges, peeled and sectioned
- 3 tbsps. slivered almonds, toasted
- 3 tbsps. sweetened shredded coconut, toasted

Direction

- Place a small saucepan on the stove and turn on to medium heat, mix marmalade and sugar; stir and cook until sugar has melted. Get saucepan away from heat. Mix in soda and grape juice. Put on top of orange sections; toss to cover. Place inside the refrigerator, covered, overnight. Remove oranges to a serving dish using a slotted spoon. Drizzle with coconut and almonds.

Nutrition Information

- Calories: 234 calories
- Total Carbohydrate: 55 g
- Cholesterol: 0 mg
- Total Fat: 2 g
- Fiber: 5 g
- Protein: 3 g
- Sodium: 21 mg

138. Spicy Gazpacho Salad

"The addition of greens makes a simple, refreshing and cool soup become tasty fork food."
Serving: 10 servings. | Prep: 25m | Ready in: 25m

Ingredients

- 3 cups chopped and seeded tomatoes
- 1 medium cucumber, seeded and chopped
- 1 medium green pepper, chopped
- 4 green onions, chopped
- 1 celery rib, thinly sliced
- 1 tomatillo, husk removed, seeded and chopped
- 1/2 cup red wine vinaigrette
- 2 tbsps. lemon juice
- 2 tbsps. Worcestershire sauce
- 2 garlic cloves, minced
- 1 tsp. coarsely ground pepper

- 1 tsp. hot pepper sauce
- 1/2 tsp. kosher salt
- 1 bunch romaine, torn

Direction

- Mix the first 6 ingredients in a big bowl. Whisk together salt, pepper sauce, pepper, garlic, Worcestershire sauce, lemon juice and vinaigrette in a small bowl. Drizzle over tomato mixture and toss to coat.
- Right before serving, put romaine into a big serving bowl. Place vegetable mixture on top, then toss to combine.

Nutrition Information

- Calories: 67 calories
- Total Carbohydrate: 7 g
- Cholesterol: 0 mg
- Total Fat: 4 g
- Fiber: 2 g
- Protein: 2 g
- Sodium: 333 mg

139. Summertime Tomato Salad

"This salad is very easy and quick to make to serve as a perfect side dish or cool summer snack."
Serving: 2 | Prep: 15m | Ready in: 8h15m

Ingredients

- 1/2 cup vegetable oil
- 1/4 cup white vinegar
- 1/2 tsp. white sugar
- 1/2 tsp. ground black pepper
- 1 tsp. Dijon mustard
- 2 tsps. seasoned salt
- 3 tomatoes, diced
- 2 onions, diced

Direction

- In a bowl, whisk together seasoned salt, mustard, pepper, sugar, vinegar and vegetable oil, then put into the bowl with onion and tomato and toss to coat. Cover and chill overnight.

Nutrition Information

- Calories: 572 calories;
- Total Carbohydrate: 20.4 g
- Cholesterol: 0 mg
- Total Fat: 55.1 g
- Protein: 3 g
- Sodium: 994 mg

140. Terrific Taco Salad

"Here's a recipe of a taco salad that didn't use a meat. This one is made with BOCA Veggie Ground Crumbles."
Serving: Makes 2 servings. | Prep: 15m | Ready in: 15m

Ingredients

- 1 cup frozen BOCA Veggie Ground Crumbles
- 1/4 cup TACO BELL® Thick & Chunky Medium Salsa
- 3 cups torn lettuce
- 1/2 cup rinsed canned black beans
- 1/2 cup frozen corn , thawed
- 1/3 cup thin red pepper strips
- 1 Tbsp. chopped fresh cilantro
- 1 Tbsp. lime juice

Direction

- In a skillet, cook salsa and crumbles over medium heat for 5 minutes, stirring often until cooked through (160°F).
- Arrange lettuce in each of the 2 plates. Top each with the crumble mixture and the remaining ingredients.

Nutrition Information

- Calories: 190
- Total Carbohydrate: 30 g
- Cholesterol: 0 mg
- Total Fat: 1 g
- Fiber: 9 g
- Protein: 19 g

- Sodium: 480 mg
- Sugar: 4 g
- Saturated Fat: 0 g

141. Thai Shrimp Salad

"A yummy salad with lean meat, cucumber, grilled shrimp and onions. Cilantro, mint, lime and sesame are made into a dressing for that flavorful and aromatic Thai twist."
Serving: 4 servings. | Prep: 25m | Ready in: 35m

Ingredients

- 1/4 cup lime juice
- 2 tbsps. sesame oil
- 2 tbsps. reduced-sodium soy sauce
- 1 tbsp. sesame seeds, toasted
- 1 tbsp. minced fresh mint
- 1 tbsp. minced fresh cilantro
- 1/8 tsp. crushed red pepper flakes
- 1 lb. uncooked large shrimp, peeled and deveined
- 1/4 tsp. salt
- 1/4 tsp. pepper
- 1 sweet onion, sliced
- 1 medium cucumber, peeled and sliced
- 4 cups torn leaf lettuce

Direction

- Mix all the first 7 ingredients together in a big bowl and put aside. Insert shrimps seasoned with pepper and salt onto 4 skewers.
- Use tongs to slightly rub an oiled paper towel on the grill rack. Put the shrimp skewers on the grill on medium heat then cover and grill for 2 to 4 minutes per side or until the shrimp turns pink in color.
- Mix the leftover dressing and put in the cucumbers, grilled shrimps and onions. Mix well to evenly coat the cucumbers, shrimps and onions. Put lettuce on 4 salad plates and put the shrimp mixture on top.

Nutrition Information

- Calories: 202 calories

- Total Carbohydrate: 10 g
- Cholesterol: 168 mg
- Total Fat: 9 g
- Fiber: 3 g
- Protein: 21 g
- Sodium: 661 mg

142. Thai Shrimp Salad For 2

"Lean meat, cucumber, grilled shrimp and onions are a good combination for a good and delicious salad. Cilantro, mint, lime and sesame gives a Thai twist for the dressing that is best paired with this salad recipe."
Serving: 2 servings. | Prep: 25m | Ready in: 35m

Ingredients

- 2 tbsps. lime juice
- 1 tbsp. sesame oil
- 1 tbsp. reduced-sodium soy sauce
- 1-1/2 tsps. sesame seeds, toasted
- 1-1/2 tsps. minced fresh mint
- 1-1/2 tsps. minced fresh cilantro
- Dash crushed red pepper flakes
- 1/2 lb. uncooked large shrimp, peeled and deveined
- 1/8 tsp. salt
- 1/8 tsp. pepper
- 1/2 large sweet onion, sliced
- 1/2 medium cucumber, peeled and sliced
- 2 cups torn leaf lettuce

Direction

- Mix the first 7 ingredients together in a big bowl and put aside. Insert shrimps seasoned with pepper and salt onto 2 skewers.
- Use tongs to lightly rub an oiled paper towel on the grill rack. Put the shrimp skewers on the grill on medium heat then cover or broil the shrimps in the oven 4 inches away from the heat for 2 to 4 minutes per side or until the shrimp turns pink in color.
- Mix the leftover dressing and put in the cucumbers, grilled shrimps and onions. Mix well to evenly coat the cucumbers, shrimps

and onions. Put lettuce on a salad plate and put the shrimp mixture on top then serve right away, this recipe makes 2 salad plates.

Nutrition Information

- Calories: 212 calories
- Total Carbohydrate: 11 g
- Cholesterol: 138 mg
- Total Fat: 9 g
- Fiber: 3 g
- Protein: 21 g
- Sodium: 614 mg

143. Tossed Salad With Cilantro Vinaigrette

"This is not a salad that you'll see everywhere...with its unique mix of veggies that tossed with romaine."
Serving: 16 servings (3/4 cup each). | Prep: 25m | Ready in: 25m

Ingredients

- 1/3 cup olive oil
- 1/4 cup minced fresh cilantro
- 1/4 cup lime juice
- 1/8 tsp. salt
- 8 cups torn romaine
- 1 medium zucchini, chopped
- 1 medium cucumber, chopped
- 1 medium sweet yellow pepper, chopped
- 5 to 10 radishes, sliced

Direction

- Combine salt, lime juice, cilantro and oil in a small bowl.
- Mix radishes, yellow pepper, cucumber, zucchini and romaine in a big bowl. Sprinkle with dressing; coat by tossing. Serve right away.

Nutrition Information

- Calories: 53 calories
- Total Carbohydrate: 3 g

- Cholesterol: 0 mg
- Total Fat: 5 g
- Fiber: 1 g
- Protein: 1 g
- Sodium: 23 mg

144. Twisted Eggs Benedict Salad

"You can absolutely make a salad for a breakfast with all ingredients are prepared ahead except for the dressing."
Serving: 8 servings. | Prep: 20m | Ready in: 40m

Ingredients

- 4 tbsps. olive oil, divided
- 1-1/2 lbs. fresh asparagus, trimmed and chopped
- 1-1/3 cups chopped fennel bulb
- 8 oz. diced deli ham or Jones Canadian Bacon
- 6 cups baby kale salad blend (about 4 oz.)
- 1 cup chopped roasted sweet red peppers
- 3 tbsps. chopped green onion tops
- 3 tbsps. Dijon mustard
- 2 tbsps. cider vinegar
- 1/4 tsp. salt
- 1/4 tsp. pepper
- 2 quarts water
- 8 large eggs

Direction

- Heat 1 tbsp. of olive oil in a big nonstick skillet on moderate heat. Put in ham, fennel and asparagus, then sauté for 8 minutes, until vegetables are crisp-tender. Allow to cool about 3 minutes.
- Toss green onions, peppers, salad blend and vegetable mixture together. Whip the leftover oil, pepper, salt, vinegar and mustard together until smooth.
- Bring water in a big saucepan to a boil then lower the heat and simmer gently. One at a time, break eggs into a small bowl then slip eggs into water. Poach without a cover for 3 to 5 minutes, until yolks start to thicken and whites are set thoroughly.

- At the same time, toss dressing and salad together. Split the salad among 8 plates. Take the eggs out of water with a slotted spoon and put one on top of each salad.

Nutrition Information

- Calories: 199 calories
- Total Carbohydrate: 5 g
- Cholesterol: 200 mg
- Total Fat: 13 g
- Fiber: 2 g
- Protein: 14 g
- Sodium: 710 mg

145. Warm Green Bean & Potato Salad

"This tasty dish is known as Green Beans Pierre and is made of red potatoes and green beans."
Serving: 10 servings. | Prep: 10m | Ready in: 30m

Ingredients

- 1 lb. small red potatoes, quartered
- 1/4 cup olive oil
- 2 tbsps. white wine vinegar
- 1/2 tsp. salt
- 1/8 tsp. each garlic powder, ground mustard and pepper
- 1/8 tsp. each dried basil, parsley flakes and tarragon
- 1 lb. fresh green beans, cut into 2-inch pieces
- 2 medium tomatoes, coarsely chopped
- 2 tbsps. chopped onion

Direction

- In a big saucepan, put potatoes and fill with water. Boil it. Cook without a cover for 10 minutes. In the meantime, mix seasonings, vinegar, and oil together in a big bowl.
- Put green beans on potatoes, boil again. Cook until vegetables are softened, or for 3-5 minutes longer. Strain, put on the dressing

and mix to coat. Mix in onion and tomatoes. Serve while warm.

146. White Ale Potato Salad

"This recipe is very popular. It uses beer as a substitute for mayo."
Serving: 12 servings (3/4 cup each). | Prep: 15m | Ready in: 35m

Ingredients

- 2 lbs. fingerling or small red potatoes, cut into 1-inch pieces
- DRESSING:
- 1/2 cup white ale
- 3 tbsps. olive oil
- 2 tbsps. balsamic vinegar
- 2 tbsps. Dijon mustard
- 1 package Italian salad dressing mix
- SALAD:
- 4 cups fresh arugula (about 2-1/2 oz.) or chopped fresh kale
- 1-1/2 cups grape tomatoes
- 6 green onions, chopped
- 10 bacon strips, cooked and crumbled
- 1 cup crumbled Gorgonzola or feta cheese
- 1/4 cup minced fresh chives

Direction

- In a big saucepan, put potatoes and fill with water. Boil it. Decrease the heat, cook without a cover until softened, or for 12-15 minutes. Strain, move to a big bowl.
- Mix the ingredients of the dressing together in a small bowl until combined. Put on the warm potatoes and mix to coat. Let it cool slightly. Put a cover on and put in the fridge for about 1 hour until chilled.
- When serving, add bacon, green onions, tomatoes, and arugula to the potatoes, mix lightly to blend. Use chives and cheese to drizzle. Serve immediately.

Nutrition Information

- Calories: 185 calories
- Total Carbohydrate: 19 g
- Cholesterol: 15 mg
- Total Fat: 9 g
- Fiber: 2 g
- Protein: 7 g
- Sodium: 536 mg

147. Yellow Squash & Watermelon Salad

"This is oil-free salad made of fresh and bright ingredients coated with a feta and lemon juice that brings you a healthy option for any potlucks or parties."
Serving: 12 servings (3/4 cup each). | Prep: 20m | Ready in: 20m

Ingredients

- 6 cups cubed seedless watermelon
- 2 medium yellow summer squash, chopped
- 2 medium zucchini, chopped
- 1/2 cup lemon juice
- 12 fresh mint leaves, torn
- 1 tsp. salt
- 8 cups fresh arugula or baby spinach
- 1 cup (4 oz.) crumbled feta cheese

Direction

- Mix the first 6 ingredients in a big bowl. Put in cheese and arugula, then gently toss to blend, right before serving.

Nutrition Information

- Calories: 60 calories
- Total Carbohydrate: 11 g
- Cholesterol: 5 mg
- Total Fat: 2 g
- Fiber: 2 g
- Protein: 3 g
- Sodium: 297 mg

Chapter 3: Fathers Day Side Dish Recipes

***

148. Asparagus With Mustard Vinaigrette

""This is an amazing side dish, making the dish more colorful and tasty.""
Serving: 3 servings. | Prep: 25m | Ready in: 30m

Ingredients

- 1 lb. fresh asparagus, trimmed
- 3 tbsps. unsweetened pineapple juice
- 1 tbsp. balsamic vinegar
- 1 tsp. Dijon mustard
- 1 tsp. olive oil
- 1/2 tsp. minced garlic

Direction

- Heat 1/2 in. of water to a boil in a large skillet. Put in asparagus; boil with a cover for 3 minutes, then drain. Let asparagus cool enough to handle, then pat it dry. Thread some asparagus spears onto two soaked wooden skewers or parallel metal. Repeat the process with the rest of asparagus.
- Grill without covering for 2 minutes per side over medium heat, until tender-crisp.
- For vinaigrette, in a small bowl, combine the rest of ingredients. Take asparagus off skewers; drizzle vinaigrette on top.

Nutrition Information

- Calories: 46 calories
- Total Carbohydrate: 6 g
- Cholesterol: 0 mg
- Total Fat: 2 g
- Fiber: 1 g
- Protein: 2 g
- Sodium: 52 mg

149. Buttery Grilled Onions

"You can prepare this dish in advance and enjoy it later. It's very delicious and your family definitely will love it."
Serving: 6 servings. | Prep: 15m | Ready in: 45m

Ingredients

- 6 medium onions, peeled
- 6 tbsps. butter, softened
- 6 tsps. beef bouillon granules
- 1/8 tsp. garlic powder
- 1/8 tsp. coarsely ground pepper
- 6 tsps. sherry, optional
- Shredded Parmesan cheese

Direction

- Gently remove a 1x1-inch core from the middle of each onion (reserve the removed onion for later uses). On a heavy-duty foil with a double thickness, put each onion (approximately 12 inches square).
- Stir together pepper, garlic powder, bouillon, and butter; add to the onion. Sprinkle sherry over if you want. Fold around the onions with the foil and close tightly.
- Close the lid and grill over medium heat until soft, about 30-40 minutes. Gently open the foil to release the steam. Sprinkle Parmesan cheese over the onions.

150. Buttery Horseradish Corn On The Cob

"Whip up a butter and horseradish topping for grilled corn to serve for a barbeque better."
Serving: 12 servings. | Prep: 15m | Ready in: 30m

Ingredients

- 3/4 cup butter, softened
- 1/4 cup shredded pepper jack cheese
- 1/4 cup prepared horseradish
- 1 tbsp. dried parsley flakes
- 3 tsps. salt
- 2 tsps. balsamic vinegar
- 1/2 tsp. pepper
- 1/4 tsp. dried thyme
- 12 medium ears sweet corn, husks removed

Direction

- Mix the first 8 ingredients together in a small bowl until combined and spread over corn. Use a piece of heavy-duty foil with 14-inch square size to wrap each and seal tightly.
- Grill corn on moderate heat with a cover until soft while turning sometimes, about 15 to 20 minutes. Carefully open foil to let steam escape.

Nutrition Information

- Calories: 203 calories
- Total Carbohydrate: 20 g
- Cholesterol: 33 mg
- Total Fat: 14 g
- Fiber: 2 g
- Protein: 4 g
- Sodium: 732 mg

151. Campfire Cheese Hash Brown Packets

"Really a wonderful hash with this easy packet of cheese, bacon and potatoes."
Serving: 4 servings. | Prep: 15m | Ready in: 30m

Ingredients

- 1 package (28 oz.) frozen O'Brien potatoes, thawed
- 1-1/4 cups shredded cheddar cheese, divided
- 8 bacon strips, cooked and chopped
- 1/2 tsp. salt
- 1/4 tsp. pepper
- hard-boiled large eggs and pico de gallo, optional

Direction

- Prepare grill or campfire to moderately high heat. Toss together pepper, salt, bacon, 3/4 cup of cheese and potatoes.
- Split the mixture between 4 18"x12" heavy-duty nonstick foil pieces, putting food on the dull side of foil, then fold foil around potato mixture and seal tightly.
- Position over grill or campfire with packets, then cook until potatoes are soft, about 6 to 9 minutes per side. Carefully open packets to let steam escape, then sprinkle leftover cheese over top. Serve together with pico de gallo and eggs if you want.

Nutrition Information

- Calories: 329 calories
- Total Carbohydrate: 31 g
- Cholesterol: 37 mg
- Total Fat: 15 g
- Fiber: 5 g
- Protein: 14 g
- Sodium: 708 mg

152. Campfire Potatoes

"Cheesy grilled potatoes!"
Serving: 6 | Prep: 10m | Ready in: 50m

Ingredients

- 5 potatoes, thinly sliced
- 1 onion, sliced
- 6 tbsps. butter, cut into pieces
- 1/3 cup shredded Cheddar cheese
- 2 tbsps. minced fresh parsley
- 1 tbsp. Worcestershire sauce
- salt and pepper to taste
- 1/3 cup chicken broth

Direction

- Preheat outdoor grill to high heat.
- Put onion and potatoes on heavy foil piece, 20x20-in. Dot butter on.
- Mix pepper, salt, Worcestershire sauce, parsley and cheddar cheese in a medium bowl. Sprinkle mixture on potatoes.
- Fold foil edges. Use chicken broth to cover potatoes.
- Tightly seal foil. Put on preheated grill. Cook till potatoes are tender for about 35-40 minutes.

Nutrition Information

- Calories: 275 calories;
- Total Carbohydrate: 33.5 g
- Cholesterol: 37 mg
- Total Fat: 13.8 g
- Protein: 5.6 g
- Sodium: 214 mg

153. Cheese-topped Potatoes In Foil

"Cheesy potato packets."
Serving: 8 servings. | Prep: 15m | Ready in: 50m

Ingredients

- 2-1/2 lbs. potatoes (about 3 large), peeled and cut into 1/4-inch slices
- 1 medium onion, finely chopped
- 5 bacon strips, cooked and crumbled
- 1/4 cup butter, melted
- 1/2 tsp. salt
- 1/4 tsp. pepper
- 6 slices process American cheese
- Sour cream, optional

Direction

- Have the campfire or a grill ready to cook on moderate heat. Toss the potatoes together with pepper, salt, butter, bacon and onion in a big bowl. Put on a big oiled heavy-duty foil piece, approximately 36x12-inch rectangle. Fold the foil around the potatoes, sealing securely.
- Grill while covering or cook on campfire for about 15 minutes on each side till potatoes are soft. Unseal the foil cautiously to release steam; put cheese on top of potatoes. Cook for 1-2 minutes until cheese melts. If preferred, serve together with sour cream.

Nutrition Information

- Calories: 217 calories
- Total Carbohydrate: 21 g
- Cholesterol: 24 mg
- Total Fat: 11 g
- Fiber: 2 g
- Protein: 7 g
- Sodium: 454 mg

154. Corn 'n' Pepper Packets

"It's a delicious and wonderful dish packed with full of flavor."
Serving: 4 servings. | Prep: 5m | Ready in: 15m

Ingredients

- 4 medium ears sweet corn, cut into 2-inch chunks
- 1 medium green pepper, cut into 2-inch strips
- 1 medium sweet red pepper, cut into 2-inch strips
- 2 tbsps. minced fresh parsley
- 3/4 tsp. garlic salt
- 1/4 tsp. celery seed
- 1/4 tsp. pepper
- 1/4 cup butter, melted

Direction

- Mix together seasonings, parsley and vegetables in a big bowl, then put on a heavy-duty foil piece (approximately 18"x12"). Drizzle over with butter then fold foil around vegetables and seal securely.
- Grill with a cover on moderately hot heat, about 5 to 6 minutes per side. Carefully open foil to let steam escape.

Nutrition Information

- Calories: 196 calories
- Total Carbohydrate: 21 g
- Cholesterol: 31 mg
- Total Fat: 13 g
- Fiber: 4 g
- Protein: 4 g
- Sodium: 471 mg

155. Corn On The Cob With Lemon-pepper Butter

"It's a delicious and wonderful dish packed with full of flavor."
Serving: 8 servings. | Prep: 10m | Ready in: 35m

Ingredients

- 8 medium ears sweet corn
- 1 cup butter, softened
- 2 tbsps. lemon-pepper seasoning

Direction

- Peel back corn husks carefully to within 1 inch of bottoms and get rid of the silk. Rewrap corn in husks and use a kitchen string to secure. Put corn in a stockpot with cold water to cover. Soak for 20 minutes then drain.
- At the same time, mix together lemon-pepper and butter in a small bowl. Grill corn with a cover on moderate heat until softened while turning frequently, or for about 20 to 25 minutes.
- Cut string and peel back husks. Serve together butter mixture and corn.

Nutrition Information

- Calories: 280 calories
- Total Carbohydrate: 17 g
- Cholesterol: 60 mg
- Total Fat: 24 g
- Fiber: 3 g
- Protein: 3 g
- Sodium: 520 mg

156. Corn With Cilantro-lime Butter

"This lime butter is especially for grilled corn and adding some cilantro will enhance the flavors greatly."
Serving: 12 servings. | Prep: 15m | Ready in: 30m

Ingredients

- 1/2 cup butter, softened

- 1/4 cup minced fresh cilantro
- 1 tbsp. lime juice
- 1-1/2 tsps. grated lime zest
- 12 medium ears sweet corn, husks removed
- Grated cotija cheese, optional

Direction

- Combine lime zest, lime juice, cilantro, and butter in a small bowl. Form into a log, then cover with plastic wrap. Chill in the fridge until firm, 30 minutes. Wrap 1 piece of heavy-duty foil (approximately 14 inches square) around each corn ear.
- Close the lid and grill the corn over medium heat until softened, 15-20 minute; flip sometimes. In the meantime, slice lime butter into 12 slices. Take the corn away from the grill. Gently open the foil, letting the steam release. Enjoy the corn with butter and cheese (if wanted).

Nutrition Information

- Calories: 145 calories
- Total Carbohydrate: 17 g
- Cholesterol: 20 mg
- Total Fat: 9 g
- Fiber: 2 g
- Protein: 3 g
- Sodium: 67 mg

157. Dilly Grilled Veggies

"This is a versatile side dish and you can choose whatever kind of veggies you want."
Serving: 6 servings. | Prep: 15m | Ready in: 30m

Ingredients

- 2 cups sliced fresh mushrooms
- 2 cups sliced fresh zucchini
- 2 cups fresh broccoli florets
- 1/2 medium sweet red pepper, cut into strips
- 2 tbsps. olive oil
- 2 tbsps. minced fresh dill or 2 tsps. dill weed

- 1/8 tsp. garlic salt
- 1/8 tsp. pepper

Direction

- On a double thickness of heavy-duty foil (approximately 18 square inches), add vegetables. Drizzle oil over vegetables, then sprinkle with pepper, garlic salt and dill. Fold foil around the vegetables and seal it tightly.
- Grill on moderate heat with a cover until vegetables are softened, 15 minutes. Carefully open foil to let the steam escape outside.

Nutrition Information

- Calories: 61 calories
- Total Carbohydrate: 4 g
- Cholesterol: 0 mg
- Total Fat: 5 g
- Fiber: 2 g
- Protein: 2 g
- Sodium: 49 mg

158. Dilly Vegetable Medley

"This wonderful and flavorful side dish is a great combination of veggies."
Serving: 13 servings (3/4 cup each). | Prep: 25m | Ready in: 45m

Ingredients

- 1/4 cup olive oil
- 2 tbsps. minced fresh basil
- 2 tsps. dill weed
- 1/2 tsp. salt
- 1/2 tsp. pepper
- 7 small yellow summer squash, cut into 1/2-inch slices
- 1 lb. Yukon Gold potatoes, cut into 1/2-inch cubes
- 5 small carrots, cut into 1/2-inch slices

Direction

- Mix the first 5 ingredients in a very big bowl. Put in vegetables and toss to coat well.
- Put on the double thickness of heavy-duty foil, 18 inches square in size, with 1/2 of the vegetables. Fold foil around the vegetables, sealing tightly. Repeat process with the rest of vegetables.
- Grill on moderate heat with a cover until potatoes are soft, about 20 to 25 minutes while flipping one time. Carefully open foil to let steam escape.

Nutrition Information

- Calories: 91 calories
- Total Carbohydrate: 12 g
- Cholesterol: 0 mg
- Total Fat: 4 g
- Fiber: 2 g
- Protein: 2 g
- Sodium: 109 mg

159. Dinner In A Packet

"Kids don't only like eating this simple dinner, they also enjoy making it. Guide Camp provided me the recipe years ago."
Serving: 1 serving. | Prep: 10m | Ready in: 40m

Ingredients

- 1 boneless pork loin chop (4 oz.)
- 1 medium potato, sliced
- 1 large carrot, sliced
- 1/4 cup frozen peas
- 1 tbsp. onion soup mix

Direction

- Position the pork chop atop heavy-duty foil that is folded to double thickness (about 18x14 inches). Add carrot, peas, and potato on top. Add a sprinkle of soup mix. Then scrunch the foil to seal the edges tightly.

- Cover the grill on medium heat for 30-35 minutes or until meat juices are clear, while flipping occasionally. Unseal and remove foil carefully to ensure steam escapes.

Nutrition Information

- Calories: 481 calories
- Total Carbohydrate: 55 g
- Cholesterol: 91 mg
- Total Fat: 9 g
- Fiber: 8 g
- Protein: 43 g
- Sodium: 474 mg

160. Fiesta Grilled Corn

"Make this corn with basil and oregano butter and Parmesan cheese if you want an Italian flair."
Serving: 6 servings. | Prep: 25m | Ready in: 50m

Ingredients

- 1/2 cup butter, softened
- 1/4 cup minced fresh cilantro
- 2 tsps. grated lime zest
- 1/2 tsp. garlic powder
- 6 large ears sweet corn in husks
- 1/2 cup mayonnaise
- 1 tbsp. chili powder
- 1/2 tsp. paprika
- 1/2 cup crumbled queso fresco or fresh goat cheese

Direction

- Mix together garlic powder, lime zest, cilantro and butter in a small bowl, then shape the mixture into a log. Use plastic to wrap. Chill log in the fridge until firm, about 30 minutes.
- Peel back corn husks carefully to within 1 inch of bottoms and take off silk. Put in a Dutch oven and add cold water to cover. Soak in the cold water about 20 minutes, then drain. Mix together paprika, chili powder and mayonnaise in a small bowl, then spread over

corn. Rewrap the corn in husks and use kitchen string to secure.

- Grill corn with a cover on medium heat until soft while turning frequently, about 25 to 30 minutes. Serve together with slices of butter and sprinkle cheese over.

Nutrition Information

- Calories: 426 calories
- Total Carbohydrate: 29 g
- Cholesterol: 53 mg
- Total Fat: 33 g
- Fiber: 4 g
- Protein: 7 g
- Sodium: 269 mg

161. Garlic-butter Parmesan Corn

"Cheese, garlic, and butter really enhance the flavors of this grill dish."
Serving: 8 servings. | Prep: 15m | Ready in: 40m

Ingredients

- 8 medium ears sweet corn in husks
- 1/3 cup butter, cubed
- 1/2 tsp. minced garlic
- 1/4 tsp. salt
- 1/4 cup grated Parmesan cheese

Direction

- Put corn in cold water to soak for 20 minutes. In the meantime, mix together salt, garlic, and butter in a small saucepan. Stir and cook over medium heat until the butter melts; put 2 tbsps. aside.
- Gently peel back corn husks to within 1 in. of bottoms; discard the silk. Brush the rest of the butter mixture over. Wrap the corn in husks again and use a kitchen string to keep it in place.
- Close the lid and grill the corn over medium heat until soft, about 25-30 minutes, flipping sometimes. Snip the string and peel back the

husks. Drizzle the saved butter mixture over the corn and sprinkle cheese over.

Nutrition Information

- Calories: 156 calories
- Total Carbohydrate: 17 g
- Cholesterol: 22 mg
- Total Fat: 9 g
- Fiber: 2 g
- Protein: 4 g
- Sodium: 211 mg

162. Greek-style Squash

"This colorful and rapid vegetable dish really brings you the taste of sunshine."
Serving: 4 servings. | Prep: 15m | Ready in: 45m

Ingredients

- 2 small yellow summer squash, thinly sliced
- 2 small zucchini, thinly sliced
- 1 medium tomato, seeded and chopped
- 1/4 cup pitted ripe olives
- 2 tbsps. chopped green onion
- 2 tsps. olive oil
- 1 tsp. lemon juice
- 3/4 tsp. garlic salt
- 1/4 tsp. dried oregano
- 1/8 tsp. pepper
- 2 tbsps. grated Parmesan cheese

Direction

- On a double thickness of heavy-duty foil, 17"x18" in size, add onion, olives, tomato, zucchini and yellow squash. Mix together pepper, oregano, garlic salt, lemon juice and oil, then drizzle over vegetables. Fold foil around mixture, sealing tightly.
- Grill on moderate heat with a cover until vegetables are soft, about 30 to 35 minutes. Carefully open foil to let steam escape.
- Remove vegetables to a serving bowl and sprinkle cheese over top.

Nutrition Information

- Calories: 80 calories
- Total Carbohydrate: 8 g
- Cholesterol: 2 mg
- Total Fat: 5 g
- Fiber: 3 g
- Protein: 4 g
- Sodium: 479 mg

163. Grill Bread

"You can use this tasty bread as pita bread as tortillas."
Serving: 4 servings. | Prep: 15m | Ready in: 20m

Ingredients

- 4 frozen Texas-size white dinner rolls (2 oz. each), thawed
- 2 garlic cloves, minced
- 2 tbsps. olive oil
- 1/2 lb. fresh mushrooms, sliced
- 1 small onion, cut into thin wedges
- 1 medium green pepper, sliced
- 1 medium sweet yellow pepper, sliced
- 1 medium sweet red pepper, sliced
- 1/2 cup fresh snow peas
- 3/4 tsp. salt
- 1/8 tsp. pepper
- 1/2 tsp. dried oregano

Direction

- On a surface lightly scattered with flour, roll each roll out into a circle, about 8-10 inches, flipping the dough often; put aside.
- Sauté garlic in oil in a big skillet until soft. Add mushrooms, sauté for 2-3 minutes. Add oregano, pepper, salt, peas, peppers, and onion; cook until crunchy and soft, about 3 minutes.
- In the meantime, grill bread without a cover over medium-high heat until turning light brown, about 30-45 seconds each side. Stuff the vegetable mixture in and enjoy

immediately. You can reheat the bread in the microwave.

Nutrition Information

- Calories: 153 calories
- Total Carbohydrate: 19 g
- Cholesterol: 0 mg
- Total Fat: 8 g
- Fiber: 3 g
- Protein: 4 g
- Sodium: 493 mg

164. Grilled Cauliflower Wedges

"This dish is very flavorful yet making it is very easy. The cauliflower is crunchy and the red pepper flakes add bite."
Serving: 8 servings. | Prep: 10m | Ready in: 30m

Ingredients

- 1 large head cauliflower
- 1 tsp. ground turmeric
- 1/2 tsp. crushed red pepper flakes
- 2 tbsps. olive oil
- Lemon juice, additional olive oil and pomegranate seeds, optional

Direction

- Peel off the leaves and chop the stem off the cauliflower. Cut the cauliflower into 8 wedges. Combine pepper flakes and turmeric. Brush oil over the wedges, sprinkle the turmeric mixture over.
- Close the lid and broil 4-inch from heat or grill over medium-high heat for 8-10 minutes per side, until the cauliflower is soft. Drizzle more oil and lemon juice over if you want. Enjoy with pomegranate seeds.

165. Grilled Cherry Tomatoes

"Butter and herbs are really the keys of this delicious side dish."
Serving: 6 servings. | Prep: 10m | Ready in: 20m

Ingredients

- 2 pints cherry tomatoes, halved
- 2 garlic cloves, minced
- 1/2 tsp. dried oregano
- 3 tbsps. butter

Direction

- On a double thickness of heavy-duty foil, 24x12-inch in size, add tomatoes. Sauté together oregano and garlic in a small skillet with butter about 2 minutes, then pour over tomatoes. Fold foil around tomatoes, sealing tightly.
- Grill on moderate heat with a cover until tomatoes are heated through, about 4 to 5 minutes per side. Carefully open foil to let steam escape.

Nutrition Information

- Calories: 73 calories
- Total Carbohydrate: 5 g
- Cholesterol: 15 mg
- Total Fat: 6 g
- Fiber: 1 g
- Protein: 1 g
- Sodium: 67 mg

166. Grilled Corn On The Cob

"An easy way to grill corn to be tender and tasty."
Serving: 6 | Prep: 10m | Ready in: 40m

Ingredients

- 6 ears corn
- 6 tbsps. butter, softened
- salt and pepper to taste

Direction

- Preheat outdoor grill to high heat. Oil the grate lightly.
- Peel the corn husks back; remove the silk. On every corn piece, put pepper, salt and 1 tbsp. butter. Close the husks once done.
- Tightly wrap every corn ear in aluminum foil. Put it on the preheated grill. Cook, occasionally turning it for 30 minutes till corn is tender.

Nutrition Information

- Calories: 179 calories;
- Total Carbohydrate: 17.1 g
- Cholesterol: 31 mg
- Total Fat: 12.6 g
- Protein: 3 g
- Sodium: 95 mg

167. Grilled Corn With Bloody Mary Butter

"This dish is a real treat with the addition of a unique and lightly spicy spread."
Serving: 8 servings. | Prep: 15m | Ready in: 25m

Ingredients

- 1/2 cup spicy Bloody Mary mix
- 1/4 cup butter, cubed
- 3 tbsps. minced fresh cilantro
- 1 jalapeno pepper, seeded and finely chopped
- 2 tsps. hot pepper sauce
- 1 garlic clove, minced
- 1/4 tsp. salt
- 8 medium ears sweet corn, husks removed

Direction

- Mix the first 7 ingredients together in a small saucepan, then cook and stir until butter has melted.
- Grill corn with a cover on medium heat until soft while turning and basting sometimes with the butter mixture, about 10 to 12 minutes.

Nutrition Information

- Calories: 133 calories
- Total Carbohydrate: 18 g
- Cholesterol: 15 mg
- Total Fat: 7 g
- Fiber: 3 g
- Protein: 3 g
- Sodium: 193 mg

168. Grilled Dijon Summer Squash

"A great recipe for mustard-seasoned squash with a crunchy texture and delicious flavor."
Serving: 8 servings. | Prep: 20m | Ready in: 30m

Ingredients

- 1/4 cup olive oil
- 2 tbsps. red wine vinegar
- 1-1/2 tsps. minced fresh oregano or 1/2 tsp. dried oregano
- 1-1/2 tsps. Dijon mustard
- 1 garlic clove, minced
- 1/4 tsp. salt
- 1/8 tsp. pepper
- 2 medium zucchini, cut into 1/2-inch slices
- 2 medium yellow summer squash, cut into 1/2-inch slices
- 1 medium red onions, quartered
- 1 small sweet red pepper, cut into 2-inch pieces
- 1 small sweet yellow pepper, cut into 2-inch pieces
- 6 to 8 whole fresh mushrooms
- 6 cherry tomatoes

Direction

- Blend the pepper, salt, garlic, mustard, oregano, vinegar, and oil in a jar covered by a tight-fitting lid. In a shallow baking dish, arrange the vegetables. Put marinade and coat by tossing. Allow to stand for 15 minutes. Let the marinade drain and discard.

- On a vegetable grill rack, arrange the vegetables. Put a cover on and grill on medium heat until tender or 10-12 minutes.

169. Grilled Garden Veggies

"This veggies dish bring you the wonderful flavor of summer."
Serving: 8 servings. | Prep: 15m | Ready in: 30m

Ingredients

- 2 tbsps. olive oil, divided
- 1 small onion, chopped
- 2 garlic cloves, minced
- 1 tsp. dried rosemary, crushed, divided
- 2 small zucchini, sliced
- 2 small yellow summer squash, sliced
- 1/2 lb. medium fresh mushrooms, quartered
- 1 large tomato, diced
- 3/4 tsp. salt
- 1/4 tsp. pepper

Direction

- Drizzle over a double thickness of heavy-duty foil with size of 24x12-inch with 1 tbsp. of oil. Mix together 1/2 tsp. of rosemary, garlic and onion, then spoon over foil. Put tomato, mushrooms, yellow squash and zucchini on top, then drizzle leftover oil over top. Sprinkle with leftover rosemary, pepper and salt.
- Fold foil around vegetables and seal tightly, then grill on moderate heat with a cover until soft, about 15 to 20 minutes. Carefully open foil to let steam escape.

Nutrition Information

- Calories: 61 calories
- Total Carbohydrate: 6 g
- Cholesterol: 0 mg
- Total Fat: 4 g
- Fiber: 2 g
- Protein: 2 g
- Sodium: 227 mg

170. Grilled Green Beans

"A good way to use green beans."
Serving: 4 | Prep: 5m | Ready in: 45m

Ingredients

- 1 lb. fresh green beans, trimmed
- 1/4 cup olive oil
- 1 tsp. minced garlic
- 1 tsp. kosher salt

Direction

- Toss salt, garlic, olive oil and green beans to coat in a bowl. Let greens marinate for 30 minutes.
- Preheat a grill to medium heat; oil grate lightly. On grill pan, put green beans.
- On preheated grill, put grill pan. Stir and cook green beans for 10 minutes or till lightly charred.

Nutrition Information

- Calories: 156 calories;
- Total Carbohydrate: 8.3 g
- Cholesterol: 0 mg
- Total Fat: 13.6 g
- Protein: 2.1 g
- Sodium: 487 mg

171. Grilled Hash Browns

"An easy hash browns recipe."
Serving: 4 servings. | Prep: 10m | Ready in: 20m

Ingredients

- 3-1/2 cups frozen cubed hash brown potatoes, thawed
- 1 small onion, chopped
- 1 tbsp. beef bouillon granules
- Dash seasoned salt
- Dash pepper
- 1 tbsp. butter, melted

Direction

- On a 20x18" heavy-duty foil piece greased with cooking spray, arrange the potatoes. Scatter with pepper, seasoned salt, bouillon and onion; drizzle butter over.
- Fold the foil around the potatoes and seal securely. Grill with a cover for 10 to 15 minutes on indirect moderate heat or until potatoes are soft, flipping one time.

Nutrition Information

- Calories: 89 calories
- Total Carbohydrate: 14 g
- Cholesterol: 8 mg
- Total Fat: 3 g
- Fiber: 1 g
- Protein: 2 g
- Sodium: 652 mg

172. Grilled Herb Vegetables

"This is really satisfying and wonderful complement to just about any main dish."
Serving: 4 servings. | Prep: 5m | Ready in: 20m

Ingredients

- 3-1/2 cups frozen California-blend vegetables, thawed
- 1 tbsp. olive oil
- 1 tsp. Italian seasoning
- 1 tsp. minced garlic
- 1/4 tsp. salt

Direction

- Mix the entire of ingredients together in a big bowl, then remove to a double thickness of heavy-duty foil, 14"x12" in size. Fold foil over vegetables, sealing tightly.
- Grill on moderate heat with a cover until vegetables are soft, about 6 to 7 minutes per side. Carefully open foil to let steam escape.

Nutrition Information

- Calories: 59 calories
- Total Carbohydrate: 5 g
- Cholesterol: 0 mg
- Total Fat: 3 g
- Fiber: 2 g
- Protein: 2 g
- Sodium: 180 mg

173. Grilled Honey-ginger Corn

"This corn dish has a sweet honey flavor jazzed up with zippy cayenne pepper."
Serving: 4 servings. | Prep: 10m | Ready in: 25m

Ingredients

- 1/3 cup butter, softened
- 1 tbsp. minced chives
- 1 tbsp. honey
- 1/4 to 1/2 tsp. ground ginger
- 1/8 tsp. cayenne pepper
- 4 medium ears sweet corn

Direction

- Mix the first 5 ingredients together in a small bowl and spread over corn. Put on a double thickness of heavy-duty foil with each ear of corn. Fold foil around corn and seal it securely. Grill with a cover on moderate heat until soft while turning after each 5 minutes, about 15 to 20 minutes.

Nutrition Information

- Calories: 228 calories
- Total Carbohydrate: 22 g
- Cholesterol: 41 mg
- Total Fat: 16 g
- Fiber: 2 g
- Protein: 3 g
- Sodium: 168 mg

174. Grilled Loaded Potato Rounds

"My go-to recipe for outdoor potlucks."
Serving: 8 servings. | Prep: 15m | Ready in: 30m

Ingredients

- 4 large potatoes, baked and cooled
- 1/4 cup butter, melted
- 1/4 tsp. salt
- 1/4 tsp. pepper
- 1 cup (8 oz.) sour cream
- 1-1/2 cups shredded cheddar cheese
- 8 bacon strips, cooked and crumbled
- 3 tbsps. minced chives

Direction

- Cut off potatoes ends. Cut potatoes into rounds of an-inch thickness. Brush with the butter; scatter pepper and salt over. On grill rack, arrange the potatoes, buttered side facing down. Grill with a cover on moderate heat or broil for 5 to 7 minutes in a 4-inch distance away from the heat or until browned. Brush with the rest of the butter; flip. Broil or grill for an additional of 5 to 7 minutes or until browned.
- Put chives, bacon, cheese and sour cream on top.

175. Grilled Marjoram Corn

"The sweet corn husks are soaked first for precise steaming and served with a tasty marjoram butter."
Serving: 6 servings. | Prep: 20m | Ready in: 45m

Ingredients

- 6 large ears sweet corn in husks
- 1 tbsp. minced fresh marjoram or 1 tsp. dried marjoram
- 1/2 tsp. lime juice
- 1/2 cup butter, softened, divided
- 3/4 tsp. salt, divided
- 24 fresh marjoram sprigs

Direction

- In cold water, soak corn about 20 minutes. In the meantime, mix together 1/4 tsp. of salt, 1/3 cup of butter, lime juice and minced marjoram in a small bowl, then put aside.
- Peel back corn husks carefully to within 1 inch of bottoms and take off silk. Mix salt and leftover butter together, then spread the mixture over corn and put marjoram sprigs on top. Rewrap the corn in husks and use kitchen string to secure.
- Grill corn with a cover on medium heat until soft while turning sometimes, about 25 to 30 minutes. Get rid of marjoram sprigs and serve corn together with reserved butter mixture.

Nutrition Information

- Calories: 259 calories
- Total Carbohydrate: 28 g
- Cholesterol: 41 mg
- Total Fat: 17 g
- Fiber: 4 g
- Protein: 5 g
- Sodium: 473 mg

176. Grilled Onion

"It is a terrific yet simple side dish for any folks even those who don't like onions."
Serving: 4 servings. | Prep: 5m | Ready in: 30m

Ingredients

- 1 large onion, peeled
- 1 tbsp. butter
- 1 tsp. beef bouillon granules

Direction

- Hollow out the center of an onion to 1-inch deep and chop removed onion. Put in the center of onion with bouillon and butter, then place chopped onion on top. Use heavy-duty foil to wrap onion tightly.

- Grill with a cover on moderate heat until soft, about 25 to 30 minutes. Carefully open foil to let steam escape, then slice into wedges.

Nutrition Information

- Calories: 41 calories
- Total Carbohydrate: 3 g
- Cholesterol: 8 mg
- Total Fat: 3 g
- Fiber: 1 g
- Protein: 1 g
- Sodium: 227 mg

177. Grilled Onion Bloom

"It is very great to serve with any kind of meat."
Serving: 4 servings. | Prep: 10m | Ready in: 45m

Ingredients

- 1 large sweet onion (14 oz.)
- 1 tbsp. minced fresh thyme or oregano
- 2 tsps. minced fresh rosemary
- 1/2 tsp. salt
- 1/8 tsp. pepper
- 1 tbsp. butter, melted

Direction

- Cut off the top of onion to within 1/2 inch using a sharp knife, then peel onion. Cut onion into 12 to 16 wedges to within 1/2 inch of root end.
- Put onion on a double thickness of heavy-duty foil, 12 inches square in size. Open onion wedges a bit, then sprinkle pepper, salt, rosemary and thyme over top. Drizzle with butter and fold foil around onion, sealing tightly. Grill with a cover on moderate heat until soft, about 30 to 35 minutes.

Nutrition Information

- Calories: 65 calories
- Total Carbohydrate: 9 g
- Cholesterol: 8 mg

- Total Fat: 3 g
- Fiber: 2 g
- Protein: 1 g
- Sodium: 327 mg

178. Grilled Onion Potatoes

"These tasty potatoes is fixed ideally with grilled outdoors."
Serving: 5 servings. | Prep: 10m | Ready in: 60m

Ingredients

- 5 medium baking potatoes
- 1 small onion, sliced
- Salt and pepper to taste
- 1 bottle (8 oz.) zesty Italian salad dressing

Direction

- Cut each potato into 5 slices and put between slices with onion, then sprinkle pepper and salt over potato slices. Reassemble each potato and arrange them on a double layer of heavy-duty foil with size of 12 inches square.
- Pour over each potato with 2 to 4 tbsp. of salad dressing, then use foil to wrap around potatoes, sealing tightly. Grill with a cover on moderate heat until potatoes are soft, about 50 to 60 minutes.

179. Grilled Peppers And Zucchini

"This is a quick and easy versatile side dish made of colorful veggies."
Serving: 3 | Prep: 10m | Ready in: 20m

Ingredients

- 1 medium green pepper, julienned
- 1 medium sweet red pepper, julienned
- 2 medium zucchini, julienned
- 1 tbsp. butter or margarine
- 2 tsps. soy sauce

Direction

- Put on a double layer of heavy-duty foil, approximately 18x15-inch in size, with vegetables, then dot with butter. Drizzle soy sauce over top. Fold foil around vegetables, sealing tightly. Grill with a cover on moderate heat until vegetables are tender yet still crispy, about 10 to 15 minutes.

180. Grilled Pineapple

""Very simple and super great. Extra kick with hot sauce and reduces the sweetness. This can comfort with patience while the rest of the grilled feast brings together, but be informed, they go fast!""
Serving: 12 | Prep: 5m | Ready in: 15m

Ingredients

- 1 fresh pineapple - peeled, cored and cut into 1 inch rings
- 1/4 tsp. honey
- 3 tbsps. melted butter
- 1 dash hot pepper sauce
- salt to taste

Direction

- In a large resealable plastic bag, put the pineapple. Add salt, hot pepper sauce, butter, and honey. Secure bag, and jiggle to equally coat. Then let it marinate for at least 30 minutes, or ideally overnight.
- Prepare an outdoor grill by preheating to high, and put oil on the grate lightly. Then place the pineapple and grill for 2 to 3 minutes each side, or until heated well and grill marks show.

Nutrition Information

- Calories: 46 calories;
- Total Carbohydrate: 5.3 g
- Cholesterol: 8 mg
- Total Fat: 2.9 g
- Protein: 0.2 g
- Sodium: 23 mg

181.Grilled Potato Fans

"Buttery potato fans seasoned with onion, celery, garlic powder and oregano."
Serving: 6 servings. | Prep: 15m | Ready in: 55m

Ingredients

- 6 medium baking potatoes
- 2 medium onions, halved and thinly sliced
- 6 tbsps. butter, cubed
- 1/4 cup finely chopped celery
- 1 tsp. salt
- 1 tsp. dried oregano
- 1/4 tsp. garlic powder
- 1/4 tsp. pepper

Direction

- Create cuts with half-an-inch gaps in every potato using a sharp knife, retaining slices attached at the bottom. Slightly fan the potatoes. Put each on a 12" square heavy-duty foil piece. Stuff butter and onions between potato slices. Scatter with pepper, garlic powder, oregano, salt and celery. Fold the foil around the potatoes and seal securely. Grill with a cover for 40 to 45 minutes over moderately-hot heat or until soft.

Nutrition Information

- Calories: 291 calories
- Total Carbohydrate: 43 g
- Cholesterol: 31 mg
- Total Fat: 12 g
- Fiber: 5 g
- Protein: 5 g
- Sodium: 528 mg

182. Grilled Potato Packets

"It's a delicious and wonderful dish packed with full of flavor."
Serving: 4 | Ready in: 35m

Ingredients

- 2 lbs. new potatoes, scrubbed and cut into ¼-inch-thick slices
- 3 medium shallots, thinly sliced
- 2 tsps. extra-virgin olive oil
- ½ tsp. salt
- ½ tsp. freshly ground pepper

Direction

- Heat grill to moderately-high.
- At the same time, in a big bowl, add pepper, salt, oil, shallots and potatoes, then toss to coat well. Put on the counter with 2 pieces of foil with the length of 24 inches and coat them lightly with nonstick cooking spray. Place shallots and potatoes on half of each foil piece in one layer, overlapping a little bit. Leave on all sides with 2-inch border, then fold foil over and pinch the edges together to make 2 packets.
- Put packets on the grill, then cover grill and cook until potatoes are softened, or for about 12 to 15 minutes. (Be careful of steam once you open a packet to check doneness.) Serve promptly.

Nutrition Information

- Calories: 191 calories;
- Total Carbohydrate: 39 g
- Cholesterol: 0 mg
- Total Fat: 3 g
- Fiber: 4 g
- Protein: 5 g
- Sodium: 333 mg
- Sugar: 3 g
- Saturated Fat: 0 g

183. Grilled Potatoes

"It's a simple sidekick to serve with steaks or chops."
Serving: 4 servings. | Prep: 10m | Ready in: 40m

Ingredients

- 1 tbsp. olive oil
- 2 garlic cloves, minced
- 1/2 tsp. dried basil
- 1/4 tsp. salt
- 1/8 tsp. pepper
- 3 medium baking potatoes, peeled and cut into 1-inch cubes

Direction

- Mix together the first 5 ingredients in a big bowl, then put in potatoes and toss to coat well. Scoop onto a greased double thickness of heavy-duty foil (approximately 18 inch square).
- Fold foil around potato mixture and seal tightly. Grill with a cover on medium heat until potatoes are softened, while turning one time, or for 30 to 35 minutes. Carefully open foil to let steam escape.

Nutrition Information

- Calories: 126 calories
- Total Carbohydrate: 22 g
- Cholesterol: 0 mg
- Total Fat: 3 g
- Fiber: 2 g
- Protein: 2 g
- Sodium: 151 mg

184. Grilled Summer Squash

"Grilling food is very flavorful, tasty with lower fat."
Serving: 4 servings. | Prep: 15m | Ready in: 25m

Ingredients

- 2 medium yellow summer squash, sliced
- 2 medium sweet red peppers, sliced

- 1 large sweet onion, halved and sliced
- 2 tbsps. olive oil
- 2 garlic cloves, minced
- 1 tsp. sugar
- 1/4 tsp. salt
- 1/4 tsp. pepper

Direction

- Mix all ingredients together in a big bowl, then divide between 2 double thicknesses of heavy-duty foil (approximately 18"x12"). Fold foil around the vegetable mixture and seal tightly.
- Grill with a cover about 10 to 15 minutes over medium heat, until vegetables are softened. Unseal foil carefully to let steam escape.

Nutrition Information

- Calories: 124 calories
- Total Carbohydrate: 15 g
- Cholesterol: 0 mg
- Total Fat: 7 g
- Fiber: 3 g
- Protein: 3 g
- Sodium: 159 mg

185. Grilled Sweet Potato Wedges

"An easy to make crispy and delicious grilled sweet potatoes recipe."
Serving: 2 | Prep: 10m | Ready in: 15m

Ingredients

- 1 medium sweet potato, scrubbed (12 oz.)
- ¼ tsp. dried oregano, crushed
- ⅛ tsp. garlic powder
- Dash salt
- Dash ground cinnamon
- Olive oil nonstick cooking spray
- 1 tbsp. snipped fresh cilantro

Direction

- Halve the sweet potato lengthwise. Wrap it and store 1/2 for later use. Slice the leftover half in 1/2 crosswise, then slice each 1/2 lengthwise into 1-inch thick wedges. Cook the sweet potato wedges in enough boiling water to cover in a medium saucepan with cover for 8-10 minutes or just until it becomes tender, then drain well. Use paper towels to pat it dry.

- Mix together the cinnamon, salt, garlic powder and oregano in a small bowl. Use cooking spray to coat the sweet potato wedges. Evenly sprinkle the oregano mixture on top.

- Put the potato wedges on the rack of an uncovered grill directly on top of the medium coals if you're using charcoal grill. Let it grill for 3-5 minutes or until the potato wedges turn light brown and turn it once halfway through the grilling process. Sprinkle cilantro on potato pieces, then serve.

Nutrition Information

- Calories: 96 calories;
- Total Carbohydrate: 13 g
- Cholesterol: 0 mg
- Total Fat: 4 g
- Fiber: 2 g
- Protein: 1 g
- Sodium: 97 mg
- Sugar: 4 g
- Saturated Fat: 0 g

---

186. Grilled Up Sweet Potato Casserole

"Add more flavor by putting in additional mini marshmallows."
Serving: 6 servings. | Prep: 20m | Ready in: 45m

Ingredients

- 6 medium sweet potatoes (about 3-3/4 lbs.)
- 1/2 cup butter
- 3/4 tsp. ground cinnamon
- 6 tbsps. packed brown sugar
- 3/4 cup chopped pecans
- 1 cup miniature marshmallows

Direction

- Peel potatoes and cut them into 1/2-inch slices, then remove each potato to separate heavy-duty foil pieces, 12 inches square in size. Slice butter into thin slices and put between slices of potato. Sprinkle pecans, brown sugar and cinnamon over top. Fold foil around potatoes and seal tightly. Grill with a cover on moderate heat or broil 4 inches away from heat source for 18 to 22 minutes, until potatoes are soft while tuning sometimes.

- Take potatoes out of the grill and open tops of foil carefully. Sprinkle over potatoes with marshmallows; avoid sealing foil. Turn potatoes back to the grill rack and grill for 3 to 4 minutes more, until marshmallows are softened.

---

187. Grilled Vegetable Medley

"This is hearty and tasty potato dish with no-fuss."
Serving: 8-10 servings. | Prep: 10m | Ready in: 50m

Ingredients

- 12 small red potatoes, halved
- 1 medium sweet potato, peeled and cut into chunks
- 4 tbsps. butter, melted, divided
- 4 to 6 garlic cloves, minced, divided
- 2 tbsps. minced fresh parsley, divided
- 1-1/2 tsps. salt, divided
- 1/2 tsp. lemon-pepper seasoning, divided
- 3/4 lb. whole fresh mushrooms
- 1 large onion, sliced
- 1 medium green pepper, cut into 1/4-inch slices
- 1 small zucchini, cut into chunks
- 1 medium yellow summer squash, cut into chunks
- 1 cup shredded part-skim mozzarella cheese or shredded Swiss cheese
- Sour cream, optional

Direction

- On a 15"x18" heavy-duty foil piece, add potatoes and sweet potato, then drizzle 1/2 of the garlic, lemon-pepper, salt and parsley over top, sealing packet tightly. Grill with a cover for 20 minutes per side, on indirect moderately hot heat.
- In the meantime, on a 20"x18" heavy-duty foil piece, place summer squash, zucchini, green pepper, onion and mushrooms. Drizzle leftover butter over top and sprinkle over with leftover seasonings. Seal packet tightly, then grill with a cover on moderately hot heat until vegetables are tender yet still crispy, about 10 minutes per side.
- In a serving bowl, mix the contents of both packets together, then sprinkle cheese over top. Serve together with sour cream, if wanted.

---

188. Grilled Vegetable Potato Skins

"Stuffed spuds topped with a colorful vegetable mix."
Serving: 4 servings. | Prep: 30m | Ready in: 55m

Ingredients

- 2 large baking potatoes
- 1 cup sliced yellow summer squash
- 1 cup sliced zucchini
- 1/2 large sweet red pepper, julienned
- 1/2 large green pepper, julienned
- 1 small red onion, cut into 1/4-inch wedges
- 1/4 cup reduced-fat Italian salad dressing
- 1-1/2 tsps. olive oil
- 1/2 tsp. salt, divided
- 1/4 cup shredded reduced-fat cheddar cheese

Direction

- Using a fork, prick the potatoes a few times and put onto a microwavable plate. Microwave for 14 to 16 minutes on high or until softened, turning the potatoes over one time. Rest until cool enough to handle.
- In the meantime, mix onion, peppers, zucchini and squash together in a big resealable plastic bag. Put the salad dressing on top of vegetables. Enclose bag and coat by tossing; let marinate for 20 minutes.
- Halve every potato lengthwise. Scrape out the pulp, retaining a thin shell; throw the pulp away or save for other use. Brush oil on inner side of shells and scatter with a quarter tsp. of salt.
- With cooking oil, dampen one paper towel and coat grill rack lightly using tongs with long handle. Prepare grill to cook on indirect heat. Put the potato shells on grill rack, skin side facing up and grill with a cover for 10 minutes on indirect moderate heat or until golden brown.
- Let vegetables drain, setting marinade aside. Remove the vegetables to a grill basket or wok. Grill without a cover for 10 minutes over moderate heat or until softened, mixing and basting often with reserved marinade.
- Scatter cheese on potato skins. Stuff with grilled vegetables; scatter the rest of salt over. Grill for an additional of 5 minutes or until cheese melts.

Nutrition Information

- Calories: 107 calories
- Total Carbohydrate: 11 g
- Cholesterol: 4 mg
- Total Fat: 6 g
- Fiber: 3 g
- Protein: 4 g
- Sodium: 497 mg

---

189. Grilled Vegetable Skewers

"My mom and I think that grilling vegetables is the best way to have them. This recipe uses fresh herbs to highlight the summer's bountiful harvest."
Serving: 2 servings. | Prep: 10m | Ready in: 20m

Ingredients

- 1 medium ear fresh or frozen sweet corn, thawed and quartered

- 1 small zucchini, quartered
- 1/4 small red onion, halved
- 4 cherry tomatoes
- 1/4 tsp. dried basil
- 1/4 tsp. dried rosemary, crushed
- 1/4 tsp. dried thyme
- 1/8 tsp. garlic powder
- 1/8 tsp. salt
- 1/8 tsp. pepper

Direction

- Place corn on a microwaveable plate and cover with wax paper. Set microwave on high and cook for 2 minutes. Alternately cue corn, tomatoes, onions, and zucchini on two metal or water-soaked wooden skewers. Lightly spritz some cooking spray on the vegetables. Combine seasonings in a small bowl and dust over the vegetables. Moisten a piece of paper towel with oil and dab on the grill using a pair of long-handled tongs. Arrange the skewers on the grill, cover it, and grill with frequent turning over medium heat, or broil 4 in. from the heat, for 6-12 minutes until vegetables are tender.

Nutrition Information

- Calories: 69 calories
- Total Carbohydrate: 16 g
- Cholesterol: 0 mg
- Total Fat: 1 g
- Fiber: 3 g
- Protein: 3 g
- Sodium: 131 mg

190. Grilled Veggie Kabobs

"Liven up your summertime supper plate with this fresh, vibrant, yet simple side dish!"
Serving: 4 kabobs. | Prep: 20m | Ready in: 30m

Ingredients

- 2 medium ears sweet corn, husked and cut into 1-inch pieces

- 1 large sweet onion, cut into 16 wedges
- 1 each medium green, sweet red and yellow peppers, cut into 1-inch pieces
- 1 tbsp. olive oil
- 1 tsp. chili powder
- 3/4 tsp. seasoned salt
- 1/2 tsp. sugar

Direction

- Alternately skewer onion, corn, and peppers onto four metal or pre-soaked wooden skewers. Brush the kabobs with oil. Mix the salt, sugar, and chili powder, and season over the skewers. Grip a paper towel with long-handled tongs, moisten it with cooking oil, and dab on the grill rack to lightly coat it with oil. Cook in a covered, medium-heat grill, turning occasionally within the 10- to 12-minute grilling time, or until crisp on the outside and tender on the inside.

Nutrition Information

- Calories: 122 calories
- Total Carbohydrate: 21 g
- Cholesterol: 0 mg
- Total Fat: 4 g
- Fiber: 4 g
- Protein: 3 g
- Sodium: 302 mg

191. Grilled Veggie Mix

"This appealing veggie dish is really good with barbeque fare."
Serving: 10 servings. | Prep: 15m | Ready in: 45m

Ingredients

- 2 medium zucchini, cut into 1/2-inch slices
- 1 large green pepper, cut into 1/2-inch squares
- 1 large sweet red pepper, cut into 1/2-inch squares
- 1 lb. fresh mushrooms, halved
- 1 large onion, cubed
- 6 medium carrots, cut into 1/4-inch slices

- 2 cups fresh broccoli florets
- 2 cups fresh cauliflowerets
- DRESSING:
- 1/4 cup olive oil
- 1/4 cup butter, melted
- 1/4 cup minced fresh parsley
- 2 garlic cloves, minced
- 1 tsp. dried basil
- 1/2 tsp. dried oregano
- 1/2 tsp. salt

Direction

- Put down the center of 2 double-layered heavy-duty foil pieces, 18 inches square in size with vegetables. Mix together dressing ingredients and drizzle over vegetables, gently tossing to coat well.
- Fold foil around vegetable mixture, sealing tightly. Grill on moderate heat with a cover until vegetables are soft, about 15 minutes per side.

Nutrition Information

- Calories: 146 calories
- Total Carbohydrate: 12 g
- Cholesterol: 12 mg
- Total Fat: 10 g
- Fiber: 4 g
- Protein: 4 g
- Sodium: 192 mg

192. Herbed Grilled Corn On The Cob

"Last summer was the first time I've tried grilled corn and it was awesome. Now I enjoy grilled corn every summer."
Serving: 8 servings. | Prep: 20m | Ready in: 45m

Ingredients

- 8 medium ears sweet corn
- 1/2 cup butter, softened
- 2 tbsps. minced fresh basil
- 2 tbsps. minced fresh parsley

- 1/2 tsp. salt

Direction

- In a stockpot, put corn; add water to cover. Let the corn soak for 20 minutes; strain. Gently peel back the corn husks to within 1-inch of bottoms; discard the silk.
- Combine the rest of the ingredients in a small bowl; spread the mixture over the corn. Wrap the husks around the corn again; use kitchen string to keep in place.
- Close the lid and grill the corn over medium heat until soft, or about 20-25 minutes, flipping frequently. Cut the string and peel back the husks.

Nutrition Information

- Calories: 178 calories
- Total Carbohydrate: 17 g
- Cholesterol: 31 mg
- Total Fat: 12 g
- Fiber: 2 g
- Protein: 3 g
- Sodium: 277 mg

193. Horseradish-dill Grilled Corn

"This dish is so great."
Serving: 5 servings. | Prep: 30m | Ready in: 55m

Ingredients

- 5 medium ears sweet corn in husks
- 1/3 cup butter, softened
- 1 tbsp. prepared horseradish
- 1/2 tsp. salt
- 1/4 tsp. garlic powder
- 1/4 tsp. white pepper
- 1/4 tsp. snipped fresh dill
- 10 fresh dill sprigs

Direction

- Steep corn in the cold water for 60 minutes. In the meantime, in the small-sized bowl, mix snipped dill, pepper, garlic powder, salt, horseradish and butter; put aside.

- Peel the back husks out of the corn carefully to within 1 inch of the bottom; take out the silk. Spread the butter mixture on top of the corn; put two sprigs of the dill on the opposite sides of each ear. Wrap the husks one more time and secure using the kitchen string.
- With the long-handled tongs, use the cooking oil to moisten the paper towel and slightly coat grill rack. Grill the corn, with cover, on medium heat till softened, about 25 to 30 minutes, flipping occasionally. Chop the string and peel the back husks. Take out and get rid of the dill sprigs prior to serving.

Nutrition Information

- Calories: 187 calories
- Total Carbohydrate: 18 g
- Cholesterol: 32 mg
- Total Fat: 13 g
- Fiber: 3 g
- Protein: 3 g
- Sodium: 345 mg

194. Lemon-sesame Veggie Kabobs

"It's a perfect combination of sesame star and lemon! The marinade gives these plain veggie kabobs a delicious and irresistible taste."
Serving: 8 servings. | Prep: 30m | Ready in: 40m

Ingredients

- 1/4 cup lemon juice
- 1/4 cup soy sauce
- 2 tbsps. sesame oil
- 3 garlic cloves, minced
- 1 tbsp. minced chives
- 1-1/2 tsps. ground ginger
- 1 lb. medium fresh mushrooms
- 1 lb. cherry tomatoes
- 1 large sweet yellow pepper, cut into 1-inch pieces
- 1 small red onion, cut into wedges

- Hot cooked brown rice, optional

Direction

- Mix the first six ingredients in a large resealable plastic bag. Stir in tomatoes, onion, mushrooms, and pepper. Seal the bag. Flip it to coat and store inside the refrigerator for at least 1 hour. Let it drain and reserve its marinade.
- Thread all the vegetables onto the soaked wooden skewers or eight metal skewers. Grill the vegetables over medium heat while covered. You can also cook them inside the broiler, positioning them 4-inches from the heat, and cook for 6-8 minutes until tender. Be sure to flip them once and baste them constantly with the reserved marinade. It's best when served together with rice.

Nutrition Information

- Calories: 51 calories
- Total Carbohydrate: 8 g
- Cholesterol: 0 mg
- Total Fat: 2 g
- Fiber: 2 g
- Protein: 3 g
- Sodium: 156 mg

195. Lemony Vegetable Kabobs With Butter Sauce

"My kids love the food when they've had a hand in preparing it. Let yours help skewer the vibrant vegetables for grilling."
Serving: 10 servings. | Prep: 60m | Ready in: 01h10m

Ingredients

- 3 medium ears sweet corn, cut into 1/2-inch slices
- 2 large red onions, cut into wedges
- 2 medium zucchini, cut into 3/4-inch slices
- 2 medium sweet red peppers, cut into 1-inch pieces

- 1 lb. large fresh mushrooms
- 1-1/2 cups cherry tomatoes
- 1/2 cup olive oil
- 1/4 cup lemon juice
- 2 garlic cloves, minced
- 2 tsps. white wine vinegar
- 1 tsp. salt
- 1/4 tsp. pepper
- SAUCE:
- 3/4 cup butter
- 1/2 tsp. grated lemon peel
- 1/4 cup lemon juice
- 1 tsp. dried parsley flakes
- 1/2 tsp. salt

Direction

- Let 6 cups of water boil in a large saucepan. Put in the corn and cook without cover for 3 minutes. Drain the water and plunge the corn in iced water. Take the corn out and pat dry. Portion the corn and the remaining veggies into two and place each portion into its own large zip-top bag. Take a small bowl and pour oil, vinegar, and lemon juice; add the garlic, salt, and pepper and whisk until well-blended. Pour half of the mixture into each bag. Close the bag, turn several times to coat, and keep in the fridge for 8 hours or even overnight. Take 10 metal skewers and alternately skewer the vegetables. Melt butter in a small saucepan and add in the remaining ingredients, stirring well. Baste the kabobs with the sauce before grilling. Cook in a covered grill over medium heat, with occasional turning and basting, until onions and peppers are crisp outside and tender inside, about 10-12 minutes.

196. Lime And Sesame Grilled Eggplant

"It is a great eggplant dish with Asian theme seasonings."
Serving: 6 servings. | Prep: 10m | Ready in: 20m

Ingredients

- 3 tbsps. lime juice
- 1 tbsp. sesame oil
- 1-1/2 tsps. reduced-sodium soy sauce
- 1 garlic clove, minced
- 1/2 tsp. grated fresh gingerroot or 1/4 tsp. ground ginger
- 1/2 tsp. salt
- 1/8 tsp. pepper
- 1 medium eggplant (1-1/4 lbs.), cut lengthwise into 1/2-inch slices
- 2 tsps. honey
- 1/8 tsp. crushed red pepper flakes
- Thinly sliced green onion and sesame seeds

Direction

- Whisk the first 7 ingredients together in a small bowl until mixed, then brush over both sides of eggplant slices with 2 tbsp. of the juice mixture. Grill with a cover on moderate heat until tender, 4 to 6 minutes per side.
- Remove eggplant to a serving plate. Stir into leftover juice mixture with pepper flakes and honey, then drizzle over eggplant. Sprinkle sesame seeds and green onion over top.

Nutrition Information

- Calories: 50 calories
- Total Carbohydrate: 7 g
- Cholesterol: 0 mg
- Total Fat: 2 g
- Fiber: 2 g
- Protein: 1 g
- Sodium: 246 mg

197. Maple Vegetable Medley

"This dish is fresh vegetables grilled beautifully with a glaze of maple. You can enjoy this with any meat dish."
Serving: 8 servings. | Prep: 20m | Ready in: 45m

Ingredients

- 1/3 cup balsamic vinegar
- 1/3 cup maple syrup
- 1 large red onion
- 1 lb. fresh asparagus, trimmed
- 1 lb. baby carrots
- 2 medium zucchini, cut lengthwise into thirds and seeded
- 1 medium sweet red pepper, cut into eight pieces
- 1 medium sweet yellow pepper, cut into eight pieces
- 2 tbsps. olive oil
- 1 tbsp. minced fresh thyme or 1 tsp. dried thyme
- 1/2 tsp. salt
- 1/2 tsp. pepper

Direction

- To prepare the glaze, boil syrup and vinegar in a small saucepan. Lower the heat, then cook while stirring over medium heat until thickened, 6-8 minutes. Take away from heat; put aside.
- Slice onion into 8 wedges to 1/2-inch of the bottom. In a big bowl, add peppers, zucchini, carrots, asparagus, and onion. Drizzle oil over and sprinkle with seasonings; stir to blend.
- Wet a paper towel using cooking oil, then rub over the grill rack, using long-handled tongs, until lightly coat. Put the vegetables on the rack.
- Close the lid and grill over medium heat or broil 4 inches from heat, about 10 minutes per side. Brush 1/2 of the glaze over; grill until tenderly crisped, 5-8 minutes more. Brush the leftover glaze over before eating.

Nutrition Information

- Calories: 120 calories
- Total Carbohydrate: 21 g
- Cholesterol: 0 mg
- Total Fat: 4 g
- Fiber: 3 g
- Protein: 2 g
- Sodium: 201 mg

198. Onion-basil Grilled Vegetables

"Grilled vegetables recipe."
Serving: 6 servings. | Prep: 25m | Ready in: 50m

Ingredients

- 3 medium ears fresh corn, cut into 3 pieces
- 1 lb. medium red potatoes, quartered
- 1 cup fresh baby carrots
- 1 large green pepper, cut into 1-inch pieces
- 1 large sweet red pepper, cut into 1-inch pieces
- 1 envelope onion soup mix
- 3 tbsps. minced fresh basil or 1 tbsp. dried basil
- 1 tbsp. olive oil
- 1/4 tsp. pepper
- 1 tbsp. butter

Direction

- Mix together the initial 9 ingredients in a big bowl and toss until coated. Put it on a double thickness of heavy-duty foil (approximately 28x18-inches). Dot it using butter. Fold the foil surrounding the veggie mixture and tightly seal.
- Let it grill for 25 to 30 minutes on medium heat with cover or until the potatoes become tender, flipping once.

Nutrition Information

- Calories: 164 calories
- Total Carbohydrate: 28 g
- Cholesterol: 5 mg

- Total Fat: 5 g
- Fiber: 4 g
- Protein: 4 g
- Sodium: 453 mg

199. Oregano Onions

""Enjoy these soft seasoned onions together with different types of grilled meat.""
Serving: 10 servings. | Prep: 10m | Ready in: 40m

Ingredients

- 5 large onions, sliced
- 6 tsps. butter
- 1-1/2 tsps. dried oregano
- Pepper to taste

Direction

- Coat the two 22x18-inches double-layered heavy-duty foil with cooking spray. Distribute the onions among the prepared foil. Top the onion with pepper, oregano, and butter. Gently fold the foil all around the mixture. Seal the foils tightly and grill them while covered over indirect heat for 30 to 40 minutes until the onions turn tender.

Nutrition Information

- Calories: 41 calories
- Total Carbohydrate: 7 g
- Cholesterol: 0 mg
- Total Fat: 2 g
- Fiber: 0 g
- Protein: 1 g
- Sodium: 28 mg

200. Pit Stop Potatoes

"Grilled potatoes that uses disposable foil pan that means easy cleanup."
Serving: 3 servings. | Prep: 15m | Ready in: 35m

Ingredients

- 2 large potatoes, thinly sliced
- 1/4 cup chopped onion
- 1/4 cup sliced baby portobello mushrooms
- 1/4 cup chopped green pepper
- 1/2 tsp. salt
- 1/2 tsp. pepper
- 1/2 tsp. taco seasoning
- 2 tbsps. butter, cut into small cubes

Direction

- Pile the green pepper, mushrooms, onion and potatoes in an oiled non-reusable foil pan. Scatter with Southwest seasoning, pepper and salt; dot with butter.
- Wrap in foil. Grill for 20 to 25 minutes on moderate-hot heat or until potatoes are soft. Unseal foil cautiously to release steam.

Nutrition Information

- Calories: 271 calories
- Total Carbohydrate: 47 g
- Cholesterol: 20 mg
- Total Fat: 8 g
- Fiber: 5 g
- Protein: 6 g
- Sodium: 496 mg

201. Potato Packets

"A very easy to grill side dish."
Serving: 4 servings. | Prep: 10m | Ready in: 30m

Ingredients

- 2 medium potatoes, peeled and diced
- 1 cup chopped onion
- 2 tbsps. butter

- 1/2 tsp. salt
- 1/4 tsp. white pepper

Direction

- Distribute pepper, salt, butter, onion, and potatoes among 2 heavy-duty foil pieces, approximately 18x18-inch. Fold the foil around potato mixture; seal securely. Cook on a grill with a cover for 20 minutes to half an hour over moderate heat or until potatoes are soft.

Nutrition Information

- Calories: 128 calories
- Total Carbohydrate: 18 g
- Cholesterol: 15 mg
- Total Fat: 6 g
- Fiber: 2 g
- Protein: 2 g
- Sodium: 356 mg

202. Red Potato Bundles

"I haven't stopped cooking, and this is one of the recipes that is often do."
Serving: 2 servings. | Prep: 10m | Ready in: 50m

Ingredients

- 6 small red potatoes, quartered
- 1 small onion, thinly sliced
- 6 whole garlic cloves, peeled
- 2 sprigs fresh rosemary or 1 to 2 tsps. dried rosemary, crushed
- 1/2 tsp. salt
- Dash pepper
- 2 tbsps. grated Parmesan cheese
- 1/4 cup olive oil

Direction

- Add garlic, onion and potatoes on 2 heavy-duty foil pieces, approximately 12-inch square; put cheese, pepper, salt and rosemary on top.

Add on a drizzle of oil. Fold in the edges and seal securely.
- Grill with a cover for 40 to 45 minutes over moderate heat or until potatoes are soft. Cautiously unseal foil to release steam.

Nutrition Information

- Calories: 390 calories
- Total Carbohydrate: 29 g
- Cholesterol: 4 mg
- Total Fat: 29 g
- Fiber: 3 g
- Protein: 6 g
- Sodium: 694 mg

203. Roast Corn On The Cob

"Make this corn dish extra special by roasting it, all wrapped up on the grill."
Serving: 6 servings. | Prep: 5m | Ready in: 30m

Ingredients

- 6 ears fresh sweet corn
- 6 tbsps. butter
- 6 ice cubes
- Salt and pepper to taste
- Additional butter, optional

Direction

- Take off both husks and silk from corn. Put on a double thickness of heavy-duty foil approximately 18x12-inch in size with each ear of corn. Put in 1 ice cube and 1 tbsp. of butter, then wrap securely and twist ends of foil to create handles for turning.
- Grill corn with a cover on moderate direct heat for 25 minutes while turning sometimes, until soft. Carefully open the foil to let steam escape, then sprinkle pepper and salt over top. Serve together with more butter, if you want.

Nutrition Information

- Calories: 190 calories

- Total Carbohydrate: 19 g
- Cholesterol: 31 mg
- Total Fat: 13 g
- Fiber: 2 g
- Protein: 3 g
- Sodium: 107 mg

204. Roasted Corn On The Cob

"It's a great way to make a delicious dish from corn."
Serving: 8 servings. | Prep: 5m | Ready in: 30m

Ingredients

- 8 medium ears sweet corn, husks removed
- Refrigerated butter-flavored spray
- 2 tbsps. butter, melted
- 2 tbsps. prepared horseradish
- 2 tbsps. Dijon mustard
- 2 garlic cloves, minced
- 1/2 tsp. salt
- 1/8 tsp. pepper
- 1/8 tsp. paprika

Direction

- Use cooking spray to coat 8 12x10-inch pieces of foil. Put on each foil piece with an ear of corn and use butter-flavored spray to spritz corn evenly. Fold foil over corn and seal securely.
- Grill corn with a cover on moderate indirect heat or bake at 400 degrees until corn is soft, about 25 to 30 minutes. Mix together pepper, salt, garlic, mustard, horseradish and butter, then brush the mixture over corn and sprinkle paprika on top.

Nutrition Information

- Calories: 115 calories
- Total Carbohydrate: 20 g
- Cholesterol: 8 mg
- Total Fat: 4 g
- Fiber: 2 g
- Protein: 3 g

- Sodium: 291 mg

205. Root Beer Apple Baked Beans

"My bean recipe with apple and bacon has become an indispensable dish in my family dinners."
Serving: 12 servings. | Prep: 20m | Ready in: 01h05m

Ingredients

- 6 thick-sliced bacon strips, chopped
- 4 cans (16 oz. each) baked beans
- 1 can (21 oz.) apple pie filling
- 1 can (12 oz.) root beer
- 1 tsp. ground ancho chili pepper, optional
- 1 cup shredded smoked cheddar cheese, optional

Direction

- Use 32 to 36 charcoal briquettes or large wood chips to make campfire or bring grill to medium heat.
- Cook bacon in 10-inch Dutch oven over the campfire until crisp. Take bacon out and discard bacon grease. Put bacon back into the pan; mix in ancho chili pepper (if using), root beer, pie filling, and baked beans; put the lid on. Once wood chips or briquettes are covered with ash, position the Dutch oven atop 16 to 18 briquettes. Arrange the remaining 16 to 18 briquettes over the lid.
- Cook until flavors blend, for 30 to 40 minutes. Sprinkle with cheese before serving, if desired.

Nutrition Information

- Calories: 255 calories
- Total Carbohydrate: 47 g
- Cholesterol: 16 mg
- Total Fat: 5 g
- Fiber: 9 g
- Protein: 10 g
- Sodium: 778 mg

206. Santa Fe Corn On The Cob

"This recipe is a great way to use corn. It's has a Southwestern flavor, but not too spicy or hot. My family really enjoys it."
Serving: 6 servings. | Prep: 10m | Ready in: 35m

Ingredients

- 6 medium ears sweet corn in husks
- 1 tbsp. butter
- 2 garlic cloves, minced
- 1/4 cup steak sauce
- 3/4 tsp. chili powder
- 1/4 tsp. ground cumin

Direction

- Put corn in cold water to soak, about 60 minutes. In the meantime, mix garlic and butter together in a microwave-safe dish. Put a cover on and microwave on high until the garlic is soft, about 2 minutes, tossing 1 time. Mix in cumin, chili powder, and steak sauce; put aside.
- Gently peel back the husks from corn to within 1 in. of bottom; discard the silk. Brush the sauce over the corn. Wrap the husks around the corn again, use a kitchen string to keep in place.
- With long-handled tongs, soak a paper towel in cooking oil to moisten and lightly coat the rack of the grill. Close the lid and grill the corn over medium heat, flipping sometimes, about 25-30 minutes.

Nutrition Information

- Calories: 107 calories
- Total Carbohydrate: 20 g
- Cholesterol: 5 mg
- Total Fat: 3 g
- Fiber: 3 g
- Protein: 3 g
- Sodium: 223 mg

207. Savory Grilled Corn

"This recipe will make corn on the cob taste even better."
Serving: 4 servings. | Prep: 10m | Ready in: 45m

Ingredients

- 1/2 cup mayonnaise
- 2 garlic cloves, minced
- 1/2 tsp. dried minced onion
- 1/2 tsp. dried parsley flakes
- 1/2 tsp. paprika
- 1/4 tsp. salt
- 1/4 tsp. pepper
- 4 medium ears sweet corn, silk and husks removed
- 1/4 cup grated Parmesan cheese

Direction

- Mix the first 7 ingredients in a small bowl. Spread the mixture over the corn; sprinkle Parmesan cheese over. Wrap a heavy-duty foil with double thickness around each corn ear. Close the lid and grill over medium heat until the corn is soft, or about 30-35 minutes, flipping sometimes.

208. Skewered Potatoes

"A unique recipe for red potatoes. Microwaving ensures they're cooked and tender inside, while grilling gives them a crisp exterior."
Serving: 6-8 servings. | Prep: 15m | Ready in: 25m

Ingredients

- 2 lbs. small red potatoes, quartered
- 1/3 cup cold water
- 1/2 cup Miracle Whip
- 1/4 cup dry white wine or chicken broth
- 2 tsps. dried rosemary, crushed
- 1 tsp. garlic powder

Direction

- Cover potatoes in water in 2-qt. microwaveable dish. Put the lid on and microwave on high for 8-12 minutes or until tender. Stir halfway through its cooking time. Drain. Take a large bowl and mix together the remaining ingredients before adding in the potatoes, tossing gently to coat. Cover and refrigerate for an hour. Drain while saving the marinade for basting. Cue the potatoes on metal or water-soaked wooden skewers. Cook in a covered grill on hot for 6-8 minutes, until potatoes are golden brown. Turn and baste from time to time with reserved marinade.

Nutrition Information

- Calories: 189 calories
- Total Carbohydrate: 19 g
- Cholesterol: 5 mg
- Total Fat: 11 g
- Fiber: 2 g
- Protein: 2 g
- Sodium: 82 mg

209. Smokin' Spiced Corn

"A great corn dish."
Serving: 6 servings. | Prep: 15m | Ready in: 25m

Ingredients

- 3 tbsps. butter
- 1/2 cup honey
- 1 to 2 tbsps. hot pepper sauce
- 2 garlic cloves, minced
- 1/2 tsp. salt
- 1/4 tsp. smoked paprika
- 1/4 tsp. ground cumin
- 1/4 tsp. pepper
- 6 medium ears sweet corn, husks removed

Direction

- Melt butter in a small saucepan. Stir in seasonings, garlic, pepper sauce and honey until combined, then heat through. Brush some of the mixture over corn.
- With long-handled tongs, wet a paper towel with cooking oil and coat the grill rack

slightly. Grill corn with a cover on medium heat until corn is soft, about 10 to 15 minutes, while turning and basting sometimes with leftover sauce.

210. Smoky Grilled Corn

"This dish is buttery corn with a spicy and sweet taste. It goes very well with steaks."
Serving: 6 servings. | Prep: 25m | Ready in: 35m

Ingredients

- 2 tbsps. plus 1-1/2 tsps. butter
- 1/2 cup honey
- 2 large garlic cloves, minced
- 2 tbsps. hot pepper sauce
- 1/2 tsp. salt
- 1/4 tsp. pepper
- 1/4 tsp. paprika
- 6 medium ears sweet corn, husks removed

Direction

- Heat butter in a small saucepan to melt. Mix in seasonings, pepper sauce, garlic, and honey until mixed; thoroughly heat. Brush the mixture over corn.
- Use cooking oil to moisten a paper towel; lightly coat the grill rack using long-handled tongs.
- Close the lid and grill the corn until the corn is soft, about 10-12 minutes over medium heat, sometimes basting the butter mixture over and flipping. Enjoy the corn with any leftover butter mixture.

Nutrition Information

- Calories: 208 calories
- Total Carbohydrate: 41 g
- Cholesterol: 13 mg
- Total Fat: 6 g
- Fiber: 3 g
- Protein: 3 g
- Sodium: 275 mg

211. Snappy Peas 'n' Mushrooms

"This dish is so delightfully seasoned with dill."
Serving: 8-10 servings. | Prep: 10m | Ready in: 20m

Ingredients

- 1 lb. fresh sugar snap or snow peas
- 1/2 cup sliced fresh mushrooms
- 2 tbsps. sliced green onions
- 1 tbsp. snipped fresh dill or 1 tsp. dill weed
- 2 tbsps. butter
- Salt and pepper to taste

Direction

- Add mushrooms and peas onto the piece of double-layer heavy-duty foil that is roughly 18 inches square piece. Drizzle with the dill and onions; use the butter to dot. Fold the foil around the mixture and seal it securely.
- Grill, while covered, on medium hot heat for 5 minutes. Flip over; grill till the veggies soften or for 5 to 8 minute more. Open the foil gently to let the steam escape. Use pepper and salt to season.

Nutrition Information

- Calories: 40 calories
- Total Carbohydrate: 3 g
- Cholesterol: 6 mg
- Total Fat: 2 g
- Fiber: 1 g
- Protein: 2 g
- Sodium: 25 mg

212. Special Grilled Veggies

"This colorful side dish goes well with any grilled seafood, chicken or meat. Plus, it's very easy to prepare."
Serving: 4-6 servings. | Prep: 15m | Ready in: 25m

Ingredients

- 1/2 cup red wine vinegar
- 1/4 cup olive oil
- 2 garlic cloves, minced
- 1/2 tsp. lemon-pepper seasoning
- 1/2 tsp. dried basil
- 1/2 tsp. dried thyme
- 1 lb. fresh asparagus, trimmed
- 1 large red onion, sliced and separated into rings
- 1 large sweet red pepper, cut into 1-inch strips
- 1 large sweet yellow pepper, cut into 1-inch strips

Direction

- Combine the first six ingredients in a large resealable plastic bag. Put in vegetables and flip to coat. Seal and put in refrigerator for 1 hour or overnight, flipping once.
- Drain, putting aside the marinade. Arrange vegetables in a disposable foil pan with slits cut in the bottom or a grill basket. Grill without a cover for 5 minutes over medium-high heat. Flip; use reserved marinade to baste the vegetables. Grill for 5 to 8 minutes more or until the vegetables are softened.

Nutrition Information

- Calories: 121 calories
- Total Carbohydrate: 9 g
- Cholesterol: 0 mg
- Total Fat: 9 g
- Fiber: 2 g
- Protein: 2 g
- Sodium: 45 mg

213. Spiced Grilled Corn

"A fantastic corn recipe."
Serving: 8 servings. | Prep: 10m | Ready in: 20m

Ingredients

- 2 tsps. ground cumin
- 2 tsps. ground coriander
- 1 tsp. salt
- 1 tsp. dried oregano
- 1/2 tsp. ground ginger
- 1/4 tsp. ground cinnamon
- 1/4 tsp. pepper
- 1/8 tsp. ground cloves
- 2 tbsps. olive oil
- 8 medium ears sweet corn, husks removed

Direction

- Combine the initial 8 ingredients in a small bowl. Brush corn with oil and sprinkle with the spice mixture. Put each on a 14x12-inch rectangle of heavy-duty foil. Fold foil around corn and seal tightly.
- Grill corn 10-12 minutes on medium heat with a cover, turning from time to time, or until tender. Carefully open foil to let steam escape.

Nutrition Information

- Calories: 113 calories
- Total Carbohydrate: 18 g
- Cholesterol: 0 mg
- Total Fat: 5 g
- Fiber: 3 g
- Protein: 3 g
- Sodium: 310 mg

214. Spicy Grilled Eggplant

"The Cajun seasoning really enhances the flavors of this dish. It's great to enjoy with meats or pasta."
Serving: 8 servings. | Prep: 10m | Ready in: 20m

Ingredients

- 2 small eggplants, cut into 1/2-inch slices
- 1/4 cup olive oil
- 2 tbsps. lime juice
- 3 tsps. Cajun seasoning

Direction

- Brush oil over eggplant slices. Use lime juice to drizzle and Cajun seasoning to sprinkle. Allow to sit for 5 minutes.
- Close the lid and broil the eggplant 4-inch from the heat or grill on medium heat for 4-5 minutes each side until soft.

Nutrition Information

- Calories: 88 calories
- Total Carbohydrate: 7 g
- Cholesterol: 0 mg
- Total Fat: 7 g
- Fiber: 4 g
- Protein: 1 g
- Sodium: 152 mg

215. Sweet Corn 'n' Peppers

"It is really a mouthwatering grilled sweet corn."
Serving: 6 servings. | Prep: 15m | Ready in: 30m

Ingredients

- 1 medium sweet red pepper, julienned
- 1 medium green pepper, julienned
- 1 medium jalapeno pepper, seeded and julienned
- 1 medium sweet onion, cut into thin wedges
- 1/2 tsp. salt
- 1/2 tsp. pepper
- 1/8 tsp. cayenne pepper

- Dash paprika
- 6 large ears sweet corn, husks removed and halved

Direction

- Mix together onion and peppers in a small bowl. Mix together paprika, cayenne, pepper and salt, then sprinkle over the vegetables with 1/2 of the mixture; put aside. Sprinkle over corn with leftover seasoning mixture.
- On a vegetable grilling rack greased with cooking spray or in a perforated disposable aluminum pan, place corn.
- Grill on moderate heat with a cover about 10 minutes. Put in reserved vegetables, then grill with a cover until vegetables are soft while stirring sometimes and rotating corn, for 5 to 10 minutes more.

216. Three-cheese Potatoes

"This side dish has a great cheese and bacon flair."
Serving: 4-6 servings. | Prep: 15m | Ready in: 50m

Ingredients

- 3 large potatoes, peeled and cut into 1-inch cubes
- 1 medium onion, chopped
- 3 tbsps. grated Parmesan cheese
- 1 tbsp. minced chives
- 1/2 tsp. seasoned salt
- 1/4 tsp. pepper
- 2 tbsps. butter
- 1/2 cup crumbled cooked bacon
- 1/2 cup shredded part-skim mozzarella cheese
- 1/2 cup shredded cheddar cheese

Direction

- Mix the first 6 ingredients together in a big bowl, then remove to a double thickness of heavy-duty foil coated with grease, 18 inches square in size. Dot the mixture with butter.
- Fold foil around potato mixture, sealing tightly. Grill with a cover on moderate heat

until potatoes are soft, about 15 to 18 minutes per side.
- Open foil carefully, then sprinkle over potato mixture with bacon cheeses. Grill until cheese has melted, for another 3 to 5 minutes more. Carefully open foil to let steam escape.

Nutrition Information

- Calories: 293 calories
- Total Carbohydrate: 36 g
- Cholesterol: 36 mg
- Total Fat: 11 g
- Fiber: 3 g
- Protein: 13 g
- Sodium: 614 mg

217. Vegetable Kabobs

"Grilling is one of the best ways to cook fresh produce. The tangy Italian marinade in this recipe brings out the best in each of the vegetables by spicing them in just the right amount."
Serving: 4 servings. | Prep: 20m | Ready in: 30m

Ingredients

- 1 garlic clove, peeled
- 1 tsp. salt
- 1/3 cup olive oil
- 3 tbsps. lemon juice
- 1 tsp. Italian seasoning
- 1/4 tsp. pepper
- 8 medium fresh mushrooms
- 2 small zucchini, cut into 1/2-inch slices
- 2 small onions, cut into six wedges
- 8 cherry tomatoes

Direction

- Mince the garlic with salt in a small bowl to make a paste. Mix in oil, Italian seasoning, lemon juice, and pepper. Alternately skewer the different vegetables onto metal or pre-soaked wooden skewers. Arrange skewers in a shallow dish and pour the garlic mixture over them. Marinate for 15 minutes. Place kabobs in the grill, cover it, and cook over medium heat for 10-15minutes or until vegetables are just about tender. Turn frequently to cook all sides.

Nutrition Information

- Calories: 202 calories
- Total Carbohydrate: 9 g
- Cholesterol: 0 mg
- Total Fat: 18 g
- Fiber: 2 g
- Protein: 3 g
- Sodium: 598 mg

218. Veggies On The Grill

"Your homegrown vegetables will taste a lot better with this recipe."
Serving: 6 servings. | Prep: 10m | Ready in: 30m

Ingredients

- 1/3 cup vegetable oil
- 1-1/2 tsps. garlic powder
- 1/2 tsp. salt
- 1/4 tsp. pepper
- 1/8 tsp. cayenne pepper
- 3 medium carrots, halved lengthwise
- 3 large potatoes, quartered lengthwise
- 3 medium zucchini, quartered lengthwise

Direction

- Mix cayenne, pepper, salt, garlic powder, and oil together in a small bowl. Brush the mixture over the vegetables. Close the lid and grill potatoes and carrots over medium heat, for 10 minutes. Baste. Add zucchini. Close the lid and grill until the vegetables are soft, for another 10-15 minutes, basting and flipping every 5 minutes.

Nutrition Information

- Calories: 282 calories
- Total Carbohydrate: 40 g
- Cholesterol: 0 mg

- Total Fat: 12 g
- Fiber: 5 g
- Protein: 5 g
- Sodium: 222 mg

219. Very Veggie Baked Potatoes

"Alternate heavy meat dishes with these chock-full-of-vegetables baked potatoes."
Serving: 4 servings. | Prep: 25m | Ready in: 35m

Ingredients

- 4 large baking potatoes
- 2 medium yellow summer squash, sliced
- 2 small zucchini, sliced
- 1 small eggplant, sliced
- 2 medium leeks (white portion only), sliced lengthwise into quarters
- 2 tbsps. reduced-fat Italian salad dressing
- 1/8 tsp. salt
- 1 package (6-1/2 oz.) garlic-herb spreadable cheese
- 1/4 cup reduced-fat sour cream
- 1/4 cup fresh basil leaves, thinly sliced

Direction

- Scrub and pierce potatoes; put onto a microwave-safe plate. Microwave without a cover on high until tender, about 15 minutes, turning once.
- Mix together leeks, eggplant, zucchini and the squash in a large bowl. Pour in salad dressing and mix to coat. Move vegetables to a grill wok or basket. Grill without a cover over medium heat until tender for 8-12 minutes, stirring frequently. Use salt to sprinkle and keep warm.
- Blend sour cream and spreadable cheese. Cut an "X" in each potato with a sharp knife. Use a fork to fluff pulp. Spoon the grilled vegetables over potatoes; dollop with cheese mixture. Decorate with basil.

Nutrition Information

- Calories: 586 calories
- Total Carbohydrate: 87 g
- Cholesterol: 59 mg
- Total Fat: 23 g
- Fiber: 12 g
- Protein: 15 g
- Sodium: 458 mg

220. Zesty Grilled Corn

"This recipe is certainly ideal for a summer gatherings."
Serving: 6 servings. | Prep: 15m | Ready in: 30m

Ingredients

- 1/3 cup butter, cubed
- 2 tbsps. prepared mustard
- 2 tbsps. prepared horseradish
- 1 tsp. Worcestershire sauce
- 1/4 to 1/2 tsp. lemon-pepper seasoning
- 6 ears sweet corn, husked

Direction

- Melt butter in a small saucepan, then add in lemon-pepper, Worcestershire sauce, horseradish and mustard. Put on a 13"x12" piece of heavy-duty foil each ear of corn, then use butter mixture to drizzle over. Fold foil in edges and seal but leave space for expansion of steam.
- Grill without a cover on medium heat until corn is soft, about 5 to 6 minutes per side. Unwrap foil carefully.

Nutrition Information

- Calories: 173 calories
- Total Carbohydrate: 18 g
- Cholesterol: 27 mg
- Total Fat: 11 g
- Fiber: 3 g
- Protein: 3 g
- Sodium: 216 mg

Chapter 4: Fathers Day Dinner Recipes

***

221. Apple-marinated Chicken & Vegetables

"This recipe with chicken and veggies is so simple and amazing."
Serving: 6 servings. | Prep: 20m | Ready in: 45m

Ingredients

- 1 cup apple juice
- 1/2 cup canola oil
- 1/4 cup packed brown sugar
- 1/4 cup reduced-sodium soy sauce
- 3 tbsps. lemon juice
- 2 tbsps. minced fresh parsley
- 3 garlic cloves, minced
- 6 boneless skinless chicken breast halves (6 oz. each)
- 4 large carrots
- 2 medium zucchini
- 2 medium yellow summer squash

Direction

- In a small-sized bowl, stir the first seven ingredients until blended. Add the chicken and 1 cup of the marinade into a big resealable plastic bag; seal the bag and turn until coated. Keep in the refrigerator for 6 hours or overnight. Refrigerate, covered, the rest of the marinade.
- Quarter the squash, zucchini and carrots lengthwise; slice crosswise into 2-inch pieces.

Toss with half a cup of the marinade reserved earlier.

- Drain the chicken off excess liquid, getting rid of the marinade in the bag. Grill the chicken, keep covered, on medium heat or broil 4 inches away from the heat source until the thermometer reaches 165 degrees, 6 to 8 minutes per side, basting often with the rest of the marinade during the last 5 minutes of cooking process. Keep warm.
- Move the vegetables into the basket or grill wok; position onto the grill rack. Grill, keep covered, on medium heat until tender-crisp or for 10 to 12 minutes, whisking often. Serve along the chicken.

Nutrition Information

- Calories: 367 calories
- Total Carbohydrate: 19 g
- Cholesterol: 94 mg
- Total Fat: 16 g
- Fiber: 3 g
- Protein: 37 g
- Sodium: 378 mg

222. Barbecued Pork Chops With Rosemary Lemon Marinade

"I'm not "chicken" to experiment when it comes to cooking. This marinade was discovered in a cookbook for poultry and I decided to give it a try using pork chops. It became a preference! Be generous while basting pork ribs or roast using the marinade, I did, and I ended up with two additional family favorite dishes."
Serving: 4 servings. | Prep: 10m | Ready in: 25m

Ingredients

- 2 garlic cloves, minced
- 1/2 cup lemon juice
- 2 tsps. grated lemon zest
- 2 tbsps. olive oil
- 1 tbsp. minced fresh rosemary or 1 tsp. dried rosemary, crushed
- 1/8 tsp. dried basil

- 1/8 tsp. lemon-pepper seasoning
- 4 bone-in pork loin chops (1 inch thick)

Direction

- Add lemon juice, garlic, oil, zest, basil, rosemary, and pepper in a small bowl and whisk together. Fill a big resealable bag with 1/3 cup of marinade, then add in the pork. Seal and turn the bag to coat the meat evenly, then store refrigerated overnight or for a minimum of 2 hours, with occasional turns in between. Keep the remaining marinade covered and refrigerated.
- Strain out marinade, then apply remaining marinade on chops when cooking. Grill on medium heat for 4-5 minutes per side or until thermometer reading shows 145 degrees. Let the meat rest for 5 minutes then serve.

Nutrition Information

- Calories: 171 calories
- Total Carbohydrate: 3 g
- Cholesterol: 99 mg
- Total Fat: 10 g
- Fiber: 0 g
- Protein: 17 g
- Sodium: 43 mg

223. Beef Short Ribs Vindaloo

"An India-inspired beef dish that I've made a few changes to fit my tastes. The smell of the spices is great as the ribs are slow cooked all day."
Serving: 4 servings. | Prep: 30m | Ready in: 08h45m

Ingredients

- 1 tbsp. cumin seeds
- 2 tsps. coriander seeds
- 1 tbsp. butter
- 1 medium onion, finely chopped
- 8 garlic cloves, minced
- 1 tbsp. minced fresh gingerroot
- 2 tsps. mustard seed
- 1/2 tsp. ground cloves

- 1/4 tsp. kosher salt
- 1/4 tsp. ground cinnamon
- 1/4 tsp. cayenne pepper
- 1/2 cup red wine vinegar
- 4 bay leaves
- 2 lbs. bone-in beef short ribs
- 1 cup fresh sugar snap peas, halved
- Hot cooked rice and plain yogurt

Direction

- In a small, dry frying pan over medium heat, toast coriander seeds and cumin while stirring often, until fragrant. Let cool. Use a spice grinder, or a mortar and pestle to coarsely crush seeds.
- In a big saucepan, heat butter over medium heat. Put in the ginger, garlic and onion; cook and stir for about 1 minute. Put in the crushed seeds, cayenne pepper, cinnamon, salt, cloves and mustard seed; cook and stir for 1 more minute. Allow to cool completely.
- In a big resealable plastic bag, combine the onion mixture, bay leaves and vinegar. Put in ribs; seal the bag and flip to coat. Let it refrigerate overnight.
- Move the rib mixture into a 4-quart slow cooker. Cook with cover on Low for 8-10 hours, or till meat becomes soft. Mix in peas; cook for 8-10 minutes more, or until peas become crisp-tender. Scoop off fat; eliminate bay leaves. Serve rib mixture along with yogurt and rice.

Nutrition Information

- Calories: 266 calories
- Total Carbohydrate: 13 g
- Cholesterol: 62 mg
- Total Fat: 15 g
- Fiber: 3 g
- Protein: 21 g
- Sodium: 180 mg

224. Bourbon Brat Skewers

"This recipe is listed on one of our VIP party lists. They love how the veggies were marinated well in a bourbon sauce and served with a grilled bratwurst."
Serving: 6 skewers. | Prep: 20m | Ready in: 35m

Ingredients

- 1/2 cup reduced-sodium soy sauce
- 1/2 cup bourbon
- 3 tbsps. brown sugar
- 1 tsp. seasoned salt
- 1/4 tsp. cayenne pepper
- 2 cups whole mushrooms
- 2 medium sweet red peppers, cut into 1-inch pieces
- 1 medium green pepper, cut into 1-inch pieces
- 1 medium onion, cut into wedges
- 1 package (16 oz.) Johnsonville® Original Brats, cut into 1-inch slices

Direction

- Mix the first five ingredients in a large resealable plastic bag. Put in vegetables. Seal the bag and flip it to coat. Store it inside the fridge for at least 60 minutes.
- Drain the vegetables, reserving the marinade. Thread the vegetables and bratwurst alternately on the six metal or soaked wooden skewers.
- Pour some reserved marinade over the threaded ingredients. Grill over medium heat, covered for 15-20 minutes, or until the vegetables are tender and the bratwurst is no longer pink. Make sure to turn and baste them often with the reserved marinade during the last 5 minutes.

Nutrition Information

- Calories: 346 calories
- Total Carbohydrate: 17 g
- Cholesterol: 56 mg
- Total Fat: 22 g
- Fiber: 3 g
- Protein: 15 g

- Sodium: 1998 mg

225. Caribbean Grilled Ribeyes

"Impress everyone with this lovely grilled steak that goes really well with seafood on the side!"
Serving: 4 servings. | Prep: 10m | Ready in: 20m

Ingredients

- 1/2 cup Dr Pepper
- 3 tbsps. honey
- 1/4 cup Caribbean jerk seasoning
- 1-1/2 tsps. chopped seeded habanero pepper
- 1/2 tsp. salt
- 1/2 tsp. pepper
- 4 beef ribeye steaks (3/4 lb. each)

Direction

- In a blender, put in all the first 6 ingredients together then put the lid on and blend until the mixture is well-combined. Place the mixture in a big ziplock plastic bag. Put in the steaks then seal the ziplock bag and turn to coat the steaks with the marinade. Keep in the fridge for no less than 2 hours.
- Drain the marinated steaks and throw away the marinade mixture. Put the marinated steaks on a grill over medium heat then cover and grill or put the steaks on a broiler and let it broil 3-4 inches away from the heat for 4-6 minutes on both sides until the preferred meat doneness is achieved (a thermometer inserted in the meat should indicate 160°F for medium, 170°F for well-done and 145°F for medium-rare).

Nutrition Information

- Calories: 762 calories
- Total Carbohydrate: 4 g
- Cholesterol: 202 mg
- Total Fat: 54 g
- Fiber: 0 g
- Protein: 61 g
- Sodium: 442 mg

226. Caribbean-spiced Pork Tenderloin With Peach Salsa

"This recipe is a favorite because of depth in flavors and the array of colors bursting out. It is simple to make and quick. Peach season is the best period to make this, but you can substitute with pineapple or strawberries instead."
Serving: 4 servings (1-1/3 cups salsa). | Prep: 15m | Ready in: 35m

Ingredients

- 3/4 cup chopped peeled fresh peaches
- 1 small sweet red pepper, chopped
- 1 jalapeno pepper, seeded and chopped
- 2 tbsps. finely chopped red onion
- 2 tbsps. minced fresh cilantro
- 1 tbsp. lime juice
- 1 garlic clove, minced
- 1/8 tsp. salt
- 1/8 tsp. pepper
- 2 tbsps. olive oil
- 1 tbsp. brown sugar
- 1 tbsp. Caribbean jerk seasoning
- 1 tsp. dried thyme
- 1 tsp. dried rosemary, crushed
- 1/2 tsp. seasoned salt
- 1 pork tenderloin (1 lb.)

Direction

- Mix the initial 9 ingredients in a small bowl and leave aside. Mix brown sugar, oil, thyme, jerk seasoning, seasoned salt, and rosemary in another small bowl. Apply on pork.
- Keep covered and grill the meat on medium heat for 9-11 minutes per side or until thermometer reading shows 145 degrees. Let the meat sit for 5 minutes before cutting into slices. Consume with salsa as a side.

Nutrition Information

- Calories: 229 calories
- Total Carbohydrate: 9 g
- Cholesterol: 63 mg

- Total Fat: 11 g
- Fiber: 1 g
- Protein: 23 g
- Sodium: 522 mg

227. Chicken & Vegetable Kabobs

"Hubby and I especially love grilling vegetables in the summer. This recipe makes for a delicious and great-looking dish!"
Serving: 4 servings. | Prep: 20m | Ready in: 30m

Ingredients

- 1 lb. boneless skinless chicken breasts, cut into 1-1/2-inch cubes
- 1 medium sweet red pepper, cut into 1-1/2-inch pieces
- 1 medium zucchini, cut into 1-1/2-inch pieces
- 1 medium red onion, cut into thick wedges
- 2/3 cup sun-dried tomato salad dressing, divided

Direction

- Toss chicken and vegetables in a large bowl with 1/3 cup of dressing. Coat the pieces with the dressing. Take four metal or pre-soaked wooden skewers and alternately cue chicken and vegetables on them. Cook in a covered grill over medium heat, or broil 4 in. from the heat, for 8-10 minutes or until chicken is cooked through, turning and basting intermittently with remaining dressing at during the final 3 minutes.

Nutrition Information

- Calories: 228 calories
- Total Carbohydrate: 11 g
- Cholesterol: 63 mg
- Total Fat: 10 g
- Fiber: 2 g
- Protein: 24 g
- Sodium: 515 mg

228. Chicken Chili Enchiladas

"Cheesy enchiladas make a daily meal into a tasty fiesta."
Serving: 2 servings. | Prep: 20m | Ready in: 40m

Ingredients

- 1 medium onion, thinly sliced
- 1 tbsp. butter
- 3 oz. cream cheese, cubed
- 2 tbsps. canned chopped green chilies
- 1/8 tsp. salt
- 4 flour tortillas (8 inches)
- 2 tbsps. canola oil
- 3/4 cup shredded cooked chicken
- 1 tbsp. 2% milk
- 1 cup shredded Monterey Jack cheese
- Chopped green onions and sliced ripe olives, optional

Direction

- Sauté onion in butter in a small frying pan till softened. Take it away from the heat. Mix in salt, chilies and cream cheese until thoroughly blended.
- In another frying pan over medium heat, cook both sides of tortillas in oil till lightly browned and warmed. Drain on paper towels. Spoon a quarter of cream cheese mixture down the center of each tortilla. Top with chicken. Roll up, then arrange seam side-down in an 8-inch square baking dish greased with cooking spray.
- Bake while uncovered at 350° for about 15 minutes. Brush the tops with milk; dust with cheese. Bake for 5-10 minutes more or until cheese becomes melted. Top with olives and green onions if wanted.

Nutrition Information

- Calories: 877 calories
- Total Carbohydrate: 61 g
- Cholesterol: 145 mg
- Total Fat: 52 g
- Fiber: 2 g
- Protein: 44 g

- Sodium: 1261 mg

229. Chicken Enchilada Casserole

"This enchiladas recipe is easy to make at home. You can add some cilantro and jalapenos on top to enhance the flavors of the dish."
Serving: 6 servings. | Prep: 30m | Ready in: 60m

Ingredients

- 1 large onion, chopped
- 1 medium green pepper, chopped
- 1 tsp. butter
- 3 cups shredded cooked chicken breast
- 2 cans (4 oz. each) chopped green chilies
- 1/4 cup all-purpose flour
- 1-1/2 to 2 tsps. ground coriander
- 2-1/2 cups reduced-sodium chicken broth
- 1 cup (8 oz.) reduced-fat sour cream
- 1 cup (4 oz.) reduced-fat Monterey Jack or reduced-fat Mexican cheese blend, divided
- 12 corn tortillas (6 inches), warmed

Direction

- Sauté green pepper and onion with butter in a small skillet until soft. Mix onion mixture, green chilies, and chicken together in a big bowl.
- Mix coriander and flour together in a small saucepan. Pour in broth, whisking until smooth. Stir and cook over medium heat until the mixture boils. Stir and cook until thickened, about another 1-2 minutes. Take away from heat, then mix in 1/2 cup cheese and sour cream. Mix into the chicken mixture with 3/4 cup sauce.
- Down the middle of each tortilla, put 1/3 cup chicken mixture. Roll up and put in a greased 13x9-inch baking dish with the seam side turning down. Add the leftover sauce on top and sprinkle the leftover cheese over. Bake without a cover at 350° until fully heated, about 30-35 minutes.

Nutrition Information

- Calories: 383 calories
- Total Carbohydrate: 37 g
- Cholesterol: 82 mg
- Total Fat: 12 g
- Fiber: 5 g
- Protein: 33 g
- Sodium: 710 mg

230. Chili 'n' Cheese Enchiladas

"This dish is very flavorful and outstanding."
Serving: 6 servings. | Prep: 30m | Ready in: 50m

Ingredients

- 1 lb. ground beef
- 1-1/2 cups chopped onions, divided
- 1 package (1-1/4 oz.) chili seasoning
- 1 can (8 oz.) tomato sauce
- 1 can (6 oz.) tomato paste
- 1 can (16 oz.) chili beans, undrained
- 1/2 cup water
- 2-1/2 cups shredded cheddar cheese
- 6 flour tortillas (6 inches), warmed
- 1 jar (8 oz.) picante sauce

Direction

- Cook 1/2 cup of onion and beef together in a big ovenproof skillet on moderate heat until meat is not pink anymore, then drain. Stir in water, chili beans, tomato paste, tomato sauce and chili seasoning, then simmer about 15 minutes without a cover.
- In the meantime, mix leftover onion and 2 cups of cheese together. Split the cheese mixture on tortillas evenly. Roll up each and arrange on top of the chili mixture, seam-side facing down. Put leftover cheese and picante sauce on top.
- Bake at 350 degrees until heated through, about 20 to 25 minutes.

231. Chipotle Chicken Fajitas

"This fajita dish is so amazing."
Serving: 5 servings. | Prep: 30m | Ready in: 40m

Ingredients

- 1 bottle (12 oz.) chili sauce
- 1/4 cup lime juice
- 4 chipotle peppers in adobo sauce
- 1 lb. boneless skinless chicken breasts, cut into strips
- 1/2 cup cider vinegar
- 1/3 cup packed brown sugar
- 1/3 cup molasses
- 4 medium green peppers, cut into 1-inch pieces
- 1 large onion, cut into 1-inch pieces
- 1 tbsp. olive oil
- 1/8 tsp. salt
- 1/8 tsp. pepper
- 10 flour tortillas (8 inches)
- 1-1/2 cups chopped tomatoes
- 1 cup shredded Mexican cheese blend

Direction

- Add chipotle peppers, lime juice and chili sauce into a food processor; keep covered and process until blended. Remove half a cup into the big resealable plastic bag; put in the chicken. Seal the bag and coat by turning; keep in the refrigerator for 1 to 4 hours.
- Add the rest of the marinade into a small-sized bowl; put in molasses, brown sugar and vinegar. Keep covered and refrigerated.
- On six metal or soaked wooden skewers, alternately thread the veggies and chicken. Use the oil to brush over the veggies-chicken skewers; sprinkle pepper and salt over. Grill, while covered, on medium heat until a thermometer reaches 170 degrees or for 10 to 16 minutes, flipping once in a while.
- Remove the veggies and chicken out of the skewers and into a big bowl; put in half a cup

molasses-chipotle mixture and coat by tossing. Keep warm.
- Grill the tortillas, while uncovered, on medium heat until warm or for 45 to 55 seconds per side. Add the rest of the molasses-chipotle mixture, cheese, tomatoes, and chicken mixture on top.

Nutrition Information

- Calories: 748 calories
- Total Carbohydrate: 113 g
- Cholesterol: 70 mg
- Total Fat: 19 g
- Fiber: 3 g
- Protein: 34 g
- Sodium: 1966 mg

232. Chipotle Pork Tenderloins

"Pork with avocado and strawberries on the side."
Serving: 9 servings (5 cups salsa). | Prep: 20m | Ready in: 40m

Ingredients

- 1 cup sliced onion
- 1/2 cup chipotle peppers in adobo sauce, chopped
- 1/4 cup lime juice
- 1-1/2 tsps. minced garlic
- 3 pork tenderloins (1 lb. each)
- STRAWBERRY SALSA:
- 5 cups sliced fresh strawberries
- 1/4 cup thinly sliced green onions
- 1/4 cup minced fresh cilantro
- 1/4 cup lime juice
- 1/4 tsp. salt
- 1 medium ripe avocado, peeled and chopped

Direction

- Mix together the chipotle peppers, onion, garlic and lime juice in a big closable plastic bag; put in pork. Close bag tightly and mix well to coat; chill on fridge for 1 hour.

- Place drip pan on top of grill. Drain pork and throw out marinade. Grill with cover on, on indirect medium heat until an instant-read thermometer shows 145°, 20-27 minutes. Let it sit for 5 minutes before cutting.
- For preparing salsa; mix the lime juice, strawberries, green onions, salt and cilantro in a big glass bowl. Slowly stir in avocado. Serve pork with salsa on the side.

Nutrition Information

- Calories: 246 calories
- Total Carbohydrate: 11 g
- Cholesterol: 84 mg
- Total Fat: 9 g
- Fiber: 3 g
- Protein: 31 g
- Sodium: 173 mg

233. Cincinnati Chili Dogs

"Give a new take on Cincinnati chilies. Add in cocoa powder and cinnamon to these chilies and pour over hotdogs for that sweet kick. A perfect tasty snack to bring on potlucks, tailgates and sports day."
Serving: 10 servings. | Prep: 20m | Ready in: 04h20m

Ingredients

- 1-1/2 lbs. ground beef
- 2 small yellow onions, chopped and divided
- 2 cans (15 oz. each) tomato sauce
- 1-1/2 tsps. baking cocoa
- 1/2 tsp. ground cinnamon
- 1/4 tsp. chili powder
- 1/4 tsp. paprika
- 1/4 tsp. garlic powder
- 2 tbsps. Worcestershire sauce
- 1 tbsp. cider vinegar
- 10 hot dogs
- 10 hot dog buns, split
- Shredded cheddar cheese

Direction

- Cook ground beef in a large skillet over medium heat setting until the beef turns brown and is starting to crumble then drain excess oil.
- Mix one chopped up onion and cooked beef together in a 3-quartz slow cooker then put in the next 8 ingredients. Cover the slow cooker and cook on low heat for about 2 hours then add in the hotdogs. Cover and continue cooking the mixture for another 2 hours on low heat until cooked through.
- Put hotdogs on bun and top off with the remaining chopped onion and grated cheese then serve.

Nutrition Information

- Calories: 419 calories
- Total Carbohydrate: 29 g
- Cholesterol: 67 mg
- Total Fat: 24 g
- Fiber: 3 g
- Protein: 23 g
- Sodium: 1135 mg

234. Citrus-marinated Chicken

"This summer recipe is familiar to picnic day or family gathering meals. Love to serve this juicy and tasty chicken!"
Serving: 6 servings. | Prep: 10m | Ready in: 20m

Ingredients

- 1/2 cup lemon juice
- 1/2 cup orange juice
- 6 garlic cloves, minced
- 2 tbsps. canola oil
- 1 tsp. salt
- 1 tsp. ground ginger
- 1 tsp. dried tarragon
- 1/4 tsp. pepper
- 6 boneless skinless chicken breast halves (6 oz. each)

Direction

- In a large resealable plastic bag, blend the first 8 ingredients. Put in the chicken; close the bag and shake to coat. Marinate in the refrigerator for a minimum of 4 hours.
- Drain chicken, discard marinade. Cover and grill chicken over medium heat or broil 4-inch stayed from the heat about 5 to 7 minutes per side, until a thermometer shows 170°.

Nutrition Information

- Calories: 195 calories
- Total Carbohydrate: 1 g
- Cholesterol: 94 mg
- Total Fat: 5 g
- Fiber: 0 g
- Protein: 34 g
- Sodium: 161 mg

235. Cola Barbecue Ribs

"Appreciate the smoky integrity of a late spring grill throughout the entire year by setting up these clammy and delicate ribs, nasty climate or not."
Serving: 4 servings. | Prep: 10m | Ready in: 09h10m

Ingredients

- 1/4 cup packed brown sugar
- 2 garlic cloves, minced
- 1 tsp. salt
- 1/2 tsp. pepper
- 3 tbsps. liquid smoke, optional
- 4 lbs. pork spareribs, cut into serving-size pieces
- 1 medium onion, sliced
- 1/2 cup cola
- 1-1/2 cups barbecue sauce

Direction

- Mix pepper, salt, garlic and brown sugar and liquid smoke (if desired) in a small bowl; rub over ribs.
- In a greased 5 to 6-quarts slow cooker, layer onion and ribs; drizzle cola over ribs. Cover and cook for 8 to 10 hours on low, until the ribs are soft. Drain liquid. Pour the sauce on top of ribs and cook for another hour.

Nutrition Information

- Calories: 999 calories
- Total Carbohydrate: 34 g
- Cholesterol: 255 mg
- Total Fat: 66 g
- Fiber: 2 g
- Protein: 64 g
- Sodium: 1650 mg

236. Corn N Bean Burritos

"This dish is a good one for summertime because it is cooked in the microwave, you don't have to worry about heating up your kitchen. You can add extra-lean beef, chicken, or pork if desired."
Serving: 8 servings. | Prep: 20m | Ready in: 20m

Ingredients

- 1 can (4 oz.) chopped green chilies, drained
- 1/3 cup lime juice
- 2 tbsps. white vinegar
- 2 tbsps. honey
- 2 tsps. Dijon mustard
- 2 garlic cloves, minced
- 1 tsp. grated lime zest
- 1/2 tsp. ground cumin
- 1 can (15 oz.) black beans, rinsed and drained
- 2 cups frozen corn, thawed
- 1 can (16 oz.) vegetarian refried beans
- 1 medium cucumber, peeled, seeded and diced
- 3/4 cup salsa
- 1/4 cup chopped green onions
- 2 tbsps. minced fresh cilantro
- 8 flour tortillas (8 inches), warmed

Direction

- Mix the first eight ingredients in a big plastic resealable bag; add corn and black beans. Close bag and flip to coat; place in refrigerator overnight. Drain marinade and discard. Put corn and beans in a big microwave-safe pan. Add cilantro, salsa, refried beans, onions, and cucumber. Cover; set microwave on high and cook through, 5-6 minutes. Put 3/4 cup in the middle of each tortilla. Fold sides and ends; roll up to cover filling.

Nutrition Information

- Calories: 305 calories
- Total Carbohydrate: 56 g
- Cholesterol: 0 mg
- Total Fat: 4 g
- Fiber: 8 g
- Protein: 12 g
- Sodium: 825 mg

237. Crab & Shrimp Stuffed Sole

"A good combination of lemony sauce with seafood stuffing in this complicated fish cookout."
Serving: 4 servings. | Prep: 25m | Ready in: 40m

Ingredients

- 1 can (6 oz.) crabmeat, drained, flaked and cartilage removed
- 1/2 cup chopped cooked peeled shrimp
- 1/4 cup soft bread crumbs
- 1/4 cup butter, melted, divided
- 2 tbsps. whipped cream cheese
- 2 tsps. minced chives
- 1 garlic clove, minced
- 1 tsp. grated lemon peel
- 1 tsp. minced fresh parsley
- 4 sole fillets (6 oz. each)
- 1-1/2 cups cherry tomatoes
- 2 tbsps. dry white wine or chicken broth
- 2 tbsps. lemon juice
- 1/2 tsp. salt

- 1/2 tsp. pepper

Direction

- Mix together parsley, lemon peel, garlic, chives, cream cheese, 2 tbsp. of butter, bread crumbs, shrimp and crab in a small bowl. Spoon on each fillet with 1/4 cup of stuffing, then roll it up and use toothpicks to secure.
- Put each fillet on a double thickness of heavy-duty foil, 18"x12" in size. Mix together leftover butter, pepper, salt, lemon juice, wine and tomatoes, then spoon over fillets. Fold foil around the fish, sealing tightly.
- Grill on moderate heat with a cover until it is easy to use a fork to flake fish, about 12 to 15 minutes. Carefully open foil to let steam escape.

Nutrition Information

- Calories: 363 calories
- Total Carbohydrate: 6 g
- Cholesterol: 184 mg
- Total Fat: 16 g
- Fiber: 1 g
- Protein: 46 g
- Sodium: 728 mg

238. Dijon Grilled Pork Chops

"Pork chops marinated in a tangy and sweet sauce. Best served with mashed potatoes and applesauce."
Serving: 4 | Prep: 10m | Ready in: 8h25m

Ingredients

- 6 tbsps. Dijon mustard
- 6 tbsps. brown sugar
- 3 tbsps. unsweetened apple juice
- 3 tbsps. Worcestershire sauce
- 4 (8 oz.) bone-in pork loin chops

Direction

- In a bowl, combine Worcestershire sauce, mustard, apple juice, and brown sugar until smooth. Transfer 2/3 of the marinade in a big ziplock bag. Put in pork chops to cover with marinade; press out the air then seal. Refrigerate for 8hrs to overnight to marinate. Use a plastic wrap to cover the leftover marinade then place in the refrigerator.

- Take the pork chops out of the bag and get rid of the marinade.
- Set grill to medium heat; grease the grate lightly.
- Place pork chops on the grill. Cook for 4-5mins on each side until the center is not pink; use the reserved marinade to baste occasionally. An inserted instant-read thermometer in the middle should register 63°C or 145°Fahrenheit. Set the pork chops aside for 5mins then serve.

Nutrition Information

- Calories: 425 calories;
- Total Carbohydrate: 28.5 g
- Cholesterol: 127 mg
- Total Fat: 10.9 g
- Protein: 49.5 g
- Sodium: 830 mg

239. Enchiladas El Paso

"Serve these enchiladas within one day made for best taste."
Serving: 10 servings. | Prep: 20m | Ready in: 45m

Ingredients

- 1 lb. lean ground beef (90% lean)
- 1/2 cup chopped onion
- 1 can (14-1/2 oz.) diced tomatoes, drained
- 1 can (6 oz.) tomato paste
- 1/2 cup water
- 3 tsps. chili powder
- 1-1/4 tsps. salt
- 1/4 tsp. pepper
- 10 flour tortillas (8 inches), warmed
- 2 cups shredded cheddar cheese

Direction

- Cook onion and beef together in a big skillet on moderate heat until beef is not pink anymore, then drain. Stir in pepper, salt, chili powder, water, tomato paste and tomatoes.
- Spoon down the center of each tortilla with 1/3 cup of the meat sauce, then put 2 tbsp. of cheese on top. Roll up tortilla and arrange on a grease-free 13"x9" baking dish, seam-side facing down. Put leftover meat sauce and cheese on top.
- Place on a cover and chill overnight, or bake at 375 degrees, covered, about 25 minutes. Take off the cover and bake until heated through, about 3 to 5 minutes.
- To use chilled enchiladas: Take out of the fridge about half an hour prior to baking, then bake following directions.

Nutrition Information

- Calories: 283 calories
- Total Carbohydrate: 34 g
- Cholesterol: 38 mg
- Total Fat: 8 g
- Fiber: 3 g
- Protein: 19 g
- Sodium: 799 mg

240. Fantastic Chicken Fajitas

"My family really likes this fajitas dish. It's actually my attempt my re-create the dish that my husband and I really love at a Mexican restaurant."
Serving: 5 servings. | Prep: 10m | Ready in: 20m

Ingredients

- 5 tbsps. canola oil, divided
- 2 tbsps. Worcestershire sauce
- 1 tbsp. soy sauce
- 1 tbsp. lemon juice
- 1 tsp. white wine vinegar
- 1/4 tsp. salt
- 1/8 tsp. pepper

- 1-1/4 lbs. boneless skinless chicken breasts, cut into thin strips
- 10 flour tortillas (7 inches), warmed
- Shredded cheddar cheese
- Guacamole

Direction

- Mix pepper, salt, vinegar, lemon juice, soy sauce, Worcestershire sauce, and 4 tbsps. oil together in a big resealable plastic bag. Add chicken, then close the bag and flip to blend. Chill for a minimum of 30 minutes.
- Strain and dispose the marinade. Sauté chicken with the leftover oil in a big skillet until no pink remained, about 8 minutes. Enjoy in tortillas with guacamole and cheese.

241. Flank Steak Fajitas

"These fajitas have a filling made of flank steak. The slow cooker makes the flank steak very tender. This recipe is great for anyone who loves Mexican food."
Serving: 8-10 servings. | Prep: 10m | Ready in: 08h10m

Ingredients

- 1-1/2 to 2 lbs. beef flank steak, cut into thin strips
- 1 can (10 oz.) diced tomatoes and green chilies, undrained
- 2 garlic cloves, minced
- 1 jalapeno pepper, seeded and chopped
- 1 tbsp. minced fresh cilantro or parsley
- 1 tsp. chili powder
- 1/2 tsp. ground cumin
- 1/4 tsp. salt
- 1 medium sweet red pepper, julienned
- 1 medium green pepper, julienned
- 8 to 10 flour tortillas (7 to 8 inches)
- Sour cream, salsa and shredded cheddar cheese, optional

Direction

- In a 3-quart slow cooker, put the beef. Mix salt, cumin, chili powder, cilantro, jalapeno, garlic,

and tomatoes together in a small bowl; add to the beef. Put the lid on and cook for 7-8 hours on low.
- Mix in green peppers and red peppers. Cook until the peppers and meat are soft, about another 60 minutes. If you want, thicken the juices.
- Down the middle of each tortilla, put approximately 1/2 cup beef mixture with a slotted spoon; fold over the filling with the sides. Enjoy with cheese, salsa, and sour cream if you like.

Nutrition Information

- Calories: 231 calories
- Total Carbohydrate: 23 g
- Cholesterol: 33 mg
- Total Fat: 8 g
- Fiber: 1 g
- Protein: 17 g
- Sodium: 416 mg

242. Fold-over Tortilla Bake

"This taco is a bit different that can be used at dinner or potlucks."
Serving: 6 servings. | Prep: 20m | Ready in: 40m

Ingredients

- 1 lb. ground beef
- 1 cup chopped onion
- 2 cans (14-1/2 oz. each) stewed tomatoes
- 1 cup enchilada sauce
- 1 to 2 tsps. ground cumin
- 1/2 tsp. salt
- 1/4 tsp. pepper
- 12 flour or corn tortillas (6 inches)
- 6 oz. cream cheese, softened
- 1 can (4 oz.) chopped green chilies, drained
- 1 cup shredded Monterey Jack cheese
- minced fresh cilantro, optional

Direction

- Cook onion and ground beef in a big skillet till beef is not pink anymore; drain. Mix in seasonings, enchilada sauce and tomatoes. Boil. Lower the heat and simmer, while covered, for 5 minutes. Add 1/2 of the meat sauce into one 13x9-in. baking dish. Put aside.
- Wrap the stack of tortillas in the foil; keep warmed at 350 degrees for 8 to 10 minutes. Spread warm tortillas with cream cheese and add chilies on top. Fold tortillas in half. Arrange folded tortillas on top meat sauce; add leftover sauce on top.
- Keep it covered and baked at 350 degrees for 15 minutes. Drizzle with cheese; bake till cheese becomes melted for 5 minutes more. Add cilantro on top if you want.

Nutrition Information

- Calories: 473 calories
- Total Carbohydrate: 38 g
- Cholesterol: 69 mg
- Total Fat: 25 g
- Fiber: 2 g
- Protein: 27 g
- Sodium: 1138 mg

---

243. Green Chili Ribs

"This one is a must-try!"
Serving: 8 servings. | Prep: 20m | Ready in: 05h20m

Ingredients

- 4 lbs. pork baby back ribs
- 2 tbsps. ground cumin, divided
- 2 tbsps. olive oil
- 1 small onion, finely chopped
- 1 jar (16 oz.) salsa verde
- 3 cans (4 oz. each) chopped green chilies
- 2 cups beef broth
- 1/4 cup minced fresh cilantro
- 1 tbsp. all-purpose flour
- 3 garlic cloves, minced

- 1/4 tsp. cayenne pepper
- Additional minced fresh cilantro

Direction

- Cut the ribs into serving-size pieces; then rub one tbsp. of the cumin over. Heat oil in large skillet over medium-high heat. Working in batches, brown the ribs. Put ribs into a 6 quarts slow cooker.
- Put onion into the same pan; cook while stirring until onion soften, about 2 to 3 minutes. Put remaining cumin, cayenne, garlic, flour, a quarter cup cilantro, broth, green chilies and salsa verde into slow cooker. Cover and cook on low until meat soften, about 5 to 6 hours. Sprinkle with more cilantro.

Nutrition Information

- Calories: 349 calories
- Total Carbohydrate: 8 g
- Cholesterol: 81 mg
- Total Fat: 25 g
- Fiber: 1 g
- Protein: 24 g
- Sodium: 797 mg

---

244. Grilled Fajita Rolled Steak

"I like the fajitas recipe with chipotle, but a black pepper marinade also works well."
Serving: 4 servings. | Prep: 20m | Ready in: 40m

Ingredients

- 1 beef sirloin tip steak (1 inch thick and 1 lb.)
- 1 cup chipotle marinade
- 1 package (14 oz.) frozen pepper strips
- 1 tbsp. canola oil
- 2 oz. cream cheese, softened

Direction

- Flatten steak with the thickness of 1/4-inch. In a large resealable plastic bag, pour marinade and add steak. Close bag and turn to coat. Store in refrigerator for 4 hours or overnight, flipping occasionally.

- Sauté pepper strips in oil in a large skillet, until tender. Take off from the heat. Drain and remove marinade from steak. Spread steak with cream cheese on top to within 1 in. of edges. Spread half of the peppers on the top. Roll up jelly-roll style, beginning with a long side; tie with kitchen string.
- Grill over medium heat, covered, until achieves desired doneness (a thermometer should read 145deg for medium-rare; 160deg for medium; and 170deg for well-done), for 20-25 minutes; turning occasionally. Stand for 10 minutes before cutting. Remove toothpicks. Enjoy with remaining pepper strips.

Nutrition Information

- Calories: 284 calories
- Total Carbohydrate: 13 g
- Cholesterol: 89 mg
- Total Fat: 14 g
- Fiber: 1 g
- Protein: 25 g
- Sodium: 867 mg

245. Grilled Fajitas

"Enjoy summer with these fajitas made even more flavorful by a special marinade."
Serving: 4 servings. | Prep: 20m | Ready in: 30m

Ingredients

- 1 beef flank steak (about 1 lb.)
- 1 envelope onion soup mix
- 1/4 cup canola oil
- 1/4 cup lime juice
- 1/4 cup water
- 2 garlic cloves, minced
- 1 tsp. grated lime zest
- 1 tsp. ground cumin
- 1/2 tsp. dried oregano
- 1/4 tsp. pepper

- 1 medium onion, thinly sliced
- Green, sweet red and/or yellow peppers, julienned
- 1 tbsp. canola oil
- 8 flour tortillas (8 inches), warmed
- Sour cream and lime wedges, optional

Direction

- Mix the first 9 ingredients together in a big ziplock bag; put in steak. Seal and flip the bag to coat steak. Let it chill in the refrigerator for 4 hours or overnight.
- Drain steak and get rid of the marinade. On high heat, grill steak until it reaches the preferred doneness (an inserted thermometer in the steak should register 170° Fahrenheit for well-done, 160 degrees F for medium done, and 145° Fahrenheit for medium rare).
- If desired, cook and stir peppers and onion in a small oiled pan for 3-4 minutes until tender-crisp. Cut the steak following the grain into thin strips. Put the strips over the tortillas and add vegetables on top; roll tortillas. If desired, add lime wedges and sour cream to serve.

Nutrition Information

- Calories: 576 calories
- Total Carbohydrate: 59 g
- Cholesterol: 54 mg
- Total Fat: 23 g
- Fiber: 4 g
- Protein: 31 g
- Sodium: 741 mg

246. Grilled Fajitas With Pico De Gallo

"This is a good dish to make when you don't have much time. It does not need to be marinated to long before grilling, and the vegetable relish is made with only a few ingredients. It is a scrumptious meal."
Serving: 4 servings. | Prep: 15m | Ready in: 30m

Ingredients

- 3 tbsps. lime juice, divided
- 2 tbsps. canola oil
- 2 garlic cloves, minced
- 1 beef top sirloin steak (3/4 inch thick and 1 lb.)
- 3/4 cup diced zucchini
- 3/4 cup chopped tomato
- 1/3 cup picante sauce
- 8 flour tortillas (8 inches), warmed

Direction

- Mix garlic, 2 tbsps. lime juice, and oil in a big plastic resealable bag; add the steak. Close bag and flip to coat; for 30 minutes, refrigerate.
- For the pico de gallo, mix remaining lime juice, zucchini, picante sauce, and tomato in a small bowl; set it aside.
- Drain marinade and discard. Grill the steak, covered, on medium heat until doneness desired is achieved, 6-8 minutes per side. Thermometer should say these temps for each doneness, 145 degrees for medium-rare, 160 degrees for medium, and 170 degrees for well-done.
- Slice the steak thinly across the grain; put on tortillas. Put on pico de gallo; roll up and enjoy immediately.

Nutrition Information

- Calories: 518 calories
- Total Carbohydrate: 56 g
- Cholesterol: 63 mg
- Total Fat: 19 g
- Fiber: 1 g
- Protein: 31 g

- Sodium: 635 mg

247. Grilled Maple-glazed Spareribs

"There will be no leftovers once everyone tastes this dish featuring maple syrup."
Serving: 6 servings. | Prep: 15m | Ready in: 01h45m

Ingredients

- 3 lbs. pork spareribs, cut into serving-size pieces
- 1 cup maple syrup
- 3 tbsps. thawed orange juice concentrate
- 3 tbsps. ketchup
- 2 tbsps. soy sauce
- 1 tbsp. Worcestershire sauce
- 1 tbsp. Dijon mustard
- 1 tsp. curry powder
- 1 garlic clove, minced
- 2 green onions, minced
- 1 tbsp. sesame seeds, toasted

Direction

- In an oiled 15-in x 10-in x 1-inch baking dish, arrange ribs with its meat side up; use foil to cover tightly. Bake ribs for 1 1/4 hrs in 350 degrees F oven until tender; drain ribs.
- While baking, mix the following 9 ingredients together in a saucepan; boil on medium heat. Lower heat and let it simmer without cover for 15 minutes, mix from time to time.
- Grease the grill rack using a paper towel moistened with cooking oil and long-handled tongs. On medium heat, grill ribs for 15-20 minutes or broil 4 inches from heat for 15-20 minutes; spread glaze over ribs from time to time. Serve with sesame seeds on top.

248. Grilled Marinated Pork Tenderloin

"This flavorful pork tenderloin with different spices is a healthy substitute for steak. It is easy to prepare too!"
Serving: 6 servings (2/3 cup sauce). | Prep: 15m | Ready in: 40m

Ingredients

- 3/4 cup canola oil
- 1/3 cup soy sauce
- 1/4 cup white vinegar
- 2 tbsps. lemon juice
- 2 tbsps. Worcestershire sauce
- 1 tbsp. minced fresh parsley
- 1 garlic clove, minced
- 1/4 tsp. salt
- 1/4 tsp. pepper
- 2 pork tenderloins (1 lb. each)
- MUSTARD SAUCE:
- 1/2 cup mayonnaise
- 2 tbsps. Dijon mustard
- 2 tsps. prepared horseradish
- 1 tsp. Worcestershire sauce
- 1/8 tsp. crushed red pepper flakes, optional

Direction

- Mix the first 9 ingredients together in a big ziplock bag; put pork in. seal and flip the bag to coat the pork. Place in the refrigerator overnight.
- Set grill on indirect heat. Drain the pork and get rid of the marinade. Grease the grill rack lightly with a paper towel moistened with cooking oil and long-handled tongs.
- On indirect medium heat, grill tenderloins for 25 to 40 mins, covered, until an inserted thermometer registers 160 degrees F. Set aside for 5 mins then slice.
- Mix the sauce ingredients together in a small bowl. Serve tenderloins with the sauce.

Nutrition Information

- Calories: 442 calories
- Total Carbohydrate: 2 g
- Cholesterol: 91 mg
- Total Fat: 33 g
- Fiber: 0 g
- Protein: 31 g
- Sodium: 781 mg

249. Grilled Marinated Sirloin

"The juicy and lovely taste of this grilled sirloin dish is all in its marinade with lime juice in it. Always a hit!"
Serving: 6 servings. | Prep: 10m | Ready in: 30m

Ingredients

- 1/4 cup lime juice
- 1 green onion, finely chopped
- 2 tbsps. paprika
- 2 tbsps. canola oil
- 1 tbsp. finely chopped jalapeno pepper
- 1-1/2 tsps. sugar
- 2 garlic cloves, minced
- 1 tsp. dried oregano
- 1 tsp. grated lime zest
- 1/2 tsp. salt
- 1 beef top sirloin steak (about 1-1/2 lbs.)

Direction

- Mix all the initial 10 ingredients together in a small bowl. In a big bowl, put in 1/2 of the marinade mixture. Put in the steak and coat with the marinade. Cover the bowl and keep in the fridge for up to 4 hours. Cover the remaining marinade and keep in the fridge as well to baste the steak with while grilling.
- Slightly grease the grill rack with oil. Put the marinated steak on the prepared grill over medium heat then cover and let it grill for 8 to 10 minutes on every side until the preferred meat doneness is achieved (a thermometer inserted on the meat should indicate 145°F for medium-well, 140°F for medium and 135°F for

medium-rare). On the last 2 minutes of grilling, use the reserved marinade to baste the steak.

Nutrition Information

- Calories: 200 calories
- Total Carbohydrate: 4 g
- Cholesterol: 63 mg
- Total Fat: 11 g
- Fiber: 1 g
- Protein: 22 g
- Sodium: 245 mg

250. Grilled Pork Chops With Pineapple

"Marinate these chops with Asian-flavored recipe."
Serving: 2 servings. | Prep: 10m | Ready in: 20m

Ingredients

- 1 can (8 oz.) sliced pineapple
- 1/2 cup reduced-sodium soy sauce
- 3 tbsps. lemon juice
- 2 tsps. brown sugar
- 2 tsps. Sriracha Asian hot chili sauce or 1 tsp. hot pepper sauce
- 2 garlic cloves, minced
- 2 boneless butterflied pork chops (1/2 inch thick and 5 oz. each)
- 1 tsp. sugar
- 1/4 tsp. ground cinnamon

Direction

- Drain pineapple, set aside juice; reserve pineapple. Blend together the lemon juice, brown sugar, soy sauce, chili sauce, garlic and reserved pineapple juice in a big closable plastic bag; put in pork chops. Close bag and mix well until coated; chill for 2 hours.
- Drain pork and throw out marinade. Use tongs with long handles to moisten a paper towel with oil; slightly rub the grill rack. Grill without cover over medium heat, 4 to 5

minutes per side or broil 4 inches away from the heat until an instant read thermometer inserted in the meat shows 145°. Let it sit 5 minutes just before serving.

- Blend cinnamon and sugar and drizzle on each sides of pineapple rings. Cook on Grill for 1 to 2 minutes per side until browned. Serve pork with sauce.

Nutrition Information

- Calories: 266 calories
- Total Carbohydrate: 19 g
- Cholesterol: 68 mg
- Total Fat: 8 g
- Fiber: 1 g
- Protein: 28 g
- Sodium: 230 mg

251. Grilled Sausages With Summer Vegetables

"The combination of veggies and grilled sausage is totally perfect."
Serving: 12 servings. | Prep: 35m | Ready in: 60m

Ingredients

- 3/4 cup peach preserves
- 1/2 cup reduced-sodium soy sauce
- 3 tbsps. minced fresh gingerroot
- 3 tbsps. water
- 3 garlic cloves, minced
- Dash hot pepper sauce, optional
- 4 medium sweet red peppers
- 1 medium eggplant
- 3 small zucchini
- 2 small yellow summer squash
- 12 Johnsonville® Hot Italian Sausage Links (4 oz. each)

Direction

- In a blender, add the first 5 ingredients, then add pepper sauce, if wanted. Place on a cover and process until combined.

- Halve peppers lengthwise and get rid of their seeds. Cut eggplant lengthwise into slices with the thickness of 1/2 inch. Quarter the zucchini and yellow squash lengthwise. In a big bowl, add in all vegetables and drizzle 1/2 cup of sauce over top, tossing to coat.
- On a grill rack coated with grease, add vegetables, then grill on moderate heat with a cover until softened and charred slightly, about 8 to 10 minutes, flipping once, then allow to cool a little bit. Lower the heat of grill to moderately low heat.
- Slice vegetables into bite-sized pieces and toss together with one more 1/4 cup of sauce, then keep warm.
- Grill sausages on moderately low heat with a cover until a thermometer reaches 160 degrees for pork sausages or 165 degrees for turkey sausages, about 15 to 20 minutes while turning sometimes. Take sausages out of the grill and toss together with leftover sauce. Serve together with vegetables.

Nutrition Information

- Calories: 362 calories
- Total Carbohydrate: 24 g
- Cholesterol: 60 mg
- Total Fat: 22 g
- Fiber: 3 g
- Protein: 17 g
- Sodium: 1099 mg

252. Grilled Steaks With Marinated Tomatoes

"Bring out the natural goodness of tomatoes by marinating the beef overnight. Pair with glazed green beans and cheesy potatoes for a perfect meal."
Serving: 6 servings. | Prep: 25m | Ready in: 45m

Ingredients

- 1/4 cup light beer
- 3 tbsps. raspberry vinaigrette
- 3 tbsps. olive oil
- 1 tbsp. torn fresh basil
- 1 tbsp. cider vinegar
- 2 tsps. garlic powder
- 2 tsps. coriander seeds, crushed
- 1-1/2 tsps. minced fresh oregano
- 1 tsp. sugar
- 1/2 tsp. salt
- 1/2 tsp. pepper
- 3 large tomatoes, sliced
- RUB:
- 2 tsps. Montreal steak seasoning
- 2 tsps. chili powder
- 1 tsp. salt
- 1 tsp. celery seed
- 1 tsp. smoked paprika
- 1/2 tsp. pepper
- 2 beef top sirloin steaks (1 inch thick and 1 lb. each)

Direction

- Mix the initial 11 ingredients together in a bowl until well combined. In a 13-in x 9-in dish, arrange tomatoes and add the beer mixture on; cover. Let it chill in the refrigerator for at least an hour.
- Combine the rub seasonings together and massage over steaks. On medium heat, grill steaks while covered or broil four inches from heat for 8-10 minutes per side until it reaches the preferred doneness (an inserted thermometer in the steak should register 170 degrees F for well-done, 160 degrees F for medium, and 145 degrees F for medium rare). Set aside for 5 minutes; slice into thirds.
- Arrange the sliced steaks on a dish and add tomatoes on top. Drizzle with the leftover beer mixture.

Nutrition Information

- Calories: 321 calories
- Total Carbohydrate: 7 g
- Cholesterol: 61 mg
- Total Fat: 17 g
- Fiber: 2 g
- Protein: 34 g
- Sodium: 962 mg

253. Grilled Teriyaki Pork Tenderloin

"This elegant and scrumptious grilled pork tenderloin recipe is perfect for your entree"
Serving: 4 servings. | Prep: 10m | Ready in: 30m

Ingredients

- 3/4 cup honey mustard
- 3/4 cup teriyaki marinade
- 1 pork tenderloin (1 lb.)
- 2 garlic cloves, minced
- 1 green onion, chopped

Direction

- Mix teriyaki marinade and mustard in a small bowl, add 1 cup into a large resealable plastic bag. Put in garlic and pork, sealing bag and turning to coat. Keep in refrigerator for 6 hours or overnight. Refrigerate the remaining marinade covered.
- Set grill for indirect heat with a drip pan. Use cooking oil to moisten a paper towel; rub on to coat grill rack lightly with long-handled tongs. Drain and dispose of marinade from pork.
- In a drip pan, place pork, cover and grill for 25-40 minutes over indirect medium-hot heat (or desired doneness) for medium-rare, a thermometer should read 145deg; medium, 160deg. Baste with reserved marinade turning several times. Before slicing, let stand 5 minutes. Top with onion.

Nutrition Information

- Calories: 222 calories
- Total Carbohydrate: 19 g
- Cholesterol: 64 mg
- Total Fat: 6 g
- Fiber: 1 g
- Protein: 25 g
- Sodium: 957 mg

254. Grilled Teriyaki Salmon

"Savor the sweet-and-sour flavor of this quick and easy salmon recipe that features maple syrup and teriyaki sauce."
Serving: 4 servings. | Prep: 20m | Ready in: 30m

Ingredients

- 3/4 cup reduced-sodium teriyaki sauce
- 1/2 cup maple syrup
- 4 salmon fillets (6 oz. each)
- Mixed salad greens, optional

Direction

- Mix the maple syrup and teriyaki sauce in a small bowl. Transfer 1 cup of the mixture in a large ziplock bag and place the salmon inside. Seal and turn to coat the salmon. Let it chill in the refrigerator for 15 minutes. Take the remaining marinade, cover and refrigerate.
- Discard the marinade and drain the salmon. Coat the grill rack lightly using a paper towel moisten with cooking oil and a long-handled tong.
- On medium heat, grill the salmon while covered, or broil within 4 inches from heat for 8-12 minutes until the salmon flakes easily with a fork. Use the reserved marinade to baste occasionally. Serve the salmon over lettuce salad, if desired.

Nutrition Information

- Calories: 362 calories
- Total Carbohydrate: 12 g
- Cholesterol: 100 mg
- Total Fat: 18 g
- Fiber: 0 g
- Protein: 35 g
- Sodium: 422 mg

255. Grilled Tilapia With Mango

""My wife really liked the mix of Parmesan with mango in this tilapia dish that I came up with for her. Having this with nice iced tea out on the patio is a wonderful experience.""

Serving: 4 servings. | Prep: 10m | Ready in: 20m

Ingredients

- 4 tilapia fillets (6 oz. each)
- 1 tbsp. olive oil
- 1/2 tsp. salt
- 1/2 tsp. dill weed
- 1/4 tsp. pepper
- 1 tbsp. grated Parmesan cheese
- 1 medium lemon, sliced
- 1 medium mango, peeled and thinly sliced

Direction

- Layer oil over the fillets with a brush before sprinkling them with pepper, dill and salt. Use cooking oil to dampen a paper towel then use long-handled tongs to coat the grill rack by rubbing the towel over it gently. With a cover on, grill the tilapia with a cover on for 5 minutes. Flip it over then place mango, lemon and cheese over the top. Continue grilling for another 4 to 6 minutes. Use a fork to test if the fish comes off easily. If it does, the dish is ready.

Nutrition Information

- Calories: 213 calories
- Total Carbohydrate: 10 g
- Cholesterol: 84 mg
- Total Fat: 5 g
- Fiber: 1 g
- Protein: 32 g
- Sodium: 377 mg

256. Grilled Tuna

""Since tuna is available almost year-round, take advantage of it and make a tuna steak out of it. Choose your fish wisely though, discard those with dark streaks or spots in the flesh and keep those with reddish color. Ocean fishes tend to be dry. Soak the tuna in oil and avoid over-grilling it. You want it served medium-rare so carefully watch your timing. If necessary, use a kitchen timer.""

Serving: 4 | Prep: 10m | Ready in: 1h16m

Ingredients

- 4 (6 oz.) albacore tuna steaks, 1 inch thick
- 3 tbsps. extra virgin olive oil
- salt and ground black pepper to taste
- 1 lime, juiced
- 1/2 cup hickory wood chips, soaked

Direction

- Mix olive oil and tuna steaks together in a big Ziplock bag. Seal the Ziplock bag and turn to coat the tuna steaks, keep in the fridge for an hour.
- Set the grill on medium heat and preheat. Once the coals are very hot, spread a handful of mesquite or hickory wood chips on top of the hot coals for flavor.
- Lightly grease the grill grate. Put pepper and salt on the marinated tuna steak to taste and put on the preheated grill and grill for roughly 6 minutes, turn once to cook both sides. Put the grilled tuna steak on a serving plate and squeeze some fresh lime juice on top. Serve right away.

Nutrition Information

- Calories: 281 calories;
- Total Carbohydrate: 1.8 g
- Cholesterol: 77 mg
- Total Fat: 11.8 g
- Protein: 40 g
- Sodium: 644 mg

257. Hearty Beef Enchiladas

"Set out a bowl of diced tomatoes, diced onions, and shredded cheddar cheese if you want something to decorate."
Serving: 28 servings. | Prep: 30m | Ready in: 50m

Ingredients

- 4 lbs. ground beef
- 4 medium onions, chopped
- 4 cans (16 oz. each) chili beans, undrained
- 4 cans (10 oz. each) enchilada sauce, divided
- 1 jar (16 oz.) salsa, divided
- Canola oil
- 28 corn or flour tortillas (8 inches)
- 4 cups shredded cheddar cheese
- 2 cans (2-1/4 oz. each) sliced ripe olives, drained

Direction

- Cook onions and beef together in a stock pot on moderate heat until beef is not pink anymore, then drain. Stir in 1 cup of salsa, 2 cans of enchilada sauce and beans, then put aside.
- Heat 1/4 inch of oil in a small skillet, then dip into hot oil with each tortilla just until limp, about 3 seconds per side, then transfer to paper towels to drain.
- Put 2/3 cup of the beef mixture on top of each tortilla, then roll it up and arrange in 4 13"x9" baking dishes coated with grease, seam-side facing down. Drizzle leftover salsa and enchilada sauce over top, then sprinkle with olives and cheese.
- Bake at 350 degrees without a cover until bubbly, about 20 to 25 minutes.

Nutrition Information

- Calories: 340 calories
- Total Carbohydrate: 32 g
- Cholesterol: 49 mg
- Total Fat: 14 g
- Fiber: 2 g
- Protein: 21 g

- Sodium: 555 mg

258. Honey-grilled Chicken Breasts

"This grilled chicken dish is absolutely amazing and delicious with full of delightful and interesting flavors."
Serving: 8 servings. | Prep: 15m | Ready in: 25m

Ingredients

- 1/2 cup orange juice
- 1/3 cup honey
- 1/4 cup lemon juice
- 1/4 cup reduced-sodium soy sauce
- 2 tbsps. minced fresh gingerroot
- 12 garlic cloves, minced
- 1/2 tsp. pepper
- 1/4 tsp. salt
- 8 boneless skinless chicken breast halves (6 oz. each)

Direction

- Mix the first 8 ingredients in a small bowl. Pour into a big resealable plastic bag with 1/2 cup of marinade, then put in chicken. Seal and turn to coat, then chill about 8 hours to overnight. Cover and chill the leftover marinade.
- Drain and get rid of marinade. Moisten a paper towel with cooking oil and coat the grill rack lightly with long handled tongs. Grill chicken with a cover on medium or broil 4 inches from source of heat until a thermometer reaches 170 degrees while basting often with reserved marinade, about 5 to 7 minutes per side.

Nutrition Information

- Calories: 221 calories
- Total Carbohydrate: 10 g
- Cholesterol: 94 mg
- Total Fat: 4 g
- Fiber: 0 g

- Protein: 35 g
- Sodium: 331 mg

259. Honey-soy Pork Chops

"Summer is always a unique season for casual and relaxed meals, for the patriotic holidays of summertime, and especially for great outdoors' picnics. All these occasions go perfectly with this recipe."
Serving: 4 servings. | Prep: 10m | Ready in: 20m

Ingredients

- 1/4 cup lemon juice
- 1/4 cup honey
- 2 tbsps. reduced-sodium soy sauce
- 1 tbsp. sherry or unsweetened apple juice
- 2 garlic cloves, minced
- 4 boneless pork loin chops (4 oz. each)

Direction

- Mix the initial 5 ingredients in a small bowl. Fill a big resealable bag with 1/2 cup of the mixture, then add the pork chops. Seal the bag and flip several times to coat the meat, then store refrigerated for 2-3 hours. Keep the remaining marinade covered and refrigerated for use for basting the meat later.
- Strain out the marinade and discard. Dampen a paper towel with cooking oil: using a pair of long-handled tongs, and give the grill rack a light coat.
- Cover and grill the pork on medium heat or let broil on the heat for 4-5 minutes per side or until thermometer reading shows 145 degrees, while applying the remainder of the marinade on the meat by basting. Let the meat rest for 5 minutes before it is ready to be served.

Nutrition Information

- Calories: 176 calories
- Total Carbohydrate: 6 g
- Cholesterol: 55 mg
- Total Fat: 6 g
- Fiber: 0 g

- Protein: 22 g
- Sodium: 132 mg

260. Jim's Secret Family Recipe Ribs

"This delicious rib recipe is worthy to be passed down in the next generations to come."
Serving: 8 servings. | Prep: 20m | Ready in: 03h30m

Ingredients

- 2 racks pork baby back ribs (about 5 lbs.)
- 1/4 cup soy sauce
- 1/4 cup dried oregano
- 2 tbsps. onion powder
- 2 tsps. garlic powder
- 1 liter lemon-lime soda
- 1/2 cup unsweetened pineapple or orange juice, optional
- BARBECUE SAUCE:
- 1/2 cup granulated or packed brown sugar
- 1/2 cup hot water
- 1 cup ketchup
- 1/4 cup honey mustard
- 1/4 cup barbecue sauce of choice
- 3 tbsps. lemon juice
- 1-1/2 tsps. white vinegar

Direction

- Rub soy sauce over ribs. Mix together garlic powder, onion powder, and oregano; massage mixture on both sides of meat then place in a big and shallow roasting pan. Cover and let it chill in the refrigerator overnight.
- Preheat the oven to 225 degrees F. If desired, pour lemon-lime juice or soda in the roasting pan and not over the ribs. Bake for 3 hours while covered until tender.
- Prepare barbecue sauce while baking by letting sugar dissolve in hot water; stir in the remaining ingredients. If necessary, add in lemon-lime juice or soda to thin mixture. Keep a cup of sauce for serving.

- Take the ribs out of the oven and get rid of the juices. Spread barbecue sauce on both sides of ribs. On low direct heat, place ribs on a greased grill rack and grill while covered for 10 minutes until cooked through. Occasionally flip and baste with the leftover sauce. Slice ribs into bite-size pieces and serve with the reserved sauce.

Nutrition Information

- Calories: 483 calories
- Total Carbohydrate: 31 g
- Cholesterol: 102 mg
- Total Fat: 27 g
- Fiber: 1 g
- Protein: 30 g
- Sodium: 1107 mg

261. Kielbasa Chicken Kabobs

"Use orange juice in place of pineapple juice, or beef instead of chicken. Mushrooms or just about any vegetable complement these kabobs."
Serving: 16 kabobs. | Prep: 20m | Ready in: 40m

Ingredients

- 3/4 cup unsweetened pineapple juice
- 1/4 cup cider vinegar
- 1/4 cup canola oil
- 2 tbsps. sugar
- 2 tbsps. soy sauce
- 1/2 tsp. garlic powder
- 1/4 tsp. lemon-pepper seasoning
- 2 lbs. boneless skinless chicken breasts, cut into 1-inch cubes
- 1 lb. Johnsonville® Fully Cooked Polish Kielbasa Sausage Rope, thickly sliced
- 1 can (20 oz.) unsweetened pineapple chunks, drained
- 2 medium green peppers, quartered
- 2 cups grape tomatoes
- 2 medium red onions, quartered

Direction

- Mix the first seven ingredients in a small bowl. Take 1/2 cup and cover and refrigerate for basting later. Portion the remaining marinade between two large zip top plastic bags. Place chicken in one bag and the vegetables, kielbasa, and pineapples in the other. Close the bags and turn several times to coat. Let marinate in the fridge for at least 2 hours. Take 16 metal or pre-soaked wooden skewers and alternately thread the chicken, vegetables, kielbasa, and pineapples. With a pair of long-handled tongs, dip a paper towel in cooking oil and dab the towel on the grates for a light coating of oil. Arrange the kabobs on the grates, cover the grill, and cook over medium heat. You may also broil 4 in. from the heat. Cook, turning and basting frequently, for 10-15 minutes or until chicken is not pink anymore.

Nutrition Information

- Calories: 376 calories
- Total Carbohydrate: 17 g
- Cholesterol: 101 mg
- Total Fat: 20 g
- Fiber: 2 g
- Protein: 32 g
- Sodium: 762 mg

262. Lemony Grilled Salmon

"Try something easy by grilling salmon on lemon slices! It makes the salmon flaky, moist and the fragrance smells good."
Serving: 4 servings. | Prep: 10m | Ready in: 25m

Ingredients

- 1/2 cup honey
- 1/4 cup lemon juice
- 1/4 cup unsweetened pineapple juice
- 2 tsps. teriyaki sauce
- 1 tsp. grated lemon peel
- 1/2 tsp. minced garlic

- 1/4 tsp. crushed red pepper flakes
- 4 salmon fillets (6 oz. each), skin removed
- 8 lemon slices (3/4 inch thick)

Direction

- In a small bowl, mix the first 7 ingredients. Put 2/3 cup of the mixture into a big closable plastic bag; put in the salmon. Close the bag and mix to coat; chill for at least 2 hours. Cover and chill the remaining marinade for basting.
- Drain and remove marinade. Use tongs with long handles to lightly coat the grill rack with oil—moist paper towel with cooking oil. Place lemon slices on the rack. Put each salmon fillet above 2 lemon slices.
- Grill salmon, with lid on. Cook over medium heat for 5 minutes. Dab with the reserved marinade. Grill for 10-15 minutes until fish flakes easily with fork, basting from time to time with the remaining marinade.

263. Lip-smackin' BBQ Chicken

"A delicious barbecue chicken to satisfy your friends."
Serving: 12 servings. | Prep: 01h15m | Ready in: 01h40m

Ingredients

- 2 cups ketchup
- 1 cup cider vinegar
- 1 cup water
- 1/4 cup packed brown sugar
- 1/4 cup reduced-sodium soy sauce
- 1/4 cup molasses
- 1/4 cup honey
- 2 tbsps. prepared mustard
- 3 tsps. ground cumin
- 1/4 tsp. salt
- 1/4 tsp. pepper
- 6 lbs. assorted bone-in chicken pieces

Direction

- Blend the first 11 ingredients in a large saucepan; boil. Turn down the heat; uncover

and bring to a simmer, stirring from time to time, until thick, 1-1 1/2 hours. Remove 1/2 of the sauce and save to brush the chicken. Save the remaining sauce warm to serve.
- Cover and grill the chicken over medium heat, brushing during the last 10 minutes with the saved sauce and turning from time to time, until the chicken juices run clear, 25-35 minutes. Serve along with the remaining sauce.

Nutrition Information

- Calories: 402 calories
- Total Carbohydrate: 27 g
- Cholesterol: 104 mg
- Total Fat: 17 g
- Fiber: 0 g
- Protein: 34 g
- Sodium: 871 mg

264. Meat Loaf Burritos

"Leftover meat loaf is disguised in this delicious burritos."
Serving: 6 burritos. | Prep: 5m | Ready in: 15m

Ingredients

- 1 tbsp. butter
- 1 can (15 oz.) pinto beans, rinsed and drained
- 2 cups crumbled cooked meat loaf (3 slices)
- 6 flour tortillas (6 inches), warmed
- Shredded cheddar cheese, shredded lettuce, chopped tomatoes and salsa, optional

Direction

- In a skillet, melt butter. Put half of the beans and use a fork to mash it. Stir in remaining beans and meat loaf, then heat through.
- Onto each tortilla, spoon about 1/2 cup of meat loaf mixture. If desired, put cheese on top. Fold sides and bottom up over filling. If desired, serve with salsa, tomatoes and lettuce.

Nutrition Information

- Calories: 251 calories
- Total Carbohydrate: 37 g
- Cholesterol: 31 mg
- Total Fat: 5 g
- Fiber: 4 g
- Protein: 13 g
- Sodium: 691 mg

265. Open-faced Turkey Tacos

"If you're craving for spicy tacos, just put in more salsa."
Serving: 10 servings. | Prep: 20m | Ready in: 20m

Ingredients

- 1 lb. lean ground turkey
- 1 medium onion, chopped
- 1 can (16 oz.) fat-free refried beans
- 1 jar (16 oz.) salsa
- 10 flour tortillas (6 inches), warmed
- 2 cups shredded lettuce
- 2 medium tomatoes, chopped
- 2 medium green peppers, chopped
- 2 medium sweet red peppers, chopped
- 10 tbsps. fat-free sour cream

Direction

- Cook the onion and turkey in a large skillet over medium heat until the meat is not pink anymore; then drain. Put in salsa and beans; cook while stirring until heated through. Fill each tortilla with 1/2 cup of the turkey mixture. Add sour cream, peppers, tomatoes, and lettuce on top.

Nutrition Information

- Calories: 265 calories
- Total Carbohydrate: 32 g
- Cholesterol: 38 mg
- Total Fat: 7 g
- Fiber: 6 g
- Protein: 16 g
- Sodium: 674 mg

266. Orange BBQ Baby Back Ribs

"I would much rather spend the summertime with my family out by the pool, so I don't bother with extensive, complex recipes. That's why I came up with this fresh citrus twist on BBQ. The Orange BBQ sauce also works perfectly on chicken fondue as well."
Serving: 4 servings. | Prep: 02h15m | Ready in: 02h30m

Ingredients

- 4 lbs. pork baby back ribs
- 1 bottle (18 oz.) honey barbecue sauce
- 1 cup orange juice
- 2 tbsps. grated orange zest

Direction

- On a rack inside a shallow roasting pan, set the ribs with the bone side down. Cover it up and bake at 325°F until it becomes tender or for 2 to 2-1/2 hours. Drain it.
- Mix the orange juice, zest and barbecue sauce in a small bowl and put 1 cup aside for serving. Use some cooking oil to moisten a paper towel then use long-handled tongs to coat the grill rack lightly. Set the ribs down on direct heat, basting with a bit of the sauce. Cover it up and grill it on medium heat until it browns or for 15 to 20 minutes, basting the ribs and turning it over every now and then. Serve it together with the reserved sauce.

Nutrition Information

- Calories: 1011 calories
- Total Carbohydrate: 53 g
- Cholesterol: 245 mg
- Total Fat: 61 g
- Fiber: 0 g
- Protein: 51 g
- Sodium: 1415 mg

267. Orange-glazed Salmon

"Serve the guests with this special treat consisting of tender grilled salmon fillets in a delicious glaze. The marinade is simple to prepare and gives a big impact."
Serving: 6 servings. | Prep: 10m | Ready in: 30m

Ingredients

- 1/2 cup barbecue sauce
- 1/3 cup thawed orange juice concentrate
- 7 tsps. soy sauce
- 4-1/2 tsps. sherry or apple juice
- 4-1/2 tsps. Dijon mustard
- 1 tbsp. minced fresh gingerroot
- 2 tsps. brown sugar
- 2 tsps. red wine vinegar
- 1-1/2 tsps. canola oil
- 1/2 tsp. minced garlic
- 1 salmon fillet (2 lbs. and 3/4 inch thick)

Direction

- Mix the first 10 ingredients in a small bowl. Save half a cup of the marinade for basting. Cover and place in a refrigerator. Transfer the leftover marinade to a large plastic bag that is sealable. Place salmon, seal the bag and flip to coat. Chill for 1 hour while flipping often.
- Drain and get rid of the marinade. Use cooking oil to moisten a paper towel with long-handled tongs and then coat the grill rack lightly. Transfer the salmon with the skin side down onto the grill rack. Grill while covered on medium heat for five minutes. Scoop the reserved marinade atop the fish. Grill for about 15 to 20 minutes or until the fish easily flakes using a fork while basting often.

Nutrition Information

- Calories: 333 calories
- Total Carbohydrate: 10 g
- Cholesterol: 89 mg
- Total Fat: 18 g
- Fiber: 0 g
- Protein: 31 g
- Sodium: 601 mg

268. Pepper Pork Fajitas For 2

"This is a very bright and delightful dish made of many kinds of bell peppers."
Serving: 2 servings. | Prep: 20m | Ready in: 25m

Ingredients

- 1 tbsp. cornstarch
- 1/2 lb. boneless pork, cut into 1/4-inch slices
- 1/4 each medium green, sweet yellow, red and orange pepper, julienned
- 1/4 cup sliced onion
- 1-1/2 tsps. canola oil
- 1/4 cup salsa
- 2 flour tortillas (8 inches), warmed
- 1/4 cup shredded cheddar cheese
- 2 tbsps. sour cream

Direction

- In a big resealable plastic bag, add cornstarch. Put several pieces of pork at a time into bag and shake to coat well. Cook together onion, peppers and pork in a big skillet with oil on moderate heat until vegetables are soft and pork is not pink anymore. Stir in salsa and heat through.
- Put down the center of each tortilla with approximately 3/4 cup of filling, then put sour cream and shredded cheese on top. Fold in sides of tortillas.

Nutrition Information

- Calories: 461 calories
- Total Carbohydrate: 37 g
- Cholesterol: 92 mg
- Total Fat: 20 g
- Fiber: 1 g
- Protein: 32 g
- Sodium: 510 mg

269. Peppered T-bone Steaks

"I usually grill thin slices of potato together with the meat. These juicy and well-marinated steaks are great when served with spinach and red onion salad for a great meal and cheesecake for a delicious dessert."
Serving: 2 servings. | Prep: 10m | Ready in: 20m

Ingredients

- 3 tbsps. steak sauce
- 4-1/2 tsps. minced fresh thyme or 1 tsp. dried thyme
- 1/4 tsp. coarsely ground pepper
- 1/4 tsp. cayenne pepper
- 2 beef T-bone steaks (1 inch thick and 3/4 lb. each)
- 1/2 tsp. salt

Direction

- Mix thyme, cayenne, pepper, and steak sauce in a small bowl. Top the steak with salt and drizzle 2 tsp. of the steak sauce mixture on the side of the steaks.
- Wet a paper towel with cooking oil. Use the long-handled tongs to wipe the coated towel into the grill rack. Place the steak, sauce side down, into the grill rack. Cover the steak and grill it over medium heat or broil the steak 4-inches away from the heat source for 6 minutes. Coat the steak with the remaining sauce and flip. Continue to grill the steak for 4-6 minutes until it already reached its desired doneness. Thermometer readings according to its desired doneness are the following: 145°F for medium-rare; 160°F for medium; and 170°F for well-done.

270. Pineapple Shrimp Kabobs

"Get those grills ready to make these kebabs. Serve them up on your next upcoming backyard party."
Serving: 4 servings. | Prep: 10m | Ready in: 20m

Ingredients

- 1/4 cup each reduced-sodium soy sauce, balsamic vinegar and honey
- 1 garlic clove, minced
- 1 lb. uncooked medium shrimp, peeled and deveined
- 1 large green pepper, cut into 1-inch pieces
- 1 can (8 oz.) pineapple, chunks, drained

Direction

- Mix garlic, soy sauce, vinegar and honey together in a small bowl. Put 1/3 cup of the marinade aside. Insert the shrimps, pineapple and green pepper alternately onto 8 skewers. Put in the kebabs and the leftover marinade into the big Ziplock plastic bag. Keep it in the fridge for 1 hour. Cover the leftover marinade and keep in the fridge as well.
- Drain the marinated kebabs and throw marinade. Use tongs to lightly rub an oiled paper towel on the grill rack. Put the kebabs on an open grill on medium heat or broil the kebabs in the oven 4 inches away from the heat for 5 to 8 minutes or until the shrimp turns pink in color, turn the kebabs from time to time to cook both sides and baste with leftover marinade each turn.

Nutrition Information

- Calories: 168 calories
- Total Carbohydrate: 19 g
- Cholesterol: 138 mg
- Total Fat: 2 g
- Fiber: 1 g
- Protein: 19 g
- Sodium: 443 mg

271. Pineapple-glazed Pork Tenderloin

"This dish is really satisfying and you can roast in the oven for shorter time."
Serving: 6 servings. | Prep: 10m | Ready in: 03h10m

Ingredients

- 3 pork tenderloins (about 3/4 lb. each), cut in half crosswise
- 1/2 tsp. salt
- 1/2 tsp. pepper
- 1 jar (12 oz.) pineapple preserves
- 1/2 cup frozen pineapple juice concentrate, thawed
- 2 garlic cloves, minced
- 1 tbsp. Dijon mustard
- 1 tsp. dried rosemary, crushed
- 2 tbsps. cornstarch
- 1 tbsp. cold water

Direction

- Sprinkle pepper and salt over pork, then put into a 3- to 4- quart slow cooker. Whisk the next 5 ingredients together, then pour over pork. Cook on low with a cover for 2 to 3 hours, until meat is tender and a thermometer reaches 145 degrees.
- Take away from the heat and allow to stand for a minimum of 5 minutes prior to slicing. Keep warm. Whisk water and cornstarch together, then put into cooking juices. Cook for 15 minutes, until thickened. Serve together with pork.

272. Pork Chops With Glaze

"These beautiful glazed chops are given a special touch with the addition of rosemary that makes it perfect for any meal."
Serving: 8 servings. | Prep: 15m | Ready in: 25m

Ingredients

- 1/2 cup ketchup

- 1/4 cup packed brown sugar
- 1/4 cup white vinegar
- 1/4 cup orange juice
- 1/4 cup Worcestershire sauce
- 2 garlic cloves, minced
- 1/2 tsp. dried rosemary, crushed
- 8 bone-in pork loin chops (3/4 inch thick and 7 oz. each)

Direction

- Combine the initial 7 ingredients in a small bowl. Fill a big Ziploc bag with 3/4 cup of marinade. Add in the pork chops, then seal and turn the bag to coat meat evenly. Store refrigerated overnight or for 8 hours. Keep the remaining marinade covered and refrigerated.
- Strain out pork and discard marinade. Apply a light coat of grease on grill rack.
- Cover and grill pork on medium heat or leave to broil at 4 inches from heat source for 4-6 minutes per side or until thermometer reading shows 145 degrees, while applying copious amounts of remaining marinade by brushing during the final 3 minutes. Leave to rest for 5 minutes then serve.

Nutrition Information

- Calories: 246 calories
- Total Carbohydrate: 11 g
- Cholesterol: 86 mg
- Total Fat: 8 g
- Fiber: 0 g
- Protein: 30 g
- Sodium: 284 mg

273. Pork Chops With Honey-balsamic Glaze

"A good dish for those who love pork chops."
Serving: 4 servings. | Prep: 10m | Ready in: 30m

Ingredients

- 4 bone-in pork loin chops (1 inch thick and 10 oz. each)
- 1/2 tsp. crushed red pepper flakes
- 1/2 tsp. salt
- 1/2 tsp. pepper
- 2 tbsps. olive oil
- GLAZE:
- 1/2 cup balsamic vinegar
- 1/2 cup honey
- 3 green onions, chopped
- 2 garlic cloves, minced
- 1 tsp. minced fresh rosemary or 1/4 tsp. dried rosemary, crushed
- 1/8 tsp. salt
- 1/8 tsp. pepper
- 1/4 cup butter, cubed

Direction

- Sprinkle pepper, salt and pepper flakes over pork chops. Heat oil in a big skillet on moderate heat. Put in pork and cook until meat achieves desired doneness (for medium-rare, a thermometer should reach 145 degrees or 160 degrees for medium), about 5 to 7 minutes per side. Take chops out and keep warm.
- Whisk together pepper, salt, rosemary, garlic, green onions, honey and vinegar in the same skillet, then bring mixture to a boil. Lower heat and simmer without a cover until thickened a little bit while stirring sometimes, about 6 to 8 minutes. Take away from the heat and whisk in butter until melted, then serve together with pork chops.

Nutrition Information

- Calories: 715 calories
- Total Carbohydrate: 41 g
- Cholesterol: 169 mg
- Total Fat: 41 g
- Fiber: 1 g
- Protein: 46 g
- Sodium: 557 mg

274. Quick Garlic-lime Chicken

"This chicken dish is so great and simple to make."
Serving: 6 servings. | Prep: 5m | Ready in: 15m

Ingredients

- 1/3 cup soy sauce
- 1/4 cup fresh lime juice
- 1 tbsp. Worcestershire sauce
- 1/2 tsp. ground mustard
- 2 garlic cloves, minced
- 6 boneless skinless chicken breast halves (4 oz. each)
- 1/2 tsp. pepper

Direction

- In a big resealable plastic bag, mix together the first five ingredients. Put in chicken; seal the bag and turn until coated. Keep in the refrigerator for no less than half an hour.
- Drain off and get rid of the marinade. Sprinkle over the chicken with pepper. Grill; keep covered, on medium heat until the thermometer reaches 170 degrees or for 4 to 7 minutes per side.

Nutrition Information

- Calories: 130 calories
- Total Carbohydrate: 1 g
- Cholesterol: 63 mg
- Total Fat: 3 g
- Fiber: 0 g
- Protein: 23 g
- Sodium: 330 mg

275. Rustic Ribeyes

"These succulent ribeyes are absolutely fantastic yet still simple to make."
Serving: 6 servings. | Prep: 15m | Ready in: 20m

Ingredients

- 3/4 cup Worcestershire sauce
- 3 tbsps. lime juice
- 1 tbsp. brown sugar
- 1 tbsp. instant coffee granules
- 3/4 tsp. ground mustard
- 1/2 to 3/4 tsp. crushed red pepper flakes
- 1/4 tsp. smoked sweet paprika
- 3 beef ribeye steaks (1 inch thick and 1 lb. each)
- 2 tbsps. canola oil
- 6 tbsps. unsalted butter

Direction

- Mix the first 7 ingredients together in a small bowl, then put aside 1/4 cup of mixture to make sauce. Add the rest of marinade into a 2-gallon resealable plastic bag, then put in beef, seal bag and turn to coat the beef well. Chill for a maximum of 8 hours, then drain beef and get rid of the marinade.
- Set the oven to 375 degrees to preheat. Brown beef in a big nonstick skillet on moderately high heat, in batches, with oil. Remove to a 15"x10"x1" baking pan coated with grease. Bake without a cover until meat achieves desired doneness (for medium-rare, a thermometer should reach 145 degrees; medium, 160 degrees and 170 degrees for well-done), about 4 to 6 minutes.
- In the meantime, put into the same skillet with reserved marinade and butter, then cook and stir on low heat until mixed. Serve together with steaks.

Nutrition Information

- Calories: 626 calories
- Total Carbohydrate: 10 g
- Cholesterol: 150 mg
- Total Fat: 47 g
- Fiber: 0 g
- Protein: 41 g
- Sodium: 439 mg

276. Saucy Barbecue Drumsticks

"The sauce of this recipe is both simple and quick. Just combine ketchup, brown mustard and honey, the result wouldn't disappoint you."
Serving: 8 servings (2 cups sauce). | Prep: 25m | Ready in: 40m

Ingredients

- 2 cups ketchup
- 2/3 cup honey
- 1/3 cup packed brown sugar
- 2 tbsps. finely chopped sweet onion
- 2 tbsps. spicy brown mustard
- 4 garlic cloves, minced
- 1 tbsp. Worcestershire sauce
- 1 tbsp. cider vinegar
- 16 chicken drumsticks

Direction

- Combine the first eight ingredients in a large saucepan; heat to a boil. Lower the heat; simmer, without covering, for 15 to 20 minutes until the flavors are well-blended, stirring on occasion. Save 2 cups of sauce for later.
- On a lightly oiled grill rack, cover and grill the chicken over medium heat about 15 to 20 minutes, until a thermometer shows 170° to 175°, turning on occasion and coating with the leftover sauce during final 5 minutes. Use with reserved sauce.

Nutrition Information

- Calories: 422 calories
- Total Carbohydrate: 49 g
- Cholesterol: 95 mg
- Total Fat: 12 g
- Fiber: 0 g
- Protein: 29 g

- Sodium: 909 mg

277. Sausage Bean Burritos

"This zippy burrito recipe has a creative way to use sausage for a dinner."
Serving: 10 burritos. | Prep: 20m | Ready in: 55m

Ingredients

- 3/4 lb. Jones No Sugar Pork Sausage Roll sausage
- 1/2 cup chopped green pepper
- 1/3 cup chopped onion
- 1 can (15 oz.) black beans, rinsed and drained
- 1-1/2 cups cooked long grain rice
- 1-1/2 cups salsa, divided
- 10 flour tortillas (7 inches)
- 1 cup shredded cheddar cheese, divided

Direction

- Over medium heat, cook onion, green pepper, and sausage in a large saucepan until meat is not pink anymore. Let it drain. Mix in 1 cup of salsa, rice and beans. Combine well.
- On the middle of the tortillas, spread about half of the sausage mixture and drizzle with 1 tbsp. of cheese. Roll the tortilla up and place in an oiled 13inx9in baking dish, seam side facing down. Put remaining salsa on top.
- Put cover on and bake for 30 minutes at 350°. Remove the cover and drizzle the rest of the cheese. Bake again until cheese melts, about another 5 to 10 minutes.

Nutrition Information

- Calories: 335 calories
- Total Carbohydrate: 41 g
- Cholesterol: 24 mg
- Total Fat: 13 g
- Fiber: 3 g
- Protein: 12 g
- Sodium: 705 mg

278. Slow Cooker Garlic-sesame Beef

"It's a yummy treat!"
Serving: 6 servings. | Prep: 15m | Ready in: 05h15m

Ingredients

- 6 green onions, sliced
- 1/2 cup sugar
- 1/2 cup water
- 1/2 cup reduced-sodium soy sauce
- 1/4 cup sesame oil
- 3 tbsps. sesame seeds, toasted
- 2 tbsps. all-purpose flour
- 4 garlic cloves, minced
- 1 beef sirloin tip roast (3 lbs.), thinly sliced
- Additional sliced green onions and toasted sesame seeds
- Hot cooked rice

Direction

- Mix first 8 ingredients in a big resealable plastic bag. Put in beef; then seal the bag; coat by turning. Place in the refrigerator for 8 hours or overnight.
- Put marinade and beef into a 3-quart slow cooker. Cover and cook on low, until the meat becomes tender, about 5 to 7 hours.
- Take out the beef with a slotted spoon to a big serving plate. Then sprinkle more sesame seeds and green onions on top. Serve together with rice.

Nutrition Information

- Calories: 384 calories
- Total Carbohydrate: 11 g
- Cholesterol: 145 mg
- Total Fat: 16 g
- Fiber: 0 g
- Protein: 47 g
- Sodium: 471 mg

279. Slow-cooked Steak Fajitas

"Since we like Mexican food, I was delighted when I found this spicy dish. I use my slow cooker to simmer the beef and it comes out tender every time."
Serving: 12 servings. | Prep: 10m | Ready in: 08h40m

Ingredients

- 1 beef flank steak (1-1/2 lbs.)
- 1 can (14-1/2 oz.) diced tomatoes with garlic and onion, undrained
- 1 jalapeno pepper, seeded and chopped
- 2 garlic cloves, minced
- 1 tsp. ground coriander
- 1 tsp. ground cumin
- 1 tsp. chili powder
- 1/2 tsp. salt
- 1 medium onion, sliced
- 1 medium green pepper, julienned
- 1 medium sweet red pepper, julienned
- 1 tbsp. minced fresh cilantro
- 2 tsps. cornstarch
- 1 tbsp. water
- 12 flour tortillas (6 inches), warmed
- 3/4 cup fat-free sour cream
- 3/4 cup salsa

Direction

- Slice the steak into thin strips across the grain; put in a 5-qt. slow cooker. Add the chili powder, jalapeno, salt, cumin, tomatoes, coriander, and garlic. Cover; set to low and cook for 7 hours. Add cilantro, onion, and peppers. Cover; cook until beef is tender, 1-2 hours. Mix water and cornstarch until smooth; slowly stir into slow cooker. Cover; set to high and cook until slightly thick, 30 minutes. Use a slotted spoon to put a 1/2 cup of meat mixture in the middle of each tortilla. Fold the tortilla bottom over filling and roll it up. Serve with salsa and sour cream.

Nutrition Information

- Calories: 273 calories
- Total Carbohydrate: 35 g
- Cholesterol: 23 mg
- Total Fat: 11 g
- Fiber: 2 g
- Protein: 21 g
- Sodium: 494 mg

280. Smoked Honey-peppercorn Salmon

""Recipe for a delightful grilled salmon.""
Serving: 4 servings. | Prep: 20m | Ready in: 01h05m

Ingredients

- 1 cup packed brown sugar
- 1 cup water
- 1/3 cup salt
- 1 tbsp. minced fresh gingerroot
- 2 bay leaves
- 1 tsp. ground allspice
- 1/2 cup cold water
- 1 salmon fillet (1 lb.)
- 1/4 cup honey
- 1 tbsp. whole peppercorns, crushed
- 2 cups soaked hickory wood chips

Direction

- Add the first 6 ingredients in a small saucepan; mix. Bring to a boil. Cook and stir till salt and brown sugar dissolve. Remove from the heat. Pour cold water in for cooling the brine to room temperature.
- In a large resealable plastic bag, lay salmon; pour into bag with cooled brine carefully. Squeeze out as much air as possible; seal bag and turn to cover. Let sit for 4 hours in the refrigerator, occasionally turning.
- Strain and discard brine; rinse and pat dry salmon. Use honey to spread over fillet; use peppercorns to drizzle on.
- Add wood chips to grill following the directions of manufacturer. On greased grill rack, lay salmon, skin-side down. Cover and grill for 45-50 minutes over indirect medium heat till fish easily flakes with a fork.

281. Soft Fish Tacos

"This Tacos is totally awesome and excellent!"
Serving: Makes 6 servings

Ingredients

- 1/4 cup mayonnaise
- 1/4 cup ketchup
- 1/4 cup crema mexicana*
- 1 cup all purpose flour
- 1 tsp. fine sea salt
- 1/2 tsp. ground pepper
- 1 cup dark beer, room temperature
- 13/4 lbs. halibut, cut into 5x3/4-inch strips
- 1 lime, halved crosswise
- 12 white corn tortillas
- Vegetable oil (for deep-frying)
- 1 1/2 cups shredded red cabbage
- 2 large tomatoes, chopped
- Lime wedges
- Bottled hot pepper sauce

Direction

- To make sauce: In a bowl, combine the entire of ingredients together, then use pepper and salt to season.
- To make batter and fish: Whisk together in a bowl with pepper, salt and flour, then add in beer and whisk until batter is smooth. Allow to stand about 15 minutes.
- Sprinkle pepper and salt over fish, then squeeze over each strip with some lime juice. Allow to stand about 15 minutes, then mix fish into the batter.
- Set the oven to 200 degrees F to preheat. Heat a skillet on moderate heat. Stack two tortillas together and sprinkle water on top. Put into the skillet with wet side facing down, then heat for a minute. Sprinkle water on top, then turn stack of tortillas over and heat for another minute. Move stack to a big heavy-duty foil sheet. Repeat process and enclose tortillas in foil, then put into the oven.
- In a medium skillet, add oil to reach 1-inch depth. Attach deep-fry thermometer and heat oil to 350 degrees F. Slide into the hot oil with four fish strips, then fry for 4 minutes, until turning golden. Remove fish to a baking sheet lined with paper towel, then put into oven. Repeat.
- Fill 2 strips of fish into each warm tortilla, then put sauce, tomato, cabbage, a dash of hot pepper sauce and squeeze of lime on top.

Nutrition Information

- Calories: 567
- Total Carbohydrate: 43 g
- Cholesterol: 129 mg
- Total Fat: 19 g
- Fiber: 4 g
- Protein: 51 g
- Sodium: 715 mg
- Saturated Fat: 3 g

282. Spicy Lemon Chicken Kabobs

"I use Meyer lemons for these, but regular lemons should still lend these easy chicken kabobs its unique smoky zest."
Serving: 6 servings. | Prep: 15m | Ready in: 25m

Ingredients

- 1/4 cup lemon juice
- 4 tbsps. olive oil, divided
- 3 tbsps. white wine
- 1-1/2 tsps. crushed red pepper flakes
- 1 tsp. minced fresh rosemary or 1/4 tsp. dried rosemary, crushed
- 1-1/2 lbs. boneless skinless chicken breasts, cut into 1-inch cubes
- 2 medium lemons, halved
- Minced chives

Direction

- Put together 3 tbsps. oil, wine, lemon juice, rosemary, and pepper flakes in a large re-sealable plastic bag. Add the chicken in the bag, seal the bag, turn to coat the chicken, and refrigerate for up to 3 hours. Drain the chicken and dispose of its marinade. Skewer chicken onto six metal or water-soaked wooden skewers then grill in a covered medium-hot grill until meat is not pink anymore, turning once during its 10- to 12-minute grilling time. Grill lemons with the cut side down, 8-10 minutes or until browned. Squeeze lemon juice over the skewers, drizzle with oil, and top with chives.

Nutrition Information

- Calories: 182 calories
- Total Carbohydrate: 2 g
- Cholesterol: 63 mg
- Total Fat: 8 g
- Fiber: 1 g
- Protein: 23 g
- Sodium: 55 mg

283. Steak And Black Bean Burritos

Serving: 2 servings. | Prep: 15m | Ready in: 25m

Ingredients

- 4 oz. beef flank steak
- 1/8 tsp. salt
- 1/8 tsp. pepper
- 1/2 tsp. canola oil
- 2 flour tortillas (8 inches), warmed
- 1/2 cup cold cooked rice
- 1/2 medium ripe avocado, peeled and diced
- 1/2 cup canned black beans, rinsed and drained
- 2 tbsps. sour cream
- 1 tbsp. salsa
- 1 tbsp. finely chopped onion
- 1-1/2 tsps. minced fresh cilantro

Direction

- Drizzle pepper and salt on the steak. Over medium high heat, cook the steak in oil in a

small skillet coated with cooking spray until you achieve your desired doneness of the steak, about 3-4 minutes on each side. A thermometer should read 145° for medium rare, 160° for medium and 170° for well-done.
- Cut the steak thinly across the grain. Put in the middle of the tortillas. Put cilantro, onion, sour cream, beans, avocado, salsa and rice on top. Roll up the tortillas then serve immediately.

Nutrition Information

- Calories: 449 calories
- Total Carbohydrate: 51 g
- Cholesterol: 37 mg
- Total Fat: 18 g
- Fiber: 6 g
- Protein: 21 g
- Sodium: 589 mg

284. Steak With Chipotle-lime Chimichurri

"What's good about chimichurri is that it goes well with any grilled food, be it fish, meat or poultry. Enjoy this steak recipe with your own homemade chimichurri!"
Serving: 8 servings. | Prep: 20m | Ready in: 30m

Ingredients

- 2 cups fresh parsley leaves
- 1-1/2 cups fresh cilantro leaves
- 1/2 medium red onion, coarsely chopped
- 1 to 2 chipotle peppers in adobo sauce
- 5 garlic cloves, sliced
- 1/2 cup olive oil
- 1/4 cup white wine vinegar
- 1 tsp. grated lime zest
- 1/4 cup lime juice
- 3 tsps. dried oregano
- 1-1/4 tsps. salt, divided
- 3/4 tsp. pepper, divided
- 2 lbs. beef flat iron steaks or 2 beef top sirloin steaks (1 lb. each)

Direction

- To prepare the chimichurri: In a food processor, put in all of the first 5 ingredients and pulse until the ingredients are chopped finely. Mix in the oregano, lime juice, 1/4 tsp. of pepper, 1/2 tsp. of salt, vinegar, oil and lime zest then blend until well-combined. Place the mixture in a bowl then cover and keep in the fridge until it's time to serve.
- Season the steaks with the remaining pepper and salt. Put the seasoned steaks on a grill over medium heat then cover and let it grill for 5-8 minutes on both sides until the preferred meat doneness is achieved (a thermometer inserted in the meat should indicate 160°F for medium, 170°F for well-done and 145°F for medium-rare). Before cutting the steaks, allow it to rest for 5 minutes. Serve it together with the chimichurri.

Nutrition Information

- Calories: 336 calories
- Total Carbohydrate: 4 g
- Cholesterol: 73 mg
- Total Fat: 26 g
- Fiber: 1 g
- Protein: 22 g
- Sodium: 462 mg

285. Sweet 'n' Spicy Country Ribs

"These tender ribs have the best sauce that everyone will keep running back to."
Serving: 6 servings. | Prep: 15m | Ready in: 55m

Ingredients

- 3/4 cup unsweetened apple juice
- 1/2 cup canola oil
- 1/2 cup cola
- 1/4 cup packed brown sugar
- 1/4 cup honey
- 1 tbsp. minced garlic
- 1 tbsp. Worcestershire sauce
- 2 tsps. Liquid Smoke, optional
- 1 tsp. salt
- 1 tsp. dried thyme
- 1 tsp. pepper
- 1/2 tsp. cayenne pepper
- 1/2 tsp. ground nutmeg
- 3 to 4 lbs. boneless country-style pork ribs

Direction

- Mix together seasonings, apple juice, Worcestershire sauce, oil, garlic, cola, honey, brown sugar, and an optional liquid smoke.
- Reserve a cup and half marinade in a big ziplock bag; place the ribs inside. Seal and flip the bag to coat the ribs. Let it chill in the refrigerator for 5 hrs up to overnight, turn bag once. Keep the remaining marinade covered for basting and store in the refrigerator.
- Drain ribs and get rid of the marinade. Grease the grill rack using a paper towel moistened with cooking oil and long-handled tongs. Use a drip pan to ready the grill for indirect heat; arrange ribs on top the drip pan. Grill for 10 minutes per side on indirect medium heat, baste from time to time.
- Grill for another 20-25 minutes until tender, flip and baste occasionally using the leftover marinade.

286. Tangy Shrimp Kabobs

"A total of 2 grams of fat in a pair of kabobs – unbelievable! Yet this easy, sweet-and-sour shrimp, pineapple, and veggie kabobs are just that, and they are easy to make, too! The marinade and basting sauce is a healthy tomato-based mixture."
Serving: 6 servings. | Prep: 25m | Ready in: 40m

Ingredients

- 1 can (20 oz.) unsweetened pineapple chunks
- 1 can (8 oz.) tomato sauce
- 1/2 cup fat-free Italian salad dressing
- 4-1/2 tsps. brown sugar
- 1 tsp. prepared mustard

- 1-1/2 lbs. uncooked large shrimp, peeled and deveined
- 12 pearl onions
- 1 large sweet red pepper, cut into 1-inch pieces
- 1 large green pepper, cut into 1-inch pieces
- Hot cooked rice, optional

Direction

- Save 1/4 cup of juice from the pineapples. Set aside the fruit without the juice. In a small bowl, mix together the reserved pineapple juice, tomato sauce, mustard, brown sugar, and Italian dressing. Put 3/4 cup of this marinade in a large re-sealable plastic bag and add the shrimps. Close the bag, turn several times to coat, and keep in the refrigerator for 3 hours, turning the bag from time to time. Keep the remaining mixture in a covered container in the refrigerator, to use as later as a sauce. Boil 6 cups of water in a Dutch oven. Put in the onions and keep boiling for 2 minutes; add the peppers and boil for 2 more minutes. Drain completely and rinse vegetables in cold water. Peel the onions and refrigerate both the onions and the peppers until grilling time. Boil 3/4 cup of the reserved tomato sauce in a small saucepan. Lower the heat and let it simmer without the lid for 5 minutes, or until sauce thickens a little. Keep the sauce warm. Take the marinated shrimps out of the bag, discarding marinade. Alternately skewer the shrimps and vegetables on 12 metal or pre-soaked wooden skewers. Arrange on an oiled rack, cover the grill, and cook on medium heat for 3-5 minutes per side or until shrimps are cooked, occasionally brushing with the tomato sauce mixture. Alternative to grilling is broiling 4 in. away from the heat. Take the warm sauce and drizzle over the kabobs before serving. May be served with rice, if desired.

Nutrition Information

- Calories: 194 calories
- Total Carbohydrate: 24 g
- Cholesterol: 138 mg
- Total Fat: 2 g
- Fiber: 3 g
- Protein: 20 g
- Sodium: 474 mg

287. Teriyaki Shish Kabobs

"In my teenage years, my father was working for an airline and we lived in the island of Guam in the South Pacific. My mother used to prepare these skewers often because we liked them a lot. A friend gave her the recipe. Now I cook it for my family, and they enjoy these as well."
Serving: 8 servings. | Prep: 20m | Ready in: 35m

Ingredients

- 1 cup sugar
- 1 cup reduced-sodium soy sauce
- 1 cup ketchup
- 2 tsps. garlic powder
- 2 tsps. ground ginger
- 2 lbs. beef top sirloin steak, cut into 1-1/2-inch cubes
- 2 to 3 small zucchini, cut into 1-inch slices
- 1/2 lb. medium fresh mushrooms
- 1 large green or sweet red pepper, cut into 1-inch pieces
- 1 small onion, cut into 1-inch pieces
- 2 cups cubed fresh pineapple

Direction

- Combine the first five ingredients to make the marinade. Pour half of the marinade over the beef inside a large re-sealable plastic bag. Seal the bag and turn several times to coat. Keep the remaining marinade in a covered container and refrigerate. Place the bag with the beef in the fridge to marinate overnight. Thread the beef and pineapples together onto a set of skewers, and thread the vegetables on a separate set. Discard the marinade used with the beef. Over medium heat in a covered grill, cook the skewers for 12-15 minutes until the vegetables are soft and the beef is done to liking. Turn from time to time to cook evenly.

Boil the reserved marinade for a minute with occasional stirring in a small saucepan. Slide the vegetables, beef, and pineapples off the skewers before serving, and put out the sauce on the side.

Nutrition Information

- Calories: 306 calories
- Total Carbohydrate: 38 g
- Cholesterol: 46 mg
- Total Fat: 5 g
- Fiber: 2 g
- Protein: 27 g
- Sodium: 1203 mg

288. Vegetable Beef Kabobs

"A main entrée of Kansas beef that has been grilled outdoors. A family favorite."
Serving: 6 servings. | Prep: 10m | Ready in: 25m

Ingredients

- 1-1/2 lbs. beef top sirloin steak
- 2/3 cup white wine or beef broth
- 1/3 cup soy sauce
- 2 tbsps. vegetable oil
- 1 tsp. minced fresh gingerroot or 1/4 tsp. ground ginger
- 1 garlic clove, minced
- 1/2 tsp. dried tarragon
- 18 small whole onions
- 3 to 4 small zucchini, cut in 1-inch slices
- 2 large sweet red peppers, cut in 1-inch pieces

Direction

- Cube beef into 1-1/4-in. size pieces. Place beef in a large re-sealable plastic bag. In a bowl, pour in the wine, soy sauce, and oil, and add in the garlic, ginger, and tarragon. Pour 2/3 cup of this over the beef. Seal the bag and let marinate in room temperature for half an hour. Keep remaining marinade on the side for basting later. Drain the beef, discarding its marinade. Alternately thread the meat,

zucchini, onions, and peppers on six metal or pre-soaked wooden skewers. Grill for 10-12 minutes at medium heat, turning and basting from time to time, until meat is cooked to liking.

289. Vegetable Steak Kabobs

"One of the best, most versatile marinades that I've tried. Great on beef, pork, chicken, and vegetables."
Serving: 6 servings. | Prep: 20m | Ready in: 30m

Ingredients

- 1/2 cup olive oil
- 1/3 cup red wine vinegar
- 2 tbsps. ketchup
- 2 to 3 garlic cloves, minced
- 1 tsp. Worcestershire sauce
- 1/2 tsp. each dried marjoram, basil and oregano
- 1/2 tsp. dried rosemary, crushed
- 1 beef top sirloin steak (1-1/2 lbs.), cut into 1-inch cubes
- 1/2 lb. whole fresh mushrooms
- 2 medium onions, cut into wedges
- 1-1/2 cups cherry tomatoes
- 2 small green peppers, cut into 1-inch pieces

Direction

- Whisk together Worcestershire sauce, vinegar, oil, ketchup, garlic, and seasonings in a small bowl. Place the beef in a large zip-top bag and pour 1/2 cup of the marinade. Zip the bag and turn multiple times to coat. Take another large zip-top bag and add in the onions, tomatoes, mushrooms, peppers, and the remaining marinade. Close the bag and turn several times. Let marinate in the fridge for at least 8 hours or even overnight. Discard the marinade from the beef, and keep that from the vegetables to use for basting. Alternately thread beef and vegetables on six metal or water-soaked wooden skewers. Place the kabobs on the grill, cover the grill, and cook over medium heat or broil 4 in. from heat for

10-15 minutes, or until vegetables are cooked through but still crisp and beef is done to liking. Turn occasionally within the cooking time and baste with reserved marinade at the last 5 minutes.

Nutrition Information

- Calories: 234 calories
- Total Carbohydrate: 10 g
- Cholesterol: 69 mg
- Total Fat: 10 g
- Fiber: 2 g
- Protein: 26 g
- Sodium: 99 mg

---

290. White Cheddar Scalloped Potatoes

"Serve this rich, saucy entree with a salad and homemade French bread."
Serving: 10 servings. | Prep: 40m | Ready in: 01h50m

Ingredients

- 1/4 cup butter
- 1 medium onion, finely chopped
- 1/4 cup all-purpose flour
- 1 tsp. salt
- 1 tsp. dried parsley flakes
- 1/2 tsp. dried thyme
- 1/2 tsp. pepper
- 3 cups 2% milk
- 1 can (10-3/4 oz.) condensed cream of mushroom soup, undiluted
- 1 cup (8 oz.) sour cream
- 8 cups thinly sliced peeled potatoes
- 3-1/2 cups cubed fully cooked ham
- 2 cups shredded sharp white cheddar cheese

Direction

- Set the oven to 375 degrees and preheat. Heat butter in a big saucepan on moderate-high heat. Put in onion, then cook and stir until soft. Stir in seasonings and flour until combined,

then whisk in milk gradually. Bring the mixture to a boil while stirring frequently, then cook and stir until thickened, about 2 minutes. Mix in soup. Take away from the heat and stir in sour cream.
- Layer in a 13"x9" baking dish coated with grease with half of each of following ingredients: potatoes, ham, cheese and sauce, then repeat layers.
- Bake with a cover for half an hour, and then bake more for 40 to 50 minutes without a cover, until potatoes are soft.

Nutrition Information

- Calories: 417 calories
- Total Carbohydrate: 37 g
- Cholesterol: 88 mg
- Total Fat: 20 g
- Fiber: 3 g
- Protein: 22 g
- Sodium: 1267 mg

---

291. Zesty Grilled Chops

"Grill these pork chops in summer or broil them in winter. Either way, everyone will enjoy this dish."
Serving: 6 servings. | Prep: 10m | Ready in: 20m

Ingredients

- 3/4 cup soy sauce
- 1/4 cup lemon juice
- 1 tbsp. chili sauce
- 1 tbsp. brown sugar
- 1 garlic clove, minced
- 6 bone-in pork loin or rib chops (about 1-1/2 inches thick)

Direction

- Mix the initial 5 ingredients together in a big ziplock bag. Keep 1/3 cup of the mixture to use for brushing later on. Place pork chops in the bag; seal and flip to cover chops with marinade. Place in the refrigerator overnight.

- Drain pork and get rid of the marinade. On medium heat, grill while covered for 6-8 minutes on each side or broil 4 inches from the heat for 6-8 min on each side until the thermometer registers 145 degrees F. Use the reserved mixture to brush chops regularly on the final 5 mins of cooking. Set aside for 5 minutes, serve.

Nutrition Information

- Calories: 246 calories
- Total Carbohydrate: 1 g
- Cholesterol: 82 mg
- Total Fat: 11 g
- Fiber: trace g
- Protein: 34 g
- Sodium: 598 mg

292. Zesty Grilled Ham

"It will make your kids eat much like ham."
Serving: 4 servings. | Prep: 5m | Ready in: 15m

Ingredients

- 1/3 cup packed brown sugar
- 2 tbsps. prepared horseradish
- 4 tsps. lemon juice
- 1 fully cooked bone-in ham steak (1 lb.)

Direction

- In a small saucepan, add lemon juice, horseradish and brown sugar, then bring mixture to a boil while stirring continuously. Brush over ham on both sides.
- Put ham on a grill rack coated with oil on moderate heat. Grill with a cover for 7 to 10 minutes while turning sometimes, until heated through and glazed.

Nutrition Information

- Calories: 180 calories
- Total Carbohydrate: 20 g
- Cholesterol: 44 mg

- Total Fat: 5 g
- Fiber: 0 g
- Protein: 14 g
- Sodium: 845 mg

293. Zesty Light Tacos

"This high-fiber and colorful main dish is very great for vegetarians."
Serving: 8 servings. | Prep: 15m | Ready in: 01h05m

Ingredients

- 1 cup uncooked brown rice
- 1 medium red onion, halved and sliced
- 1 medium green pepper, thinly sliced
- 1 tbsp. canola oil
- 1 can (15 oz.) black beans, rinsed and drained
- 1 can (14-1/2 oz.) diced tomatoes with mild green chilies, undrained
- 1/2 cup frozen corn
- 1/2 cup taco sauce
- 1 tsp. chili powder
- 3/4 tsp. cayenne pepper
- 8 whole wheat tortillas (8 inches), warmed
- Optional toppings: shredded lettuce, chopped tomatoes, pickled jalapeno slices, shredded reduced-fat cheddar cheese and reduced-fat sour cream

Direction

- Follow package directions to cook rice. In the meantime, sauté onion and pepper together in a big nonstick skillet with oil until soft. Stir in cayenne, chili powder, taco sauce, corn, tomatoes and beans, then heat through. Mix in cooked rice.
- Spoon down the center of each tortilla with 3/4 cup of the mixture and put on toppings if you want.

Nutrition Information

- Calories: 326 calories
- Total Carbohydrate: 57 g

- Cholesterol: 0 mg
- Total Fat: 6 g
- Fiber: 7 g
- Protein: 10 g
- Sodium: 565 mg

Chapter 5: Fathers Day Dessert Recipes

***

294. Apple Snack Squares

"A sweet cake topped with butterscotch chips and filled with apples and nuts. Fold in pecans or the walnuts depending on your own taste."
Serving: 24 | Prep: 30m | Ready in: 1h10m

Ingredients

- 2 cups white sugar
- 2 eggs
- 3/4 cup vegetable oil
- 1 tsp. vanilla extract
- 2 1/2 cups self-rising flour
- 1 tsp. ground cinnamon
- 3 cups peeled, cored, and chopped tart apple
- 1 cup chopped walnuts
- 1 cup butterscotch chips

Direction

- Set the oven to 350°F (175°C), and start preheating. Cover lightly a 9x13-inch baking dish with oil.
- In a large bowl, mix vanilla, oil, eggs and sugar and stir till well combined. Mix in the cinnamon and flour, the mixture should be thick. Fold in the nuts and chopped apple.

Spread the batter in the prepared baking dish, and sprinkle butterscotch chips on top.
- Bake in the preheated oven for 35-40 minutes, until a toothpick put in the middle goes out clean. Let it cool then cut into squares for serving.

Nutrition Information

- Calories: 258 calories;
- Total Carbohydrate: 33.8 g
- Cholesterol: 16 mg
- Total Fat: 12.6 g
- Protein: 2.6 g
- Sodium: 179 mg

295. Apple-berry Streusel Bars

"These appealing bars with nutty topping and fruity filling taste much better than they really cost."
Serving: 4 dozen. | Prep: 10m | Ready in: 55m

Ingredients

- 2-1/2 cups plus 2 tbsps. all-purpose flour, divided
- 2 cups old-fashioned oats
- 1-1/4 cups sugar
- 2 tsps. baking powder
- 1 tsp. ground cinnamon
- 1 cup butter, melted
- 3 cups thinly sliced peeled tart apples
- 1 jar (12 oz.) raspberry preserves
- 1/2 cup finely chopped walnuts

Direction

- Mix cinnamon, baking powder, sugar, oats, and 2 1/2 cups of flour in a large bowl. Whisk in the butter until just moistened. Put 2 cups of the topping aside.
- Pat the rest of the oat mixture in a 13x9-inch baking pan coated with cooking spray. Bake for 15 minutes at 375 degrees.
- Toss apples together with the remaining flour in a large bowl; add the preserves and stir. Spread over the hot crust to within 1/2 inch of

edges. Mix the saved oat mixture and nuts; dust over the fruit mixture.

- Bake until browned lightly, for 30-35 more minutes. Transfer onto a wire rack to completely cool. Slice into bars.

Nutrition Information

- Calories: 121 calories
- Total Carbohydrate: 18 g
- Cholesterol: 10 mg
- Total Fat: 5 g
- Fiber: 1 g
- Protein: 2 g
- Sodium: 56 mg

296. Banana Flip Cake

"This great cake has the taste of banana flips."
Serving: 16 servings. | Prep: 30m | Ready in: 60m

Ingredients

- 1 package yellow cake mix (regular size)
- 1 package (3.4 oz.) instant banana or vanilla pudding mix
- 1-1/2 cups 2% milk
- 4 eggs
- FROSTING:
- 1/3 cup all-purpose flour
- 1 cup 2% milk
- 1/2 cup butter, softened
- 1/2 cup shortening
- 1 cup sugar
- 1-1/2 tsps. vanilla extract
- 2 tbsps. confectioners' sugar

Direction

- Use waxed paper to line 2 15"x10"x1" baking pans coated with grease, then grease the paper and put aside.
- Mix together eggs, milk, pudding mix and cake mix in a big bowl, then beat on low speed about half a minute. Continue to beat on medium about 2 minutes.

- Spread the batter into prepped pans and bake at 350 degrees until a toothpick exits clean after being inserted into the center, about 12 to 15 minutes. Allow to cool about 5 minutes prior to inverting on wire racks to cool thoroughly. Peel off waxed paper gently.
- In the meantime, whisk together milk and flour in a small saucepan until smooth. Bring mixture to a boil, then cook and stir until thickened, about 2 minutes. Take away from the heat, then place on a cover and allow to cool to room temperature.
- Cream together sugar, shortening and butter in the bowl of a heavy-duty stand mixer until fluffy and light. Beat in vanilla. Put in milk mixture and beat on high until fluffy, about 10 to 15 minutes.
- Put on a big cutting board with one cake and spread frosting over top. Put leftover cake on top and sprinkle with more confectioners' sugar. Cut cake into slices and chill leftovers.

Nutrition Information

- Calories: 355 calories
- Total Carbohydrate: 49 g
- Cholesterol: 71 mg
- Total Fat: 16 g
- Fiber: 0 g
- Protein: 4 g
- Sodium: 372 mg

297. Banana Split Icebox Cake

"One of my friends shared this icebox cake recipe with me."
Serving: 10 servings. | Prep: 30m | Ready in: 30m

Ingredients

- 1 carton (16 oz.) frozen whipped topping, thawed
- 1 cup (8 oz.) sour cream
- 1 package (3.4 oz.) instant vanilla pudding mix
- 1 can (8 oz.) crushed pineapple, drained
- 24 whole graham crackers
- 2 medium bananas, sliced

- Toppings: chocolate syrup, halved fresh strawberries and additional banana slices

Direction

- Combine pudding mix, sour cream, and whipped topping in a large mixing bowl until incorporated. Mix in pineapple. Snip a small hole in a corner of a food-safe plastic bag or in the tip of a pastry bag. Pour pudding mixture into the bag.
- Place 4 crackers in a rectangle on a flat serving plate. Squeeze about 1 cup of pudding mixture over cracker layer; place about 1/4 cup banana slices over pudding mixture. Repeat layering process 5 more times. Cover and chill overnight.
- Top cake with more banana slices, strawberries, and chocolate syrup right before serving.

Nutrition Information

- Calories: 405 calories
- Total Carbohydrate: 60 g
- Cholesterol: 16 mg
- Total Fat: 15 g
- Fiber: 2 g
- Protein: 4 g
- Sodium: 372 mg

298. Bananas Foster On The Grill

""Preparing desserts on the grill is simple, enjoyable and delicious!""
Serving: 1 | Prep: 5m | Ready in: 10m

Ingredients

- 1/2 banana
- 2 tbsps. coffee-flavored liqueur (such as Kahlua®)
- 1 tbsp. butter
- 1 tbsp. brown sugar
- 1 tsp. ground cinnamon

Direction

- Preheat the grill to medium heat. Prepare a durable aluminium foil. On a large part of foil, put ground cinnamon, brown sugar, butter, coffee-flavored liquor and banana then bring the two sides of foil up until they touch. Seal it up by folding down twice. To seal it up even more firmly, double fold the ends of the packet. Move the packet onto the preheated grill. Leave it cooking for around 5 minutes until it is thoroughly heated. Before serving, put over vanilla ice cream.

Nutrition Information

- Calories: 318 calories;
- Total Carbohydrate: 41.9 g
- Cholesterol: 31 mg
- Total Fat: 11.8 g
- Protein: 0.9 g
- Sodium: 88 mg

299. Bavarian Chocolate-hazelnut Braid

"It is really a delightful loaf with the accompaniment of flaky crust and creamy filling."
Serving: 12 servings. | Prep: 15m | Ready in: 35m

Ingredients

- 3/4 cup (6 oz.) vanilla yogurt
- 1/3 cup sweetened shredded coconut
- 1 large egg, separated
- 1/4 tsp. almond extract
- 1 tube (8 oz.) refrigerated crescent rolls
- 1/3 cup Nutella
- 3 tbsps. sliced almonds
- 2 tbsps. confectioners' sugar

Direction

- Mix together extract, egg yolk, coconut and yogurt in a small bowl.
- On a baking sheet coated lightly with grease, unroll crescent dough into a long rectangle,

sealing seams and perforations. Roll out dough into a 14"x9" rectangle.

- Spread down the center of rectangle with Nutella, in a strip with the width of 3 inches. Put yogurt mixture on top. Cut strips on each long side with the width of 1 inch, to within 1/2 inch of filling. Fold strips alternately, beginning at one end, at an angle across the filling.
- Whisk egg white and brush over top as well as sides of the dough, then sprinkle almonds over top.
- Bake at 350 degrees until turning golden brown, about 20 to 25 minutes. Sprinkle confectioners' sugar over top and allow to cool about 10 minutes prior to cutting into slices.

Nutrition Information

- Calories: 160 calories
- Total Carbohydrate: 17 g
- Cholesterol: 18 mg
- Total Fat: 9 g
- Fiber: 1 g
- Protein: 3 g
- Sodium: 174 mg

300. Big & Buttery Chocolate Chip Cookies

"This is really the best large, chewy and thick chocolate chip cookie."
Serving: about 2 dozen. | Prep: 35m | Ready in: 45m

Ingredients

- 1 cup butter, softened
- 1 cup packed brown sugar
- 3/4 cup sugar
- 2 large eggs
- 1-1/2 tsps. vanilla extract
- 2-2/3 cups all-purpose flour
- 1-1/4 tsps. baking soda
- 1 tsp. salt
- 1 package (12 oz.) semisweet chocolate chips
- 2 cups coarsely chopped walnuts, toasted

Direction

- Beat sugars and butter together in a big bowl until combined, then beat in vanilla and eggs. Whisk together salt, baking soda and flour in a small bowl, then beat into the butter mixture gradually. Stir in walnuts and chocolate chips.
- Form the dough into balls, 1/4 cupful dough per ball. Flatten each ball to the thickness of 3/4 inch with the diameter of 2 1/2 inches, then smooth edges if needed. Put into a tightly sealed container, using parchment or waxed paper to divide layers. Chill with a cover overnight.
- To bake, put dough portions on baking sheets lined with parchment paper, spaced 2 inches apart. Allow to stand at room temperature about half an hour prior to baking. Set the oven to 400 degrees to preheat.
- Bake until edges turn golden brown, about 10 to 12 minutes; the centers will become light. Allow to cool on pans about 2 minutes, then transfer to wire racks to cool completely.

Nutrition Information

- Calories: 311 calories
- Total Carbohydrate: 35 g
- Cholesterol: 38 mg
- Total Fat: 19 g
- Fiber: 2 g
- Protein: 4 g
- Sodium: 229 mg

301. Black Walnut Brownies

"These both crispy and chewy brownies are studded with black walnuts."
Serving: 16 servings. | Prep: 10m | Ready in: 40m

Ingredients

- 1 cup sugar
- 1/4 cup canola oil
- 2 large eggs
- 1 tsp. vanilla extract

- 1/2 cup all-purpose flour
- 2 tbsps. baking cocoa
- 1/2 tsp. salt
- 1/2 cup chopped black walnuts

Direction

- Beat oil and sugar together in a small bowl until mixed, then beat in vanilla and eggs. Mix together salt, cocoa and flour, then put into the sugar mixture gradually, blending well. Mix in walnuts.
- Transfer batter into an 8-inch square baking pan coated with grease, then bake at 350 degrees until a toothpick exits clean after being inserted into the center, about 30 to 35 minutes. Allow to cool on a wire rack.

Nutrition Information

- Calories: 128 calories
- Total Carbohydrate: 16 g
- Cholesterol: 27 mg
- Total Fat: 6 g
- Fiber: 0 g
- Protein: 2 g
- Sodium: 82 mg

302. Blissful Peanut Butter-chocolate Cheesecake

"The three words that best describe this cheesecake are fun, delicious, and decadent. Just try one bite and you'll agree to this description."
Serving: 12 servings. | Prep: 60m | Ready in: 02h00m

Ingredients

- 32 Nutter Butter cookies
- 1/3 cup butter, melted
- 4 packages (8 oz. each) cream cheese, softened
- 1 cup sugar
- 3 oz. semisweet chocolate, melted
- 3 oz. bittersweet chocolate, melted
- 1 tsp. vanilla extract
- 4 eggs, lightly beaten
- PEANUT BUTTER MOUSSE:
- 1-1/2 tsps. unflavored gelatin
- 2 tbsps. cold water
- 1 cup heavy whipping cream
- 3 tbsps. creamy peanut butter
- 2 tbsps. sugar
- 2 egg yolks
- GARNISH:
- 3 oz. semisweet chocolate, chopped
- Chocolate curls and sweetened whipped cream, optional

Direction

- Place a greased 9-inches springform pan over an 18-inch double thick and heavy-duty square shaped foil. Wrap the foil tightly around the pan.
- Grind the cookies in a food processor until it appears fine crumbs. Mix in butter. Pour the mixture into the bottom and 2-inches up the sides of the greased pan. Set aside the pan.
- Whisk sugar and cream cheese in a big bowl until smooth. Stir in vanilla and melted chocolates. Whisk in eggs and beat at low speed until the egg incorporates. Spread the mixture over the crust. Place the pan in a big baking pan with an inch of hot water.
- Set the oven to 325°F and bake for 60-65 minutes until the top appears dull and the center is fixed. Remove the pan from the water bath and transfer it into a wire rack. Cool for 10 minutes. Loosen the sides of the cheesecake using a knife. Cool for 60 more minutes.
- To make a peanut butter moose, add gelatin on cold water. Set aside for 60 seconds. Place it inside the microwave and heat on the high setting for 20 to 30 seconds. Whisk and set aside for 60 seconds until the gelatin dissolves completely.
- Heat peanut butter, sugar, and cream in a small and heavy saucepan until bubbles appear on the sides of the pan. Add a bit of the hot mixture in egg yolks. Bring the mixture back into the pan and constantly stir.
- Cook the mixture on low heat, stirring constantly until it has a thick consistency and

when it coats the back of the spoon. Add the gelatin mixture. Transfer the heated mixture immediately in a bowl. Place it in ice water and whisk for 15 minutes until the mixture is thick and cold. Spread the mixture over the cheesecake. Store it inside the fridge overnight. Remove the rim from the pan.

- Melt chocolate in a microwave. Spread the melted chocolate over the cheesecake. Style the cake with whipped cream and chocolate curls.

Nutrition Information

- Calories: 792 calories
- Total Carbohydrate: 58 g
- Cholesterol: 228 mg
- Total Fat: 59 g
- Fiber: 2 g
- Protein: 15 g
- Sodium: 448 mg

303. Butter Pecan Cake

"A delightful dessert for a sweet tooth."
Serving: 12 servings. | Prep: 40m | Ready in: 01h10m

Ingredients

- 3 tbsps. butter, melted
- 1-1/3 cups chopped pecans
- 2/3 cup butter, softened
- 1-1/3 cups sugar
- 2 large eggs
- 2 cups all-purpose flour
- 1-1/2 tsps. baking powder
- 1/4 tsp. salt
- 2/3 cup whole milk
- 1-1/2 tsps. vanilla extract
- BUTTER PECAN FROSTING:
- 3 tbsps. butter, softened
- 3 cups confectioners' sugar
- 3 tbsps. whole milk
- 3/4 tsp. vanilla extract

Direction

- In a baking pan, add melted butter, then stir in pecans. Toast pecans at 350 degrees about 10 minutes, then put aside to cool.
- Cream sugar and butter together in a bowl until fluffy and light. Put in 1 egg at a time while beating well between additions. Mix together salt, baking powder and flour, then put into creamed mixture together with milk, alternately. Stir in 1 cup of toasted pecans and vanilla. Transfer batter into 2 8-inch round baking pans coated with grease and flour. Bake at 350 degrees until a toothpick exits clean after being inserted into the center, about 30 to 35 minutes. Allow to cool in pans about 10 minutes prior to transferring to wire racks to cool thoroughly.
- In the meantime, to make frosting, cream sugar and butter together. Put in vanilla and milk while beating mixture until fluffy and light. Put in more milk if necessary. Stir in leftover toasted pecans, then spread mixture between layers and over top as well as sides of cake.

Nutrition Information

- Calories: 534 calories
- Total Carbohydrate: 71 g
- Cholesterol: 80 mg
- Total Fat: 27 g
- Fiber: 2 g
- Protein: 5 g
- Sodium: 280 mg

304. Butterscotch Brownie Mix

"Just need vanilla, eggs and butter to make these delicious butterscotch brownies."
Serving: 2 dozen. | Prep: 15m | Ready in: 35m

Ingredients

- 2 cups all-purpose flour
- 3-1/2 tsps. baking powder
- 1/4 tsp. salt

- 3/4 cup chopped pecans, toasted
- 1-1/2 cups packed brown sugar
- 1/2 cup butterscotch chips
- ADDITIONAL INGREDIENTS:
- 3/4 cup butter, cubed
- 2 large eggs
- 2 tsps. vanilla extract

Direction

- Combine together salt, baking powder and flour in a small bowl. Layer in a 1-quart glass jar with flour mixture, pecans, brown sugar and butterscotch chips in the given order. Place on a cover and keep in a cool, dry area for a maximum of 3 months. Produce: 1 batch, approximately 4 cups mix.
- For brownies preparation: Set the oven to 350 degrees to preheat. Heat butter in a big saucepan on moderate heat until just melted. Take away from the heat. Whisk vanilla and eggs together until mixed. Put in blondie mix gradually and mix well, then spread mixture into a 13"x9" baking pan coated with grease.
- Bake until a toothpick exits with moist crumbs after being inserted into the center, about 20 to 25 minutes without over-baking. Allow to cool thoroughly in pan on a wire rack.

305. Cake Mix Peanut Butter Brownies

"This cookie recipe is so easy to make with the use of boxed cake mix. By adding in melted chocolate chips and peanut butter, these will taste amazing."
Serving: 4-1/2 dozen. | Prep: 10m | Ready in: 35m

Ingredients

- 1 package chocolate cake mix (regular size)
- 1/3 cup vegetable oil
- 1 egg
- 1 can (14 oz.) sweetened condensed milk
- 2 cups (12 oz.) semisweet chocolate chips, melted
- 1/2 cup peanut butter

- 1 tsp. vanilla extract

Direction

- Mix together egg, oil and cake mix in a bowl until the mixture form crumbs. Reserve one cup of mixture for topping. In a 13x9-inch baking pan coated with grease, firmly press the rest of dough and put aside.
- Stir together vanilla, peanut butter, chocolate and milk in a bowl until smooth. Layer it onto the dough. Scatter the rest of crumb mixture over top.
- Bake at 350 degrees until the batter pulls away from the baking pan, about 25 to 30 minutes. Place on a wire rack to cool. Slice into bars.

Nutrition Information

- Calories: 121 calories
- Total Carbohydrate: 16 g
- Cholesterol: 6 mg
- Total Fat: 6 g
- Fiber: 1 g
- Protein: 2 g
- Sodium: 82 mg

306. Cappuccino Truffle Brownies

"These brownies are a great combination of chocolate and good drinks."
Serving: 16 bars. | Prep: 30m | Ready in: 50m

Ingredients

- 2 oz. semisweet chocolate
- 1/2 cup butter, cubed
- 2 eggs
- 3/4 cup packed brown sugar
- 1 tsp. vanilla extract
- 3/4 cup all-purpose flour
- 1/2 tsp. baking powder
- 1/2 tsp. ground cinnamon
- FILLING:
- 1 package (8 oz.) cream cheese, softened
- 1/4 cup confectioners' sugar

- 1 tsp. instant coffee granules
- 1 tbsp. hot water
- 1 cup (6 oz.) semisweet chocolate chips
- 1/2 tsp. butter
- GLAZE:
- 1/2 cup semisweet chocolate chips
- 1 tsp. shortening
- Whole blanched almonds

Direction

- Melt butter and chocolate together in a microwave and stir mixture until smooth. Allow to cool a little bit. Beat vanilla, brown sugar and eggs together in a small bowl, then beat in chocolate mixture. Mix together cinnamon, baking powder and flour, then stir into chocolate mixture.
- Spread batter into a 9-inch square baking pan coated with grease and bake at 350 degrees until a toothpick exits clean after being inserted into the center, 20 to 22 minutes. Allow to cool on a wire rack.
- To make filling, beat together confectioners' sugar and cream cheese in a big bowl until fluffy and light. Dissolve coffee in water, then stir into cream cheese mixture. Melt butter and chips in a microwave, stirring until smooth. Beat the mixture of butter and chips into cream cheese mixture until combined. Spread cream cheese mixture over top of brownies.
- To make glaze, melt shortening and chips together in a microwave, stirring until smooth. Dip into glaze with half of each almond then arrange on a baking sheet lined with waxed paper. Allow to stand until chocolate has set, then drizzle over bars with leftover graze. Put in the center of each bar with almond, then chill leftovers.

Nutrition Information

- Calories: 265 calories
- Total Carbohydrate: 28 g
- Cholesterol: 58 mg
- Total Fat: 17 g
- Fiber: 1 g
- Protein: 3 g

- Sodium: 127 mg

307. Caramel Nut Logs

"This recipe can make a bunch."
Serving: 4-1/2 lbs.. | Prep: 30m | Ready in: 03h00m

Ingredients

- 4 cups (1-1/3 lbs.) chopped salted peanuts, divided
- 3 cups sugar, divided
- 1-1/3 cups light corn syrup, divided
- 1 cup water, divided
- 2 egg whites
- 1/4 cup butter, melted
- 2 tsps. vanilla extract
- 1/8 tsp. salt
- COATING:
- 2 cups sugar
- 1-1/2 cups half-and-half cream, divided
- 1-1/4 cups light corn syrup
- 1 tsp. vanilla extract
- 1/4 tsp. salt
- Additional chopped salted peanuts

Direction

- Use foil to line a 15x10x1-inch baking pan; use cooking spray to grease the foil. Sprinkle 2 cups peanuts on top; put aside.
- Combine 3/4 cup sugar, 2/3 cup corn syrup and 1/4 cup water in a small heavy saucepan. Heat to boil over medium heat, stir continuously. Lower the heat to medium-low. Cook, do not stir, until it reaches a hard-ball stage (candy thermometer reads 250°).
- In the meantime, beat egg whites in a heat-proof large bowl until it form stiff peaks. While the mixer is running on high speed, stream hot syrup slowly and steadily into the mix, beat continuously at high speed until thicken, for about 5 minutes. Cover and put aside.
- Combine the rest of the sugar, corn syrup and water in a large heavy saucepan. Heat to boil

over medium heat, stir continuously. Lower the heat to medium-low; cook, do not stir, until it reaches a soft-crack stage (a candy thermometer reads 290°).

- Pour hot syrup into the egg white mixture slowly; stir using a wooden spoon. Stir the butter, vanilla and salt into the mixture.
- Transfer the mixture on top of peanuts in pan; butter your fingers and press down evenly.
- To make the coating, mix together the sugar, 1/2 cup cream and corn syrup in a large saucepan. Heat to boil on medium heat, stir continuously; add in the remaining cream. Lower heat to medium-low; cook and stir until it reaches a soft-ball stage (a candy thermometer reads 242°).
- Take off from heat; stir vanilla and salt into the mixture. Pour on top of the nougat layer in the pan. Sprinkle the remaining peanuts on top, slightly pushing into the nougat. Let it cool down for no less than 2 hours or until set. Slice into 1-1/2 inch x 1-inch pieces. Roll edges in more peanuts and shape them into logs. Encase using waxed paper. For storage, keep at room temperature.

Nutrition Information

- Calories: 107 calories
- Total Carbohydrate: 18 g
- Cholesterol: 3 mg
- Total Fat: 4 g
- Fiber: 0 g
- Protein: 2 g
- Sodium: 44 mg

308. Carrot Cake Bars

"It is a moist cake made of carrot and frosted with great cream cheese frosting."
Serving: 14 | Prep: 10m | Ready in: 30m

Ingredients

- 2 cups white sugar
- 1 1/2 cups vegetable oil

- 4 eggs
- 2 cups all-purpose flour
- 2 tsps. baking soda
- 2 tsps. ground cinnamon
- 1 tsp. salt
- 3 (4 oz.) jars carrot baby food

Direction

- Set the oven to 175°C or 350°F to preheat. Coat a 15"x10" jelly roll pan with grease and flour. Sift salt, cinnamon, baking soda and flour together, then put aside.
- Beat together eggs, oil and sugar in a big bowl until smooth. Blend in flour mixture, then stir in baby food carrots.
- Spread batter into a 15"x10" jelly roll pan. In the preheated oven, bake until a toothpick exits clean after being inserted into the center, about 20 minutes. Let the cake cool.

Nutrition Information

- Calories: 412 calories;
- Total Carbohydrate: 44 g
- Cholesterol: 53 mg
- Total Fat: 25.2 g
- Protein: 3.8 g
- Sodium: 375 mg

309. Carrot Cake With Pecan Frosting

"My husband is in love with this carrot cake!"
Serving: 16 servings. | Prep: 35m | Ready in: 01h15m

Ingredients

- 1 cup shortening
- 2 cups sugar
- 4 large eggs
- 1 can (8 oz.) unsweetened crushed pineapple, undrained
- 2-1/2 cups all-purpose flour
- 2 tsps. ground cinnamon
- 1 tsp. baking powder

- 1 tsp. baking soda
- 3/4 tsp. salt
- 3 cups shredded carrots (about 6 medium carrots)
- FROSTING:
- 1 package (8 oz.) reduced-fat cream cheese
- 1/2 cup butter, softened
- 1 tsp. vanilla extract
- 3-3/4 cups confectioners' sugar
- 1 cup chopped pecans

Direction

- Set the oven to 325° and start preheating. Using parchment paper, line bottoms of 2 greased 9-in. round baking pans; grease paper.
- Cream sugar and shortening until fluffy in a large bowl. Put in eggs, 1 at a time; after each addition, whisk well. Whisk in pineapple. Whisk salt, cinnamon, baking powder, flour and baking soda in another bowl; add to creamed mixture gradually. Mix in carrots.
- Transfer batter into the greased pan. Bake 40-45 minutes or until the inserted toothpick in center comes out clean. Cool in pans 10 minutes, transfer to wire racks; get rid of paper. Cool completely.
- Beat vanilla, butter and cream cheese until blended in a large bowl. Whisk in confectioners' sugar gradually until smooth. Stir in pecans.
- Spread frosting between layers and over sides and top of cake. Chill in the fridge until serving.

Nutrition Information

- Calories: 557 calories
- Total Carbohydrate: 74 g
- Cholesterol: 72 mg
- Total Fat: 27 g
- Fiber: 2 g
- Protein: 6 g
- Sodium: 358 mg

310. Cast-iron Peach Crostata

"An open-faced fruit tart with awesome peach filling."
Serving: 10 servings. | Prep: 45m | Ready in: 01h30m

Ingredients

- 1-1/2 cups all-purpose flour
- 2 tbsps. plus 3/4 cup packed brown sugar, divided
- 1-1/4 tsps. salt, divided
- 1/2 cup cold unsalted butter, cubed
- 2 tbsps. shortening
- 3 to 5 tbsps. ice water
- 8 cups sliced peaches (about 7-8 medium)
- 1 tbsp. lemon juice
- 3 tbsps. cornstarch
- 1/2 tsp. ground cinnamon
- 1/4 tsp. ground nutmeg
- 1 large egg, beaten
- 2 tbsps. sliced almonds
- 1 tbsp. coarse sugar
- 1/3 cup water
- 1 cup fresh raspberries, optional

Direction

- Combine 1 tsp. of salt, 2 tbsps. of brown sugar and flour; cut in shortening and butter till crumbly. Slowly put in ice water; use a fork to toss till the dough holds together when pressed. Roll into a disk; use plastic to wrap. Chill in a refrigerator for 1 hour or overnight.
- Mix lemon juice and peaches. Put in the remaining salt, spices, cornstarch and the remaining brown sugar; toss gently. Allow to sit for 30 minutes.
- Set the oven at 400° and start preheating. Roll the dough out into a 13-in. circle on a lightly floured work surface; transfer to a 10-in. cast-iron skillet, letting any excess hang over the edge. Transfer the peaches into the pastry with a slotted spoon, reserving the liquid. Fold the pastry edge over the filling, pleating as you go, leave the center uncovered. Use beaten egg to brush the folded pastry; sprinkle with coarse sugar and almonds. Bake for 45-55 minutes, till

the filling is bubbly and the crust turns dark golden.
- Mix water and the reserved liquid in a small saucepan; boil the mixture. Simmer for 1-2 minutes, or till thickened; serve warm together with pie. Top with fresh raspberries if you want.

Nutrition Information

- Calories: 322 calories
- Total Carbohydrate: 49 g
- Cholesterol: 43 mg
- Total Fat: 13 g
- Fiber: 3 g
- Protein: 4 g
- Sodium: 381 mg

311.Chocolate Cheese Layered Bars

"Chocolaty and rich bars."
Serving: 2 dozen. | Prep: 20m | Ready in: 42m

Ingredients

- 1/2 cup butter, softened
- 1 cup sugar
- 2 eggs
- 1 oz. unsweetened chocolate, melted
- 1 tsp. vanilla extract
- 1 cup all-purpose flour
- 1 tsp. baking powder
- 1/2 cup chopped pecans
- CHEESE LAYER:
- 6 oz. cream cheese, softened
- 1/4 cup butter, softened
- 1/2 cup sugar
- 1 egg
- 2 tbsps. all-purpose flour
- 1/2 tsp. vanilla extract
- 1/4 cup chopped pecans
- 1 cup (6 oz.) semisweet chocolate chips
- 3 cups miniature marshmallows
- TOPPING:
- 1/4 cup butter
- 2 oz. cream cheese, softened
- 1 oz. unsweetened chocolate
- 2 tbsps. milk
- 3 cup confectioners' sugar
- 1 tsp. vanilla extract

Direction

- Cream sugar and butter till fluffy and light in big bowl. Beat eggs in; beat vanilla and chocolate in till well blended. Mix baking powder and flour; mix into chocolate mixture. Fold pecans in; put in 13x9-in. greased baking pan.
- Mix butter and cream cheese in another big bowl; beat vanilla, flour, egg and sugar in till combined well. Fold pecans in; spread on chocolate layer then sprinkle chips on top.
- Bake for 20-25 minutes till edges pull away from pan's sides at 350°. Sprinkle marshmallow on top; bake till puffed for another 2 minutes. Evenly spread on cream cheese layer. On wire rack, cool.
- Mix initial 4 topping ingredients in big saucepan; mix and cook till smooth on low heat. Put in big bowl; add vanilla and confectioners' sugar. Beat till smooth. Spread on cooled bars; keep in the fridge.

Nutrition Information

- Calories: 330 calories
- Total Carbohydrate: 43 g
- Cholesterol: 58 mg
- Total Fat: 18 g
- Fiber: 1 g
- Protein: 3 g
- Sodium: 135 mg

312. Chocolate Coconut Cake

"Sweet treat that satisfies both coconut and chocolate lovers."
Serving: 16-20 servings. | Prep: 30m | Ready in: 45m

Ingredients

- 1 package chocolate cake mix with pudding (regular size)
- 1 cup sugar
- 1 cup whole milk
- 24 large marshmallows
- 1 package (14 oz.) sweetened shredded coconut
- GLAZE:
- 1-1/2 cups sugar
- 1 cup evaporated milk
- 1/2 cup butter, cubed
- 2 cups (12 oz.) semisweet chocolate chips
- 1 cup chopped almonds

Direction

- Make cake following packaging instructions. Oil 2 13x9-inch baking pans. Line waxed paper on sides and bottom of a pan; coat using cooking spray. Distribute batter between pans. Bake for 15 to 20 minutes at 350°. Let cool.
- Boil milk and sugar in a big saucepan. Lower the heat to moderate and mix in marshmallows till smooth. Put in coconut. Scatter on top of another cake.
- Take second cake off pan with waxed paper and cautiously invert over of filling; cautiously remove waxed paper. Cool fully.
- Boil butter, milk and sugar in a separate saucepan. Take off from heat; put in chips and mix till smooth. Put in nuts. Put on top of cake; let come to room temperature. Place cover and chill overnight.

313. Chocolate Date Squares

""These moist bars were sent to my husband from his mother when he was still in the Army.""
Serving: 24 servings. | Prep: 10m | Ready in: 50m

Ingredients

- 2 cups chopped dates
- 1 cup hot water
- 1 cup sugar
- 2/3 cup shortening
- 2 eggs
- 1-1/2 cups all-purpose flour
- 1 tsp. baking soda
- 1/2 tsp. salt
- TOPPING:
- 1 cup (6 oz.) semisweet chocolate chips
- 1/2 cup packed brown sugar
- 1/2 cup chopped nuts

Direction

- Mix water and dates in a small bowl and put aside to cool without draining. In a big bowl, cream shortening and sugar until light and fluffy and add eggs while beating continuously. Then, combine flour, salt and baking soda and add slowly to the creamed mixture. Add in dates.
- Place the mixture in a 13x9-inch baking pan that was previously greased and floured. Mix the toppings and sprinkle on top. Bake at 350°F for about 40 minutes or until a toothpick comes off clean when inserted at the center and let it cool on a wire rack.

Nutrition Information

- Calories: 223 calories
- Total Carbohydrate: 34 g
- Cholesterol: 18 mg
- Total Fat: 9 g
- Fiber: 2 g
- Protein: 3 g
- Sodium: 110 mg

314. Chocolate Peanut Butter Brownies

"A delicious brownie recipe that I created."
Serving: 20 | Prep: 15m | Ready in: 45m

Ingredients

- 1/2 cup butter, softened
- 1/2 cup peanut butter
- 1/2 cup white sugar
- 1/2 cup brown sugar
- 1 egg
- 1 tsp. vanilla extract
- 1 cup all-purpose flour
- 1/2 tsp. baking soda
- 1 pinch salt
- 1/2 cup milk chocolate chips
- 2/3 cup peanut butter
- 2/3 cup confectioners' sugar
- 1/4 cup shortening
- 1/2 cup milk
- 1 tsp. vanilla extract
- 3/4 cup frozen whipped topping, thawed

Direction

- Set the oven to 325°F (165°C) to preheat. Grease a 9x9-inch baking dish.
- Cream together a tsp. of vanilla, butter, egg, brown sugar, white sugar and 1/2 cup peanut butter in a medium bowl until smooth. Mix the salt, baking soda and flour; mix into the sugar mixture. Put evenly into the greased pan.
- Bake in the prepared oven for 20 minutes until set. Take it out of the oven and garnish with chocolate chips. Let sit for a minute, then scatter the chips to create a layer.
- For topping, whip together shortening, confectioners' sugar and 2/3 cup peanut butter. Mix in the milk and 1 tsp. vanilla gradually. Stir in the whipped topping gently. Refrigerate. When brownies and topping are cooled, spread topping onto brownies, then slice into bars.

Nutrition Information

- Calories: 262 calories;
- Total Carbohydrate: 23.8 g
- Cholesterol: 23 mg
- Total Fat: 17.3 g
- Protein: 5.3 g
- Sodium: 148 mg

315. Chocolate-cherry Ice Cream Cake

"Make ahead: Keep frozen, wrapped in foil, for around a week before serving."
Serving: 12 servings. | Prep: 30m | Ready in: 30m

Ingredients

- 1-1/2 cups Oreo cookie crumbs (about 15 cookies)
- 2 tbsps. butter, melted
- 4 cups cherry ice cream, softened if necessary
- 8 Oreo cookies, coarsely chopped
- 1 cup (6 oz.) miniature semisweet chocolate chips, divided
- 4 cups fudge ripple ice cream, softened if necessary
- Sweetened whipped cream, optional
- 12 fresh sweet cherries

Direction

- Preheat an oven to 350°. Mix butter and cookie crumbs in a small bowl; press 1-in. up sides and on bottom of 9-in. greased springform pan. Bake till firm or for 8-10 minutes; cool on wire rack.
- In crust, spread cherry ice cream; freeze till firm, covered. Layer with 1/2 cup chocolate chips and chopped cookies in reversed order; spread the fudge ripple ice cream on chocolate chips. Sprinkle leftover chocolate chips; freeze, covered, till firm or for 8 hours.

- 10 minutes before serving, remove cake from freezer; use a knife to loosen sides from pan carefully. Remove pan's rim. Serve with whipped cream, if desired; top with cherries.

---

316. Chocolate-peanut Butter Cup Cookies

"Amazing treats."
Serving: 4 dozen. | Prep: 25m | Ready in: 35m

Ingredients

- 1 cup butter, softened
- 3/4 cup creamy peanut butter
- 1 cup packed brown sugar
- 1/2 cup sugar
- 2 large egg yolks
- 1/4 cup 2% milk
- 2 tsps. vanilla extract
- 2-1/3 cups all-purpose flour
- 1/3 cup baking cocoa
- 1 tsp. baking soda
- 1 cup milk chocolate chips
- 1 cup peanut butter chips
- 6 packages (1-1/2 oz. each) peanut butter cups, chopped

Direction

- Preheat an oven to 350°. Cream sugars, peanut butter and butter till fluffy and light in big bowl; beat vanilla, milk and egg yolks in. Mix baking soda, cocoa and flour; add to creamed mixture slowly. Stir well; mix peanut butter cups and chips in.
- Drop heaping tablespoonfuls on ungreased baking sheets, 2-in. apart; bake till set for 8-10 minutes. Don't overbake. Cool for 2 minutes; transfer from pans onto wire racks. Keep in airtight container.

Nutrition Information

- Calories: 170 calories
- Total Carbohydrate: 18 g
- Cholesterol: 20 mg
- Total Fat: 10 g
- Fiber: 1 g
- Protein: 3 g
- Sodium: 100 mg

---

317. Chocolaty Nanaimo Bars

"A winning recipe!"
Serving: 16 servings. | Prep: 55m | Ready in: 01h05m

Ingredients

- 1/2 cup butter, cubed
- 1/4 cup sugar
- 1/4 cup baking cocoa
- 1 large egg, lightly beaten
- 1-1/2 cups graham cracker crumbs
- 1 cup sweetened shredded coconut, toasted
- 1/2 cup chopped pecans, toasted
- FILLING:
- 1/2 cup butter, softened
- 2 tbsps. Bird's custard powder or instant vanilla pudding mix
- 2 cups confectioners' sugar
- 3 tbsps. half-and-half cream
- TOPPING:
- 1 oz. white baking chocolate, melted
- 1 cup (6 oz.) semisweet chocolate chips
- 1 tbsp. shortening

Direction

- Line parchment paper on bottom of square 9-in. baking pan. Mix and cook cocoa, sugar and butter in small heavy saucepan on medium low heat till butter melts. Take off heat.
- Whisk small amount hot mixture into egg in small bowl; put all in pan, constantly mixing. Cook, constantly mixing, till thermometer reads 160° and thick enough to coat metal spoon for 2-3 minutes. Take off heat.
- Mix pecans, coconut and cracker crumbs in; press in prepped pan. Refrigerate till cold for 30 minutes.
- Filling: Beat custard powder and butter till blended in big bowl. Beat half and half and

confectioners' sugar till smooth; spread on crust. Refrigerate till firm for 1 hour, covered.

- Topping: Use melted white chocolate to fill small resealable bag; put aside, keep warm. Melt shortening and chocolate chips in microwave; mix till smooth. Evenly spread chocolate mixture on filling.
- Cut small corner in the bag with white chocolate. Pipe parallel lines on chocolate liquid quickly, spacing lines 1/4 - 1/2-in. apart. At right angles to white chocolate lines, pull toothpick back and forth across pan, cutting through piped lined to make feather design.
- Refrigerate till topping just sets for 10 minutes, don't completely harden chocolate. Cut to bars; keep in airtight container in the fridge.

Nutrition Information

- Calories: 343 calories
- Total Carbohydrate: 37 g
- Cholesterol: 45 mg
- Total Fat: 22 g
- Fiber: 2 g
- Protein: 2 g
- Sodium: 168 mg

---

318. Coconut Cranberry Oat Bars

"These bars are so salty, sweet, tart and chock-full for a tongue-tingling combo."
Serving: 2 dozen. | Prep: 40m | Ready in: 01h10m

Ingredients

- 2 cups fresh cranberries
- 1 cup dried cranberries
- 2/3 cup sugar
- 1/2 cup water
- 2 tsps. grated lemon peel
- 1/2 cup butter, softened
- 1 cup packed brown sugar
- 1-1/4 cups all-purpose flour
- 3/4 cup old-fashioned oats
- 1/2 tsp. salt

- 1/2 tsp. baking soda
- 1/2 cup sweetened shredded coconut
- 1/2 cup chopped pecans, toasted

Direction

- Mix together lemon peel, water, sugar and cranberries in a small saucepan, then cook mixture on moderate heat for 15 minutes, until berries pop. Take away from the heat and allow to cool to room temperature.
- In the meantime, beat butter and brown sugar together in a small bowl for 2 minutes, until crumbly. Mix together baking soda, salt, oats and flour, then put into the creamed mixture gradually, mixing well. Put aside 1 cup for topping, then press the rest of crumb mixture into a 13"x9" baking dish coated with grease.
- Bake at 400 degrees until browned slightly, about 10 to 12 minutes. Spread over crust with the cranberry mixture. Mix together reserved crumb mixture, pecans and coconut, then sprinkle over the filling. Bake until filling is set, about 18 to 20 minutes more.
- Allow to cool on a wire rack, then chill for a minimum of 2 hours. Slice into bars.

Nutrition Information

- Calories: 168 calories
- Total Carbohydrate: 28 g
- Cholesterol: 10 mg
- Total Fat: 7 g
- Fiber: 1 g
- Protein: 1 g
- Sodium: 111 mg

---

319. Coffee 'n' Cream Brownies

"These rich brownies are perfect when topped with a chocolate glaze and creamy coffee-enhanced filling."
Serving: 16 servings. | Prep: 35m | Ready in: 60m

Ingredients

- 1/2 cup butter, cubed
- 3 oz. unsweetened chocolate, chopped

- 2 large eggs
- 1 cup sugar
- 1 tsp. vanilla extract
- 2/3 cup all-purpose flour
- 1/4 tsp. baking soda
- FILLING:
- 1 tsp. instant coffee granules
- 3 tbsps. heavy whipping cream
- 1 cup confectioners' sugar
- 2 tbsps. butter, softened
- GLAZE:
- 1 cup (6 oz.) semisweet chocolate chips
- 1/3 cup heavy whipping cream

Direction

- Melt chocolate and butter in a microwave while stirring until smooth. Allow to cool a bit. Beat together vanilla, sugar and eggs in a small bowl, then stir in the chocolate mixture. Mix baking soda and flour together, then stir into chocolate mixture.
- Spread into an 8-inch square baking pan coated with grease, then bake at 350 degrees until a toothpick exits clean after being inserted into the center, about 25 to 30 minutes; avoid over-baking. Allow to cool on a wire rack.
- To make filling, dissolve in cream with coffee granules. Put in butter and confectioners' sugar, beating just until fluffy and light; avoid over-beating, Spread over brownies and chill until set.
- Mix together cream and chips in a small saucepan, then cook and stir on low heat until chips are melted. Allow to cool a bit, then spread over filling carefully. Allow to stand until glaze is set, about half an hour. Slice into squares and keep in the fridge.

Nutrition Information

- Calories: 282 calories
- Total Carbohydrate: 33 g
- Cholesterol: 51 mg
- Total Fat: 17 g
- Fiber: 2 g
- Protein: 3 g

- Sodium: 91 mg

320. Cookie Pizza

"These are huge cookies with peanuts, candies, chocolate and coconut on top."
Serving: 24

Ingredients

- 1 1/2 cups all-purpose flour
- 2 tsps. baking soda
- 1 tsp. salt
- 2 1/3 cups rolled oats
- 1 cup butter
- 1 1/2 cups packed brown sugar
- 2 eggs
- 1/2 tsp. vanilla extract
- 1 1/2 cups shredded coconut
- 2 cups semisweet chocolate chips
- 1/2 cup chopped walnuts
- 1 cup candy-coated chocolate pieces
- 1 cup peanuts

Direction

- Mix together oats, salt, baking soda and flour, stirring well to mix. Cream thoroughly together vanilla, eggs, brown sugar and butter. Put into creamed mixture with flour mixture, mixing well.
- Stir in chopped nuts and 1/2 cup of coconut. Spread evenly dough in two 10-in. pizza pans coated with grease or press into 10-in. circles on baking sheets coated with grease.
- Bake at 175°C or 350°F about 10 minutes, then take out of the oven.
- Sprinkle over with peanuts, candies, leftover 1 cup of coconut and chocolate, then bake until turning golden brown, about 5 to 10 minutes more. Allow to cool in pans on wire racks, then cut cooled cookie pizza into wedges.

Nutrition Information

- Calories: 367 calories;
- Total Carbohydrate: 43.9 g

- Cholesterol: 37 mg
- Total Fat: 20.6 g
- Protein: 5.4 g
- Sodium: 287 mg

321. Cookies & Cream Brownies

"This cookie and cream cheese brownie recipe my favorite. I really love the crushed cookies topping."
Serving: 2 dozen. | Prep: 15m | Ready in: 40m

Ingredients

- 1 package (8 oz.) cream cheese, softened
- 1/4 cup sugar
- 1 large egg
- 1/2 tsp. vanilla extract
- BROWNIE LAYER:
- 1/2 cup butter, melted
- 1/2 cup sugar
- 1/2 cup packed brown sugar
- 1/2 cup baking cocoa
- 2 large eggs
- 1 tsp. vanilla extract
- 1/2 cup all-purpose flour
- 1 tsp. baking powder
- 12 Oreo cookies, crushed
- 8 Oreo cookies, coarsely chopped

Direction

- Beat cream cheese with vanilla, egg, and sugar in a small bowl until no lumps remain; put aside. To make brownie layer, combine butter, cocoa, and sugars in a large bowl. Add eggs and beat well. Combine baking powder and flour; slowly mix in to cocoa mixture. Mix in crushed cookie crumbs.
- Transfer batter into a greased 11x7-inch baking pan. Pour cream cheese mixture over batter. Scatter top with coarsely chopped cookies. Bake for 25 to 30 minutes at 350° until a toothpick comes out with moist crumbs from the center. Allow to cool entirely on a wire rack. Divide into bars. Store bars in the fridge.

Nutrition Information

- Calories: 159 calories
- Total Carbohydrate: 18 g
- Cholesterol: 47 mg
- Total Fat: 9 g
- Fiber: 1 g
- Protein: 2 g
- Sodium: 130 mg

322. Corn Ice Cream

"An ideal summer treat is made from corn, maple syrup and vanilla extract,"
Serving: 4 cups. | Prep: 40m | Ready in: 55m

Ingredients

- 2 cups 2% milk
- 3/4 cup sugar
- 1/2 cup maple syrup
- 4 large egg yolks, lightly beaten
- 1 can (14-3/4 oz.) cream-style corn
- 1 tsp. vanilla extract

Direction

- Heat syrup, sugar and milk in a large heavy saucepan until bubbles appear around sides of pan. Stir a small amount of hot mixture into egg yolks. Pour all back to the pan, whisking continuously.
- Cook while stirring over low heat until mixture reaches 160°. Immediately pour into a bowl; put in ice water and whisk for 2 minutes. Mix in vanilla and corn. Use waxed paper to press onto surface of custard. Refrigerate for a few hours or overnight.
- Strain custard and get rid of the corn. Fill cylinder of ice cream freezer 2/3 full; freeze following the manufacturer's directions. Once ice cream is frozen, remove to a freezer container; freeze before serving, about 2-4 hours.

Nutrition Information

- Calories: 221 calories
- Total Carbohydrate: 45 g
- Cholesterol: 107 mg
- Total Fat: 4 g
- Fiber: 1 g
- Protein: 4 g
- Sodium: 185 mg

323. Cranberry-port Fudge Brownies

"You adults will fall in love with this addition of wine to the sweet and yummy brownies."
Serving: 16 servings. | Prep: 25m | Ready in: 55m

Ingredients

- 4 oz. unsweetened chocolate, chopped
- 1/2 cup butter, cubed
- 1-1/2 cups sugar
- 1/2 tsp. vanilla extract
- 2 large eggs
- 3/4 cup all-purpose flour
- 1/4 tsp. salt
- 1/2 cup dried cranberries
- 1/2 cup tawny port wine

Direction

- Heat butter and chocolate in a small saucepan to melt; whisk until smooth. Take away from the heat; mix in vanilla and sugar. Pour in eggs, one at a time, stirring well between additions. Mix in salt and flour just until incorporated.
- In a separate saucepan, mix together wine and cranberries. Place over medium heat, boil, and then cook for 3 minutes until the mixture is decreased to a thin syrupy consistency. Mix into batter.
- Grease a baking pan of 9 inches square and pour in batter. Bake in 325-degree oven until a toothpick comes out clean when being put into

the center, or about 30-35 minutes (make sure not to overbake). Place on a wire rack to cool.

Nutrition Information

- Calories: 212 calories
- Total Carbohydrate: 30 g
- Cholesterol: 41 mg
- Total Fat: 10 g
- Fiber: 2 g
- Protein: 2 g
- Sodium: 88 mg

324. Dark Chocolate Mocha Brownies

" "These frosted brownies are always a hit since everyone loves dark chocolate. Ended with this recipe by modifying a recipe I've made for a long time. These brownies gone so quick that will make you wonder if you prepared enough.""
Serving: 5 dozen. | Prep: 20m | Ready in: 45m

Ingredients

- 2 cups packed brown sugar
- 1 cup butter, melted
- 3 large eggs
- 1 tbsp. instant coffee granules
- 2 tsps. vanilla extract
- 1 cup all-purpose flour
- 1 cup baking cocoa
- 1/2 tsp. baking powder
- 1/2 tsp. salt
- 6 oz. bittersweet chocolate, coarsely chopped
- FROSTING:
- 1/4 butter, melted
- 3 tbsps. sour cream
- 2 tsps. vanilla extract
- 2-3/4 to 3 cups confectioners' sugar
- 2 oz. grated bittersweet chocolate

Direction

- Mix butter and brown sugar in a large bowl. Mix in eggs, one at a time. Put in vanilla and coffee; combine well. Mix salt, baking powder, cocoa and flour; gently add to sugar mixture. Mix in chocolate. Place into a greased 13x9-inch baking pan and spread. Put in the oven and bake for 25-30 minutes at 350°F or until toothpick pricked into middle comes out clean. Place on a wire rack to cool. To make frosting, mix vanilla, sour cream and butter until turns smooth. Gently mix in sugar until frosting is smooth and reaches consistency you desire. Then frost brownies. Dust with grated chocolate.

325. Delightful Brownies

"Moist and fudgy!"
Serving: 1 dozen. | Prep: 15m | Ready in: 45m

Ingredients

- 3 tbsps. butter, softened
- 2 egg whites
- 1 jar (4 oz.) prune baby food
- 1 tsp. vanilla extract
- 2/3 cup sugar
- 1/2 cup all-purpose flour
- 1 package (1.4 oz.) sugar-free instant chocolate pudding mix
- 1/2 tsp. baking powder
- 1/4 tsp. salt
- 3/4 cup miniature semisweet chocolate chips

Direction

- Beat egg whites and butter till blended in a bowl; beat in vanilla and baby food. Mix salt, baking powder, pudding mix, flour and sugar; add to egg mixture. Mix in chocolate chips.
- Spread into 8-in. square baking pan that's coated in cooking spray; bake it at 350° till inserted toothpick in middle exits clean for 30-35 minutes. Cool on wire rack.

Nutrition Information

- Calories: 176 calories
- Total Carbohydrate: 30 g
- Cholesterol: 8 mg
- Total Fat: 6 g
- Fiber: 2 g
- Protein: 2 g
- Sodium: 338 mg

326. Dessert From The Grill

""End your meal with this beautiful dessert, which is a lb. cake with pineapple layered with sweet sauce then topped with caramel sauce over ice cream. The coals will be at the perfect temperature to make it once you are done with your grilled meal.""
Serving: 6 servings. | Prep: 10m | Ready in: 15m

Ingredients

- 1 can (20 oz.) sliced pineapple, drained
- 1 tsp. butter
- 1/2 tsp. brown sugar
- 1/4 tsp. vanilla extract
- 1/8 tsp. ground cinnamon
- 1/8 tsp. ground nutmeg
- 6 slices lb. cake
- Vanilla ice cream
- Caramel ice cream topping

Direction

- Drain the pineapple. Keep six pineapple rings and 1/3 cup of the juice and leave the rest of it for a different use. Mix the leftover pineapple juice, nutmeg, cinnamon, vanilla, brown sugar and butter together in a dish that is microwave safe. Without any cover, microwave for 1 to 2 minutes on high until it turns bubbly. On each side of the cake slices and pineapple rings, layer the mixture on with a brush. At moderate heat, grill the cake and pineapple without any cover on until they turn golden brown. Cook for 1 to 2 minutes per side, layering with the rest of the pineapple juice mixture from time to time. On every cake slice, put a scoop of ice cream and pineapple ring on top of it before drizzling using caramel topping. Serve at once.

327. Double Cherry Pie

"This cherry pie is a tasty combination of dried cherries and canned cherries."
Serving: 8 servings. | Prep: 25m | Ready in: 01h05m

Ingredients

- 3 cans (14-1/2 oz. each) pitted tart cherries, undrained
- 1 cup dried cherries
- 1/2 tsp. almond extract
- 1 cup sugar
- 1/4 cup cornstarch
- 1/4 tsp. salt
- 1/4 tsp. ground nutmeg
- Pastry for double-crust pie (9 inches)
- 1 tbsp. butter

Direction

- Strain the cherries, saving 1 cup juice. Put the cherries aside. Mix the saved juice and dried cherries together in a small saucepan. Boil it; allow to sit for 5 minutes. Strain and put aside to cool.
- Mix extract, dried cherries, and tart cherries together in a big bowl. Mix nutmeg, salt, cornstarch, and sugar together in a small bowl. Pour into the cherry mixture, mix to coat.
- Split the dough into 2 portions with 1 portion is a bit bigger than the other. Roll the bigger portion out until fitting a 9-inch pie plate. Remove the pastry to the pie plate. Snip the pastry to even with the edges. Add the filling to the crust. Dot with butter.
- Roll the leftover pastry out until fitting the top of the pie. Put on the filling. Snip, seal and flute the edges. Slit vents in the pastry. Bake at 375° until the filling is bubbling and the crust turns golden brown, about 40-45 minutes. If needed, use foil to cover the edges during the final 30 minutes to avoid over-browning. Put on a wire rack to cool.

Nutrition Information

- Calories: 473 calories
- Total Carbohydrate: 81 g
- Cholesterol: 14 mg
- Total Fat: 16 g
- Fiber: 2 g
- Protein: 4 g
- Sodium: 296 mg

328. Double Chocolate Brownies

"The decisive factor that keeps these tasty chocolate brownies chewy and dense without the butter. For additional nutrients and fiber, we've used whole-wheat pastry flour. For richness and satisfaction, we filled them with a bunch of chocolate chips."
Serving: 24 | Ready in: 1h30m

Ingredients

- 4 oz. unsweetened chocolate
- 2 tbsps. butter
- 1 cup whole-wheat pastry flour, (see Ingredient Note)
- ¼ cup unsweetened cocoa powder
- ¼ tsp. salt
- 4 large egg whites
- 3 large eggs
- 1⅓ cups packed light brown sugar
- ¾ cup unsweetened applesauce
- 2 tbsps. canola oil
- 1 tsp. vanilla extract
- ½ cup semisweet chocolate chips
- ⅓ cup chopped walnuts, or pecans (optional)

Direction

- Set oven to 350°F to preheat. Spray a 9-by-13-inch baking dish with cooking spray.
- In a double boiler, melt butter and chocolate on barely simmering water. (Or microwave in a small microwaveable bowl on Medium, mixing every half a minute, until smooth and melted.)
- In a medium bowl, mix salt, cocoa and flour.

- In a big mixing bowl, whip brown sugar, eggs and egg whites using an electric mixer. Put vanilla, oil and applesauce; whip until combined. Put the chocolate and butter mixture; whip until combined. Put the dry ingredients in and stir until just moistened. Mix in chocolate chips. Into the greased pan, scrape the batter and spread it evenly. Scatter with nuts (optional).
- Bake the brownies 20-25 mins until the top springs back when gently pressed. Take out onto a wire rack and let cool completely. Slice into bars.
- Variation:
- In Step 4, mix in 4 tsps. of instant coffee granules mixed with 2 tbsps. hot water until dissolved for a mocha flavor.

Nutrition Information

- Calories: 148 calories;
- Total Carbohydrate: 21 g
- Cholesterol: 26 mg
- Total Fat: 6 g
- Fiber: 2 g
- Protein: 3 g
- Sodium: 48 mg
- Sugar: 15 g
- Saturated Fat: 3 g

329. Double Chocolate Brownies With Pecans

"Can be given as gifts."
Serving: 8 brownies. | Prep: 15m | Ready in: 30m

Ingredients

- 1 oz. unsweetened chocolate
- 2 tbsps. butter
- 1 egg
- 1/2 cup sugar
- 1/2 tsp. vanilla extract
- 1/3 cup all-purpose flour
- 1/4 tsp. baking powder
- 1/8 tsp. salt

- 1/4 cup chopped pecans
- 1/4 cup semisweet chocolate chips

Direction

- In a microwave-safe dish or small heavy saucepan, melt butter and unsweetened chocolate; mix till smooth.
- In a small bowl, combine sugar and egg. Mix in the chocolate mixture and combine well. Mix in nuts.
- Spread into an 8x4-in. greased loaf pan. Sprinkle chocolate chips on top. Bake until toothpick comes out clean, at 350° for 15-18 minutes. Cool down on a wire rack.

Nutrition Information

- Calories: 172 calories
- Total Carbohydrate: 21 g
- Cholesterol: 34 mg
- Total Fat: 10 g
- Fiber: 1 g
- Protein: 2 g
- Sodium: 87 mg

330. Favorite Frosted Brownies

""You cannot overdo chocolate for this holiday. My tried-and-real brownies are dressed up by candy sprinkles for the occasion.""
Serving: 12-15 servings. | Prep: 15m | Ready in: 40m

Ingredients

- 1 cup butter, softened
- 2 cups sugar
- 4 large eggs
- 2 tsps. vanilla extract
- 1-3/4 cups all-purpose flour
- 6 tbsps. baking cocoa
- 1 tsp. baking powder
- 1/4 tsp. salt
- FROSTING:
- 1/2 cup butter, softened
- 1/4 cup evaporated milk

- 1 tsp. vanilla extract
- 2 tbsps. baking cocoa
- 3 cups confectioners' sugar
- Decorating sprinkles, optional

Direction

- Beat sugar and cream butter in a large bowl. Put in eggs, one at a time, whisking well after every addition. Mix in vanilla. Mix salt, baking powder, cocoa and flour; gently add to creamed mixture and combine well. Then place into a greased 13x9-inch baking pan and spread. Place in the oven and bake for 25-30 minutes at 350°F or until a toothpick pricked in the middle comes out clean. Place on a wire rack to cool. To make frosting, beat vanilla, milk, and butter in a bowl; put in cocoa. Gently mix in confectioner's sugar until become smooth. Then place over cooled brownies and spread. Garnish with sprinkles if want.

Nutrition Information

- Calories: 445 calories
- Total Carbohydrate: 64 g
- Cholesterol: 107 mg
- Total Fat: 20 g
- Fiber: 1 g
- Protein: 4 g
- Sodium: 273 mg

331. Frosted Walnut Brownie Pie

"This chocolaty treat is very amazing."
Serving: 4 servings. | Prep: 15m | Ready in: 35m

Ingredients

- 1/4 cup butter, softened
- 1/2 cup sugar
- 1 egg
- 1/2 tsp. vanilla extract
- 1/4 cup all-purpose flour
- 3 tbsps. baking cocoa
- 1/4 cup chopped walnuts

- FROSTING:
- 1/2 cup confectioners' sugar
- 1 tbsp. baking cocoa
- 2-1/2 tsps. 2% milk

Direction

- Cream sugar and butter together in a small bowl. Beat egg and vanilla into the mixture. Mix together cocoa and flour, then put into creamed mixture gradually. Mix in walnuts.
- Use cooking spray to coat a 6-inch round springform pan, then sprinkle with sugar. Put into the pan with batter and position pan on a baking sheet. Bake at 350 degrees until a toothpick exits clean after being inserted into the center, about 20 to 25 minutes. Allow to cool on a wire rack.
- Take off sides of pan. Mix frosting ingredients together in a small bowl, then spread over pie.

Nutrition Information

- Calories: 368 calories
- Total Carbohydrate: 50 g
- Cholesterol: 84 mg
- Total Fat: 18 g
- Fiber: 2 g
- Protein: 5 g
- Sodium: 134 mg

332. Frozen Peanut Butter And Chocolate Terrine

"This terrine is more flavorful with lovely accompaniment including chocolate, peanut butter and banana."
Serving: 12 servings. | Prep: 30m | Ready in: 30m

Ingredients

- 15 Nutter Butter cookies, crushed (about 2 cups)
- 1 carton (16 oz.) mascarpone cheese
- 1 cup sugar
- 2 tsps. vanilla extract

- 1 carton (8 oz.) frozen whipped topping, thawed
- 1 medium banana, sliced
- 1 cup semisweet chocolate chips, melted and cooled slightly
- 1 tbsp. baking cocoa
- 1 cup chunky peanut butter

Direction

- Use plastic wrap to line a 9"x5" loaf pan and allow edges to extend up all sides. Sprinkle 1/3 of the crushed cookies over top.
- Combine together vanilla, sugar and mascarpone cheese in a big bowl, then fold in whipped topping. Split mixture between 3 bowls evenly.
- For the first portion, fold in sliced banana, then put into loaf pan and spread evenly. Repeat cookie layer. For the second portion, stir in cocoa and melted chocolate, then put into loaf pan. Sprinkle leftover cookies over top. For the last portion, stir in peanut butter, then spread over top.
- Freeze with a cover for a minimum of 5 hours, until firm. To serve, invert terrine on a platter and take off plastic wrap, then cut into slices.

Nutrition Information

- Calories: 568 calories
- Total Carbohydrate: 49 g
- Cholesterol: 47 mg
- Total Fat: 39 g
- Fiber: 3 g
- Protein: 10 g
- Sodium: 190 mg

333. Ginger Pound Cake S'mores

"It has a unique flavor from the addition of crystallized ginger."
Serving: 8 servings. | Prep: 15m | Ready in: 20m

Ingredients

- 8 large marshmallows

- 5 oz. bittersweet chocolate candy bars, broken into eight pieces
- 8 tsps. crystallized ginger
- 16 slices lb. cake (1/4 inch thick)
- 3 tbsps. butter, softened

Direction

- Slice each marshmallow lengthwise into 4 slices. Put on each of 8 cake slices with ginger, 4 marshmallows slices and chocolate, then put leftover cake on top. Use butter to spread the outsides of cake slices.
- Grill on moderate heat with a cover until toasted, about 1 to 2 minutes per side.

Nutrition Information

- Calories: 382 calories
- Total Carbohydrate: 44 g
- Cholesterol: 144 mg
- Total Fat: 24 g
- Fiber: 2 g
- Protein: 5 g
- Sodium: 272 mg

334. Gingersnap Coconut Creams

"This spiced gingersnap cookie is the combination of macaroons and gingerbread cookies."
Serving: 4 dozen. | Prep: 35m | Ready in: 45m

Ingredients

- 1/3 cup butter, softened
- 1/3 cup packed brown sugar
- 1 large egg
- 1/3 cup molasses
- 1-1/2 cups all-purpose flour
- 1 tsp. baking soda
- 1/2 tsp. ground ginger
- 1/2 tsp. ground cinnamon
- 1/4 tsp. ground cloves
- FILLING:
- 1/4 cup butter, softened
- 3/4 cup confectioners' sugar

- 1/2 tsp. orange extract
- 1/4 cup sweetened shredded coconut

Direction

- Set the oven to 375 degrees to preheat. Cream together brown sugar and butter in a big bowl until fluffy and light. Beat in molasses and egg. Whisk together spices, baking soda and flour in a separate bowl, then beat into the creamed mixture gradually.
- Drop level teaspoonfuls of dough on baking sheets lined with parchment paper with 1 inch apart. Bake just until edges start to brown, about 6 to 8 minutes. Transfer from pans to wire racks to cool thoroughly.
- To make filling, combine together extract, confectioners' sugar and butter until combined, then stir in coconut. Spread on the bottoms of 1/2 of the cookies, then cover with leftover cookies.

Nutrition Information

- Calories: 58 calories
- Total Carbohydrate: 8 g
- Cholesterol: 10 mg
- Total Fat: 3 g
- Fiber: 0 g
- Protein: 1 g
- Sodium: 50 mg

335. Gluten-free Brownies

"These chocolate brownies are so amazing and will melt in your mouth right away."
Serving: 10 | Prep: 15m | Ready in: 55m

Ingredients

- 3/4 cup white sugar
- 6 tbsps. unsalted butter, melted
- 1 tsp. vanilla extract
- 2 eggs
- 1/4 cup cornstarch
- 1 tbsp. unsweetened cocoa powder
- 1 pinch salt

- 1 1/4 cups chopped dark chocolate

Direction

- Set the oven to 200°C or 400°F to preheat. Coat an 8-in. square baking dish lightly with grease.
- In a big bowl, mix together vanilla extract, butter and sugar, then use an electric mixer to beat the mixture until creamy and smooth. Put in 1 egg at a time, beating well between additions.
- Mix together in a bowl with salt, cocoa powder and cornstarch, then sift over sugar and butter mixture. Use a spatula or wooden spoon to beat in the entire of ingredients gradually until well blended. Fold in chopped chocolate and allow batter to rest about 5 minutes. Pour into the prepped baking dish with brownie batter.
- In the preheated oven, bake until a toothpick exits clean after being inserted into the center, about 20 minutes. Take out of the oven and allow to cool thoroughly for 15 minutes prior to cutting into squares.

Nutrition Information

- Calories: 249 calories;
- Total Carbohydrate: 32.8 g
- Cholesterol: 56 mg
- Total Fat: 13.6 g
- Protein: 2.5 g
- Sodium: 85 mg

336. Grilled Peaches And Berries

"This very fruity recipe calls for just a few ingredients grilled into deliciousness and the clean up afterwards is super easy as well!"
Serving: 2 servings. | Prep: 10m | Ready in: 30m

Ingredients

- 2 medium ripe peaches, halved and pitted
- 1/2 cup fresh blueberries
- 1 tbsp. brown sugar
- 2 tsps. lemon juice

- 4 tsps. butter

Direction

- Prepare two sheets of heavyweight foil that are doubly thick at the size of 12 inches square. On top of each, set two peach halves with the cut side facing upwards. Over each, layer with lemon juice, brown sugar and blueberries and dot with butter before folding the foil and sealing it up firmly. Over a moderately low heat, grill it with a cover on until the contents turn tender. Cook for 18 to 20 minutes then open the foil up slowly to let the steam out.

Nutrition Information

- Calories: 156 calories
- Total Carbohydrate: 23 g
- Cholesterol: 20 mg
- Total Fat: 8 g
- Fiber: 2 g
- Protein: 1 g
- Sodium: 57 mg

337. Juicy Cherry Pie

"You need to pick up fresh tart cherries for this amazing cherry pie."
Serving: 8 servings. | Prep: 35m | Ready in: 01h30m

Ingredients

- 2-1/2 cups all-purpose flour
- 1/2 tsp. salt
- 2/3 cup cold unsalted butter, cubed
- 1/3 cup shortening
- 6 to 10 tbsps. ice water
- FILLING:
- 5 cups fresh tart cherries, pitted
- 2 tsps. lemon juice
- 1/4 tsp. almond extract
- 1 cup sugar
- 1/3 cup all-purpose flour
- 1 tsp. ground cinnamon
- SUGAR TOPPING:

- 1 tbsp. 2% milk
- 1 tsp. sugar

Direction

- Combine salt and flour in a large bowl; cut in shortening and butter until mixture becomes crumbly. Slowly pour in ice water, stirring mixture using a fork until dough holds together when pressed. Split dough into 2 equal portions. Form each portion into a disk, and wrap in plastic. Chill for 60 minutes or overnight in the fridge.
- Turn oven to 375° to preheat. To make filling, put cherries into a large bowl; sprinkle almond extract and lemon juice. Combine cinnamon, flour and sugar in a small bowl. Scatter over cherries; stir gently until evenly coated.
- Roll 1 half of the dough to a 1/8-inch-thick circle on a work surface lightly dusted with flour; move into a 9-inch pie plate. Cut off excess pastry to even with rim. Pour in filling.
- Roll the rest of the dough into another 1/8-inch-thick circle; cut out stars or other shapes with cookie cutters. Lay the top pastry over the filling. Cut off excess pastry, seal, and flute the edge. Garnish on top with cutouts, if desired.
- Bake in the preheated oven for 40 minutes. To make topping, brush milk all over the top of the pie; scatter with sugar. Bake until filling is bubbly and crust turns golden brown, or for 15 to 20 minutes more. Allow the pie to cool on a wire rack.

Nutrition Information

- Calories: 521 calories
- Total Carbohydrate: 72 g
- Cholesterol: 41 mg
- Total Fat: 24 g
- Fiber: 3 g
- Protein: 6 g
- Sodium: 155 mg

338. Lemon Curd Chiffon Pie

"Refreshing and tart!"
Serving: 8 servings. | Prep: 30m | Ready in: 40m

Ingredients

- 9 whole graham crackers, broken into large pieces
- 1/2 cup chopped pecans
- 3 tbsps. sugar
- 1/4 tsp. vanilla extract
- 1/8 tsp. salt
- 5 tbsps. butter, melted
- FILLING:
- 1-1/2 cups heavy whipping cream
- 3 tbsps. sugar
- 3 tsps. vanilla extract
- 1 jar (11 oz.) lemon curd
- 1 package (8 oz.) cream cheese, softened
- 1 tbsp. grated lemon peel
- 1-1/2 tsps. unflavored gelatin
- 1/3 cup lemon juice
- 1 tbsp. limoncello
- BERRY SAUCE:
- 1/2 pint fresh raspberries
- 1/2 pint fresh blueberries
- 1/2 pint fresh strawberries
- 1/4 cup sugar
- 1 tbsp. seedless raspberry jam
- 1 tbsp. lemon juice
- 1 tbsp. raspberry liqueur

Direction

- In a food processor, add salt, vanilla, sugar, pecans and graham crackers; cover up and pulse till mixture looks like fine crumbs. Put in the butter; process until mixed.
- In a greased deep-dish pie plate of 9 inches, press the crumb mixture onto the bottom and the sides of the plate. Bake in the oven at 350° until light golden brown, about 10-12 minutes. Allow to completely cool on a wire rack.
- Mix vanilla, sugar and cream together in a small bowl. Beat until getting stiff peaks; put aside. Beat the lemon peel, cream cheese and lemon curd in a large bowl till blended; put aside.
- Sprinkle lemon juice with gelatin; allow to rest for 60 secs. Microwave on high level for 20 seconds. Stir and allow to sit for 1 minute or until the gelatin is dissolved completely. Mix in limoncello. Slowly beat into lemon mixture until well combined. Fold in whipped cream; add into the crust. Place in the fridge until set, about 3 hours.
- In a small saucepan, mix together jam, sugar and berries over medium heat. Cook and stir till the fruit is softened, about 3-5 minutes. Process berry mixture with a cover in a blender for 1-2 minutes or till blended. Strain, keeping the juice. Remove seeds.
- Pour the juice back into the saucepan; cook for 15-18 minutes, stirring occasionally, until the mixture reduces to the desired consistency. Mix in raspberry liqueur and lemon juice. Chill in the fridge for 1 hour. Drizzle with sauce and serve.

Nutrition Information

- Calories: 684 calories
- Total Carbohydrate: 69 g
- Cholesterol: 140 mg
- Total Fat: 43 g
- Fiber: 2 g
- Protein: 6 g
- Sodium: 327 mg

339. Lemon Torte

"A light and beautiful treat."
Serving: 16 servings. | Prep: 10m | Ready in: 01h10m

Ingredients

- 4 large eggs, separated
- 1 tsp. vanilla extract
- 1/4 tsp. cream of tartar
- 1-1/2 cups sugar, divided
- 2 tbsps. lemon juice
- 2 tbsps. grated lemon zest

- 2 cups heavy whipping cream, whipped, divided

Direction

- Put egg whites in big bowl; stand for 30 minutes at room temperature. Add cream of tartar and vanilla; beat at medium speed till soft peaks form. About 2 tbsp. at a time, add 1 cup sugar slowly; beat on high till sugar melts and glossy stiff peaks form.
- Spread in 13x9-in. well-greased baking dish; bake for 1 hour at 300°. On wire rack, cool.
- Meanwhile, whisk egg yolks till lemon colored in top of double boiler. Add leftover sugar, zest and lemon juice; cook on hot yet not boiling water, occasionally mixing, till thermometer reads 160° and thick. Cool down to room temperature.
- Spread 1/2 whipped cream on meringue shell; use lemon mixture to cover. Put leftover whipped cream over; cover. Refrigerate. Best created a day before serving.

Nutrition Information

- Calories: 195 calories
- Total Carbohydrate: 20 g
- Cholesterol: 94 mg
- Total Fat: 12 g
- Fiber: 0 g
- Protein: 2 g
- Sodium: 27 mg

340. Lightened-up Fudgy Brownies

"A brownie that is rich and flavorful but still low in fat is a dessert you can achieve by adding in almond extract."
Serving: 1 dozen. | Prep: 20m | Ready in: 40m

Ingredients

- 1/4 cup butter, cubed
- 1 oz. unsweetened chocolate
- 1-1/2 cups sugar
- 3 egg whites
- 1 egg

- 1/4 tsp. almond extract
- 1 cup all-purpose flour
- 2/3 cup baking cocoa
- 1/2 tsp. baking powder

Direction

- In a small saucepan, cook chocolate and butter over medium heat while stirring to melt. Take away from the heat; mix in sugar until combined. Allow to cool for 10 minutes.
- Mix together extract, egg and egg whites; whisk into chocolate mixture until incorporated. Stir together baking powder, cocoa and flour; slowly whisk into chocolate mixture little by little until combined.
- Spray a 9-inch square baking pan with cooking spray and pour in mixture. Bake in 350-degree oven until a toothpick has moist crumbs when pulled out of the middle, about 18 to 22 minutes (make sure not to overbake). Place on a wire rack to cool. Slice into bars.

Nutrition Information

- Calories: 205 calories
- Total Carbohydrate: 36 g
- Cholesterol: 28 mg
- Total Fat: 6 g
- Fiber: 2 g
- Protein: 4 g
- Sodium: 75 mg

341. Makeover Gooey Chocolate Peanut Butter Cake

"A makeover version of a desert dish with less fat yet still tastes delicious."
Serving: 24 servings. | Prep: 25m | Ready in: 01h05m

Ingredients

- 1 package chocolate cake mix (regular size)
- 1 egg
- 1/4 cup canola oil
- 1/4 cup unsweetened applesauce

- TOPPING:
- 1 package (8 oz.) reduced-fat cream cheese
- 1/2 cup creamy peanut butter
- 1/2 cup reduced-fat butter, melted
- 2 eggs
- 2 egg whites
- 1 tsp. vanilla extract
- 2 cups confectioners' sugar

Direction

- Beat the applesauce, oil, egg and cake mix in a big bowl on low speed until blended. Press it into a cooking spray coated 13x9-inch baking pan.
- Beat the peanut butter and cream cheese in a separate big bowl until it becomes smooth, then add vanilla, egg whites, eggs and butter and beat it on low until blended. Add the confectioner's sugar and stir well. Pour it on top of the crust.
- Let it bake for 40 to 45 minutes at 350 degrees or until the edges turn golden brown in color. Allow it to cool for 20 minutes on a wire rack prior to slicing. Chill the leftovers in the fridge.

Nutrition Information

- Calories: 228 calories
- Total Carbohydrate: 29 g
- Cholesterol: 38 mg
- Total Fat: 11 g
- Fiber: 1 g
- Protein: 4 g
- Sodium: 255 mg

342. Makeover Rocky Road Fudge Brownies

"A satisfying makeover recipe with less fat and fewer calories."
Serving: 2 dozen. | Prep: 20m | Ready in: 45m

Ingredients

- 1 package reduced-fat fudge brownie mix (13-inch x 9-inch pan size)
- 1/2 cup chopped pecans
- 2 cups miniature marshmallows
- 1 cup marshmallow creme
- 1/4 cup fat-free milk
- 3 tbsps. butter
- 3 tbsps. baking cocoa
- 1 oz. unsweetened chocolate
- 1 cup confectioners' sugar
- 1/2 tsp. vanilla extract

Direction

- Prepare the brownie mix following the package instructions, then mix in pecans. Spread the batter into a cooking spray coated 13x9-inch baking pan. Let it bake for 25 to 30 minutes at 350 degrees until an inserted toothpick in the middle exits clean. Sprinkle marshmallows on top. Let it cool on a wire rack.
- Mix together the chocolate, cocoa, butter, milk and marshmallow creme in a big saucepan. Cook and stir on low heat until smooth and melted.
- Move to a big bowl, then beat in vanilla and confectioners' sugar until it becomes smooth. Drizzle it on top of marshmallows.

Nutrition Information

- Calories: 180 calories
- Total Carbohydrate: 32 g
- Cholesterol: 4 mg
- Total Fat: 6 g
- Fiber: 1 g
- Protein: 2 g
- Sodium: 109 mg

343. Mini Brownie Treats

"Everybody loves these treats."
Serving: 4 dozen. | Prep: 15m | Ready in: 35m

Ingredients

- 1 package fudge brownie mix (13-inch x 9-inch pan size)
- 48 striped or milk chocolate kisses

Direction

- Make brownie mix as directed on the package for brownies with fudge-like texture. Fill two-thirds full into miniature muffin cups lined with paper.
- Bake at 350° until a toothpick comes out clean after being inserted into the middle, or for 18-21 minutes.
- Place a chocolate kiss on top immediately on each. Allow to cool for 10 minutes before taking out of pans to wire racks to cool thoroughly.

Nutrition Information

- Calories: 94 calories
- Total Carbohydrate: 12 g
- Cholesterol: 9 mg
- Total Fat: 5 g
- Fiber: 0 g
- Protein: 1 g
- Sodium: 52 mg

344. Mocha Butterscotch Cookies

"A lot of people have asked me for this cookie recipe that I adapted to make for my family."
Serving: 40 cookies. | Prep: 20m | Ready in: 30m

Ingredients

- 1 package (12 oz.) dark chocolate chips
- 2 tbsps. butter
- 2 tbsps. instant coffee granules
- 3 eggs
- 1 cup sugar
- 1/4 cup packed brown sugar
- 2 tsps. vanilla extract
- 3/4 cup all-purpose flour
- 1 tsp. baking powder
- 1/2 tsp. salt
- 1 cup butterscotch chips

Direction

- Heat coffee granules, butter and chocolate chips in a small saucepan to dissolve coffee, and melt butter and chocolate; put aside and allow to cool.
- Beat sugars and eggs in a big bowl to form a light mixture. Put in chocolate mixture and vanilla; mix until smooth. Mix together salt, baking powder and flour; blend into the egg mixture until combined. Mix in butterscotch chips and you will have a sticky dough.
- Scoop by heaping tablespoonfuls of dough and place 2 inches apart onto baking sheets lined with parchment paper. Bake in 325-degree oven until edges set and the center remains lightly soft texture (cookies will look cracked). Transfer to a wire rack. Keep in a tightly sealed container to store.

Nutrition Information

- Calories: 122 calories
- Total Carbohydrate: 17 g
- Cholesterol: 17 mg
- Total Fat: 5 g
- Fiber: 0 g
- Protein: 2 g
- Sodium: 53 mg

345. Mocha Chocolate Chip Cheesecake

"This is one of my mother's extraordinary pastries, which she regularly served on our dining table. Its taste brings back my childhood memories."
Serving: 16 servings. | Prep: 60m | Ready in: 03h00m

Ingredients

- 1-1/2 cups chocolate wafer crumbs
- 1/3 cup sugar
- 6 tbsps. butter, melted
- FILLING:
- 1/2 cup heavy whipping cream
- 1 tbsp. instant coffee granules
- 3 packages (8 oz. each) cream cheese, softened
- 1 cup sugar
- 1 tsp. vanilla extract
- 3 large eggs, lightly beaten
- 1 cup (6 oz.) miniature semisweet chocolate chips, divided

Direction

- Grease a 9-inches springform pan and place it over a double thickness of heavy-duty foil, about 18-inches square. Wrap the foil around the pan tightly.
- Mix butter, wafer crumbs, and sugar in a big bowl and spread it on the prepared pan.
- Combine the coffee granules and cream in a small saucepan. Cook the granules, stirring constantly until it dissolves completely. Allow it to cool.
- Whisk cream cheese and sugar in a big bowl until smooth. Add vanilla and the coffee mixture. Beat in eggs and whisk at low speed just until incorporated. Blend in a 3/4 cup of chocolate chips. Pour the mixture over the crust and top it with the remaining chocolate chips. Pour hot water into a big baking pan, about 1-inch of the pan. Place the springform pan into the water bath.
- Set the oven to 325°F and let it bake for 60-70 minutes until the cake's top appears dull and its center is fixed. Remove the pan from the

water bath and transfer it on a wire rack to cool for 10 minutes. Run a knife slowly around the edges of the pan to loosen the cake. Let it cool for 1 more hour. Store it inside the fridge overnight. Remove the rim from the pan before serving.

Nutrition Information

- Calories: 388 calories
- Total Carbohydrate: 33 g
- Cholesterol: 108 mg
- Total Fat: 28 g
- Fiber: 1 g
- Protein: 6 g
- Sodium: 234 mg

346. Mrs. Thompson's Carrot Cake

"The Mother of one of my patients gave me this recipe and it's the best carrot cake I've ever tried. I have always made it for your family gatherings."
Serving: 15 servings. | Prep: 30m | Ready in: 01h05m

Ingredients

- 3 cups shredded carrots
- 1 can (20 oz.) crushed pineapple, well drained
- 2 cups sugar
- 1 cup canola oil
- 4 large eggs
- 2 cups all-purpose flour
- 2 tsps. baking soda
- 2 tsps. ground cinnamon
- FROSTING:
- 1 package (8 oz.) cream cheese, softened
- 1/4 cup butter, softened
- 2 tsps. vanilla extract
- 3-3/4 cups confectioners' sugar

Direction

- Whisk the first 5 ingredients together in a big bowl until fully combined. Combine cinnamon, baking soda, and flour in a separate bowl; slowly whisk into the carrot mixture.

- Remove into an oil-coated 13x9-inch baking dish. Bake at 350° until a toothpick will come out clean when you insert it into the middle, 35-40 minutes. Put the pan on a wire rack to fully cool.
- To prepare the frosting, beat vanilla, butter, and cream cheese together in a big bowl until combined. Slowly beat in confectioners' sugar until smooth. Spread over the cake. Put in the fridge to store.

Nutrition Information

- Calories: 552 calories
- Total Carbohydrate: 80 g
- Cholesterol: 81 mg
- Total Fat: 25 g
- Fiber: 2 g
- Protein: 5 g
- Sodium: 269 mg

347. Nutty Brownies

"This recipe brings you a great treat for a quick dessert."
Serving: about 1-1/2 dozen. | Prep: 10m | Ready in: 20m

Ingredients

- 1 cup sugar
- 2 eggs
- 1/2 cup butter, melted
- 1 tsp. vanilla extract
- 3/4 cup all-purpose flour
- 1/3 cup baking cocoa
- 1/2 tsp. salt
- 1 cup chopped nuts
- Confectioners' sugar, optional

Direction

- Beat eggs and sugar together in a big bowl until well combined, then stir in vanilla and butter. Mix together salt, cocoa and flour, then put into butter mixture gradually until just blended. Mix in nuts and spread batter into a microwavable 8-inch square dish coated with grease.

- Microwave on high without a cover until top turns out dry and springs back when pressed slightly, about 3 1/2 to 4 minutes. Sprinkle confectioners' sugar over top if you want.

Nutrition Information

- Calories: 162 calories
- Total Carbohydrate: 17 g
- Cholesterol: 37 mg
- Total Fat: 10 g
- Fiber: 1 g
- Protein: 3 g
- Sodium: 124 mg

348. Oatmeal Brownies

"Using this packaged brownie mix, you won't need much time to prepare these brownies. You can use chocolate chips to substitute mini M&Ms. These rich fudgy squares go very well with ice cream and our kids love it."
Serving: 5 dozen. | Prep: 15m | Ready in: 40m

Ingredients

- 1-1/2 cups quick-cooking oats
- 1 cup M&M's minis
- 1/2 cup all-purpose flour
- 1/2 cup packed brown sugar
- 1/2 cup chopped walnuts
- 1/2 tsp. baking soda
- 1/2 cup butter, melted
- 1 package fudge brownie mix (13-inch x 9-inch pan size)

Direction

- Mix butter, baking soda, walnuts, sugar, flour, M&M's, and oats in a large bowl. Put 1 cup aside to use for the topping. Press the greased 15x10x1-inch baking pan with the rest of the mixture.
- For the brownie batter, prepare it by following the package instructions. Spread onto the crust. Sprinkle the saved oat mixture over.
- Bake it at 350° until the toothpick will come out clean once you insert it into the center,

about 25-30 minutes. Put on a wire rack to cool. Slice into bars.

Nutrition Information

- Calories: 116 calories
- Total Carbohydrate: 14 g
- Cholesterol: 15 mg
- Total Fat: 6 g
- Fiber: 1 g
- Protein: 2 g
- Sodium: 66 mg

349. Peanut Butter Blondies

"Moist chewy bars with plenty of peanut butter flavor."
Serving: 2 dozen. | Prep: 30m | Ready in: 01h05m

Ingredients

- 3/4 cup creamy peanut butter
- 2/3 cup butter, softened
- 1 cup packed brown sugar
- 1/2 cup sugar
- 2 eggs
- 1 tsp. vanilla extract
- 1-3/4 cups all-purpose flour
- 1 tsp. baking powder
- 1/3 cup milk
- 1 cup peanut butter chips
- FROSTING:
- 1/4 cup butter, softened
- 1/4 cup baking cocoa
- 2 tbsps. milk
- 1 tbsp. light corn syrup
- 1 tsp. vanilla extract
- 1-1/2 cups confectioners' sugar
- 1/3 cup peanut butter chips

Direction

- In a large bowl, cream together the sugars, butter and peanut butter until fluffy and light. Beat in the vanilla and eggs. Combine the baking powder and flour; put into creamed mixture alternating with the milk, beating

thoroughly after each time you add. Mix in chips.
- Spread the mixture into a 13x9-in. greased baking pan. Bake for 35-40 minutes at 325° until tested done with a toothpick (be careful not to overbake). Allow to cool on a wire rack.
- To make frosting, in a small bowl, combine the vanilla, corn syrup, milk, cocoa and butter. Add the confectioners' sugar slowly; beat till smooth. Use it to frost the brownies. Sprinkle chips on top. Slice into bars.

Nutrition Information

- Calories: 283 calories
- Total Carbohydrate: 35 g
- Cholesterol: 37 mg
- Total Fat: 15 g
- Fiber: 2 g
- Protein: 6 g
- Sodium: 160 mg

350. Peanut Butter Cheesecake Pizza

"This dessert is very special with a sprinkling of nuts and chips inside."
Serving: 16 slices. | Prep: 25m | Ready in: 40m

Ingredients

- 1 tube (16-1/2 oz.) refrigerated sugar cookie dough
- 1 package (8 oz.) cream cheese, softened
- 2 large eggs
- 1/2 cup sugar
- 1 cup peanut butter chips
- 1 cup chopped unsalted peanuts
- 1 cup milk chocolate chips
- 1 tsp. shortening

Direction

- Press dough on a grease-free 14-inch pizza pan, then bake at 350 degrees until turning deep golden brown, about 15 to 18 minutes.

- Beat cream cheese in a small bowl until fluffy. Put in sugar and eggs, beating until blended. Spread mixture over crust, then sprinkle peanuts and peanut butter chips over top.
- Bake until center has set, about 15 to 18 minutes. Allow to cool about 15 minutes. In the meantime, melt shortening and chocolate chips in a microwave, stirring until smooth. Drizzle mixture over pizza and chill leftovers.

Nutrition Information

- Calories: 372 calories
- Total Carbohydrate: 37 g
- Cholesterol: 53 mg
- Total Fat: 22 g
- Fiber: 2 g
- Protein: 8 g
- Sodium: 209 mg

351. Peanut Butter Chocolate Tart

"With this tart recipe, those peanut butter cups fan will be so in love!"
Serving: 16 servings. | Prep: 40m | Ready in: 40m

Ingredients

- 1 package (9 oz.) chocolate wafers
- 1/2 cup peanut butter chips
- 2 tbsps. sugar
- 1/2 cup butter, melted
- FILLING:
- 1 cup creamy peanut butter
- 1/2 cup butter, softened
- 4 oz. cream cheese, softened
- 1 cup confectioners' sugar
- 1/4 cup light corn syrup
- 1 tsp. vanilla extract
- GANACHE:
- 3/4 cup semisweet chocolate chips
- 1/2 cup heavy whipping cream
- 1-1/2 tsps. sugar
- 1-1/2 tsps. light corn syrup
- 1/4 cup chopped salted peanuts

Direction

- Put sugar, peanut butter chips and wafers in a food processor; cover, then pulse until finely crushed. Mix melted butter into the mixture. In an ungreased fluted tart pan with removable bottom (9 inches), pat the crust onto the base and sides. Chill in the refrigerator for half an hour.
- To make the filling, beat cream cheese, butter and peanut butter in a big bowl until it forms a fluffy mixture. Pour in vanilla, corn syrup and confectioners' sugar, then blend until smooth. Spread into the pie crust. Chill in the refrigerator; meanwhile, prepare the ganache.
- In a small bowl, add chocolate chips. Boil corn syrup, sugar and cream in a small saucepan. Pour into the bowl; stir until the chips melt and the mixture is smooth. Spread on top of the filling. Scatter peanuts on top. Chill for no less than two hours.

Nutrition Information

- Calories: 448 calories
- Total Carbohydrate: 37 g
- Cholesterol: 48 mg
- Total Fat: 32 g
- Fiber: 2 g
- Protein: 8 g
- Sodium: 299 mg

352. Peanut Butter Lover's Cake

""Everyone loves peanut butter, so they just enjoy it when I prepare this recipe.""
Serving: 12-14 servings. | Prep: 20m | Ready in: 45m

Ingredients

- 3 eggs
- 1-2/3 cups sugar, divided
- 1-1/2 cups milk, divided
- 3 oz. unsweetened chocolate, finely chopped
- 1/2 cup shortening
- 1 tsp. vanilla extract

- 2 cups cake flour
- 1 tsp. baking soda
- 1/2 tsp. salt
- PEANUT BUTTER FROSTING:
- 2 packages (8 oz. each) cream cheese, softened
- 1 can (14 oz.) sweetened condensed milk
- 1-1/2 cups peanut butter
- 1/4 cup salted peanuts, chopped
- 3 milk chocolate candy bars (1.55 oz. each), broken into squares

Direction

- Beat 1 egg in a small saucepan until combined. Mix in chocolate, 1/2 cup milk and 2/3 cup sugar. Stir and cook over medium heat mixture just comes to a boil and chocolate is dissolved. Separate from heat; let cool at a room temperature.
- Cream remaining sugar and shortening in large bowl until fluffy and light. Put in remaining eggs, one at a time, whisking well after every addition. Mix in vanilla. Mix the salt, baking soda and flour; cautiously add to creamed mixture alternately with remaining milk, whisking well after every addition. Mix in chocolate mixture.
- Place into three 9-inch round baking pans that are greased and floured. Put in the oven and bake for 25-30 minutes at 325°F or until a toothpick pricked in the middle comes out clean. Let cool for 10 minutes before taking from pans to wire rack to fully cool. To make frosting, whip cream cheese in a large bowl until smooth. Gently add peanut butter and milk until creamy. And spread between layers and over top and sides of cooled cake. Dust with peanuts. Decorate with candy bars. Keep in the refrigerator.

Nutrition Information

- Calories: 610 calories
- Total Carbohydrate: 64 g
- Cholesterol: 77 mg
- Total Fat: 34 g
- Fiber: 3 g
- Protein: 15 g

- Sodium: 427 mg

353. Pecan Brownies

"You can't stop eating these nutty desserts. A batch of these can be made only in minutes."
Serving: 16 brownies. | Prep: 15m | Ready in: 30m

Ingredients

- 1/2 cup butter, cubed
- 2 oz. unsweetened chocolate
- 1 cup sugar
- 2 eggs, lightly beaten
- 1 tsp. vanilla extract
- 3/4 cup all-purpose flour
- 1/2 to 1 cup chopped pecans

Direction

- Melt chocolate and butter in a saucepan over low heat. Mix in sugar; let cool slightly. Put in vanilla and eggs; stir well. Mix in pecans and flour.
- Spread into a greased 8-inch square baking tray. Bake for 15 to 20 mins at 350° or until a toothpick inserted in the middle comes out clean. Let cool on a wire rack.

Nutrition Information

- Calories: 165 calories
- Total Carbohydrate: 18 g
- Cholesterol: 42 mg
- Total Fat: 10 g
- Fiber: 1 g
- Protein: 2 g
- Sodium: 66 mg

354. Pecan Sour Cream Cake

"A pleasing touch of cinnamon is remarkable in this nice drizzled icing."
Serving: 6 servings. | Prep: 20m | Ready in: 55m

Ingredients

- 1/2 cup butter, softened
- 2/3 cup sugar
- 3 eggs
- 2 tbsps. maple syrup
- 2 tsps. vanilla extract
- 1-1/2 cups all-purpose flour
- 1/4 cup ground pecans, toasted
- 1/2 tsp. baking soda
- 3/4 cup sour cream
- FILLING:
- 1/4 cup ground pecans, toasted
- 4 tsps. brown sugar
- 1-1/2 tsps. all-purpose flour
- 1/2 tsp. ground cinnamon
- GLAZE:
- 1/2 cup confectioners' sugar
- 1/4 tsp. ground cinnamon
- 2 to 3 tsps. 2% milk

Direction

- Cream together sugar and butter in a small bowl until fluffy and light, then beat in vanilla, syrup and eggs. Mix together baking soda, pecans and flour, then put into the creamed mixture together with sour cream, alternately.
- Put into an 8-inch fluted tube pan greased with cooking spray with 2 cups of batter. Mix filling ingredients together and sprinkle over batter, then pour leftover batter on top.
- Bake at 350 degrees until a toothpick exits clean after being inserted into the center, about 35 to 40 minutes. Allow to cool about 15 minutes, then transfer from pan to wire rack to cool thoroughly. Mix glaze ingredients together and drizzle over cake.

Nutrition Information

- Calories: 549 calories
- Total Carbohydrate: 67 g
- Cholesterol: 167 mg
- Total Fat: 27 g
- Fiber: 1 g
- Protein: 9 g
- Sodium: 309 mg

355. Polka-dot Cookie Bars

""Bars are the perfect option to cater large groups of people because it will save you much more time.""
Serving: 4 dozen. | Prep: 15m | Ready in: 35m

Ingredients

- 1 cup butter, softened
- 3/4 cup sugar
- 3/4 cup packed brown sugar
- 2 eggs
- 1/2 tsp. almond extract
- 2-1/4 cups all-purpose flour
- 1/3 cup baking cocoa
- 1 tsp. baking soda
- 1/2 tsp. salt
- 1 package (10 to 12 oz.) white baking chips,divided

Direction

- Beat sugars and butter in a large bowl until creamy and light. Put in eggs, one at a time and blend well between additions. Mix in extract. Whisk together salt, baking soda, cocoa and flour; slowly pour into butter mixture. Save a quarter cup chips and mix the rest into batter.
- Grease a 15x10x1 inch baking pan and pour in the mixture. Scatter with the saved chips. Bake in 375-degree oven until a toothpick exits clean when being put into the center, about 18 to 23 minutes. Let cool on a wire rack before cutting into bars.

Nutrition Information

- Calories: 117 calories
- Total Carbohydrate: 15 g

- Cholesterol: 20 mg
- Total Fat: 6 g
- Fiber: 0 g
- Protein: 1 g
- Sodium: 99 mg

356. Raspberry Pie Squares

"A fantastic recipe to make a pie for the crowd. The combination of a flaky home-cooked pastry and the sweet-tart raspberry filling will sure to satisfy your guests."
Serving: 24 servings. | Prep: 40m | Ready in: 01h20m

Ingredients

- 3-3/4 cups all-purpose flour
- 4 tsps. sugar
- 1-1/2 tsps. salt
- 1-1/2 cups cold butter
- 1/2 to 1 cup cold water
- FILLING:
- 2 cups sugar
- 2/3 cup all-purpose flour
- 1/4 tsp. salt
- 8 cups fresh or frozen unsweetened raspberries
- 1 tbsp. lemon juice
- 5 tsps. heavy whipping cream
- 1 tbsp. coarse sugar

Direction

- Mix salt, sugar, and flour in a large bowl; slice in the butter until it is crumbly. Pour in water gradually and use a fork to toss until the dough forms into a ball.
- Split the dough in two so that one part is a bit larger than the other one; use a plastic wrap to wrap each. Chill in the fridge until easy to handle, for 1 1/4 hours.
- Set an oven to 375 degrees and start preheating. Between 2 large sheets of waxed paper, roll the larger part of dough into a 17x12-inch rectangle. Place into an ungreased 15x10x1-inch baking pan. Press the pastry onto the bottom and up the sides of the pan; trim it even with the edges.
- For the filling: Mix salt, flour, and sugar in a large bowl. Pour in lemon juice and raspberries; toss them to coat. Scoop over the pastry.
- Roll the rest of pastry out; arrange on the filling. Trim the edges and seal. Slice slits in the pastry. Brush cream over the top and dust with coarse sugar. On a baking sheet, arrange the pan. Bake until golden brown, for 40-45 minutes. Transfer onto a wire rack to let cool entirely. Slice into squares.

Nutrition Information

- Calories: 277 calories
- Total Carbohydrate: 40 g
- Cholesterol: 32 mg
- Total Fat: 12 g
- Fiber: 3 g
- Protein: 3 g
- Sodium: 254 mg

357. Really Rocky Road Brownies

"A fudgy and rich dessert that is ideal for any family get-togethers."
Serving: 4 dozen. | Prep: 20m | Ready in: 45m

Ingredients

- 8 oz. unsweetened chocolate, chopped
- 1-1/2 cups butter
- 6 large eggs
- 3 cups sugar
- 1 tbsp. vanilla extract
- 1-1/2 cups all-purpose flour
- 1 cup chopped walnuts, optional
- TOPPING:
- 2 cups miniature marshmallows
- 1 oz. unsweetened chocolate, melted

Direction

- Melt chocolate and butter in a microwavable bowl, stirring until smooth. Allow to cool a little bit. Beat eggs and sugar in a big bowl, then stir in chocolate mixture and vanilla. Mix salt and flour, then put into chocolate mixture gradually. Mix in nuts, if you want.

- Transfer mixture into 2 9-inch square baking pans coated with grease and flour, then bake at 350 degrees until a toothpick exits with moist crumbs after being inserted into the center, about 25 to 30 minutes. Avoid over-baking.
- To make topping: Sprinkle 1 cup of marshmallows over each pan, then broil for 30 to 60 seconds, until turning golden brown. Drizzle melted chocolate over top and allow to cool on a wire rack. Chill for a few hours prior to cutting.

Nutrition Information

- Calories: 135 calories
- Total Carbohydrate: 18 g
- Cholesterol: 42 mg
- Total Fat: 7 g
- Fiber: 0 g
- Protein: 1 g
- Sodium: 67 mg

358. Rhubarb-blueberry Crumble

"A delicious combination of blueberries and rhubarb!"
Serving: 8 servings. | Prep: 15m | Ready in: 55m

Ingredients

- 2/3 cup sugar
- 2 tbsps. cornstarch
- 1/4 tsp. salt
- 3 cups fresh blueberries
- 3 cups sliced fresh or frozen rhubarb, thawed
- TOPPING:
- 3/4 cup biscuit/baking mix
- 1/3 cup sugar
- 1/8 tsp. salt
- 1/3 cup cold unsalted butter, cubed
- 1/2 cup old-fashioned oats
- 1/2 cup chopped almonds

Direction

- Heat the oven to 375° to preheat. Combine salt, cornstarch and sugar together in a large bowl. Put in rhubarb and blueberries; toss to coat. Place into a greased square baking dish of 8-in.
- To make topping, combine salt, sugar and baking mix in a small bowl. Cut in butter till crumbly; mix in almonds and oats. Sprinkle the mixture over filling. Bake in the oven until it is golden brown on top and the filling is bubbling, about 40-45 minutes.

Nutrition Information

- Calories: 324 calories
- Total Carbohydrate: 49 g
- Cholesterol: 20 mg
- Total Fat: 14 g
- Fiber: 4 g
- Protein: 4 g
- Sodium: 255 mg

359. Rustic Chocolate Raspberry Tart

"A dessert for all ages."
Serving: 16 servings. | Prep: 20m | Ready in: 01h05m

Ingredients

- 5 oz. cream cheese, softened
- 6 tbsps. butter, softened
- 1-1/2 cups all-purpose flour
- FILLING:
- 2 cups fresh raspberries
- 2 tbsps. sugar
- 1 tsp. cornstarch
- 1/3 cup Nutella

Direction

- Process butter and cream cheese in a food processor until incorporated. Add flour into the mix; process just until it makes a dough. Form it into a disk and wrap in plastic. Chill in the refrigerator for 1 hour or overnight.

- Set oven to preheat at 350°. Toss together raspberries, sugar and cornstarch in a small bowl using a fork, slightly smash some of the berries.
- Roll the dough out on a lightly floured surface into a 14x8-in. rectangle. Place onto a baking sheet lined with parchment paper. Spread Nutella on top to within 1 in. of edges. Add the raspberry mixture on top. Fold the edge of the pastry toward the tart's center, pleating and pinching as necessary.
- Bake until crust is golden brown for about 45-50 minutes. Place tart onto a wire rack to cool.

Nutrition Information

- Calories: 157 calories
- Total Carbohydrate: 17 g
- Cholesterol: 20 mg
- Total Fat: 9 g
- Fiber: 2 g
- Protein: 2 g
- Sodium: 65 mg

360. Strawberry Blitz Torte

"My mom's German torte recipe."
Serving: 12 servings. | Prep: 45m | Ready in: 01h15m

Ingredients

- 4 egg whites
- 1/2 cup butter, softened
- 1/2 cup sugar
- 3 egg yolks
- 1 tsp. almond extract
- 1 cup all-purpose flour
- 1 tsp. baking powder
- 1/8 tsp. salt
- 1/3 cup 2% milk
- MERINGUE:
- 1/2 tsp. vanilla extract
- 1/4 tsp. cream of tartar
- 1 cup sugar
- 1/2 cup sliced almonds
- FILLING:
- 2 tbsps. sugar
- 1 tbsp. cornstarch
- 1 cup 2% milk
- 2 egg yolks
- 1 tbsp. butter
- 1/2 tsp. vanilla or almond extract
- 2-1/2 cups sliced fresh strawberries
- Sweetened whipped cream, optional

Direction

- Put egg whites in big bowl; stand for 30 minutes at room temperature. Preheat an oven to 325°. Line parchment paper on bottoms of 2 8-in. round greased baking pans; grease paper.
- Cream sugar and butter till fluffy and light in big bowl. One by one, add egg yolks; beat well with every addition. Beat extract in.
- Whisk salt, baking powder and flour in a separate bowl. Alternately with milk, add to creamed mixture. Beat well with every addition; put in prepped pans.
- Meringue: Use clean beaters to beat vanilla, cream of tartar and egg whites at medium speed till foamy. 1 tbsp. at a time, add sugar slowly; beat on high with every addition till sugar melts. Beat till stiff glossy peaks form. Spread on batters in pans; sprinkle almonds.
- Bake for 28-32 minutes or till meringue turn lightly brown. Completely cool in pans on wire racks (it'll crack).
- Meanwhile, for filling: Mix cornstarch and sugar in small heavy saucepan; whisk milk in. Mix and cook on medium heat till bubbly and thick. Lower heat to low; mix and cook for 2 minutes longer. Take off heat.
- Whisk small amount hot mixture to egg yolks in small bowl; put all in pan, constantly whisking. Gently boil; mix and cook for 2 minutes. Take off heat. Mix vanilla and butter in; completely cool.
- Use knife to loosen cake edges from pans. Use 2 big spatulas to remove 1 cake to serving plate carefully, meringue side up. Spread with filling gently. Put strawberries on filling. Put leftover cake layer over, meringue side up.

Serve with whipped cream, if desired. Refrigerate leftovers.

Nutrition Information

- Calories: 299 calories
- Total Carbohydrate: 41 g
- Cholesterol: 110 mg
- Total Fat: 13 g
- Fiber: 1 g
- Protein: 5 g
- Sodium: 163 mg

361. Strawberry Tarragon Crumble

"The pretty strawberry cake!"
Serving: 4 servings. | Prep: 20m | Ready in: 20m

Ingredients

- 2 cups chopped fresh strawberries
- 3 tbsps. sugar
- 2 tbsps. minced fresh tarragon
- 1 tbsp. orange juice
- TOPPING:
- 1 cup coarsely crushed graham crackers
- 8 chocolate-covered miniature pretzels, crushed
- 3 tbsps. butter, melted
- 1 tbsp. honey
- 1 tsp. vanilla extract
- 1 cup reduced-fat whipped topping
- Additional minced fresh tarragon

Direction

- Combine orange juice, tarragon, sugar and strawberries in a small bowl. Combine vanilla, honey, butter, pretzels and graham crackers in another bowl.
- Layer three tbsps. of the graham cracker mixture, a quarter cup of strawberries and two tbsps. of the whipped topping in each of 4 parfait glasses. Repeat these layers. Decorate with more tarragon.

Nutrition Information

- Calories: 321 calories
- Total Carbohydrate: 48 g
- Cholesterol: 23 mg
- Total Fat: 14 g
- Fiber: 2 g
- Protein: 2 g
- Sodium: 211 mg

362. Walnut Brownies

"These brownies are delicious and chewy."
Serving: 12

Ingredients

- 1/4 cup butter
- 6 tbsps. carob powder
- 1 cup white sugar
- 1/4 tsp. salt
- 1/2 cup all-purpose flour
- 2 tsps. vanilla extract
- 2 egg white
- 1 cup chopped walnuts

Direction

- Set the oven to 300°F (175°C) and start preheating. Grease an 8-inch square baking pan.
- Over low heat, melt margarine or butter. Place into a large mixing bowl; stir in vanilla, flour, salt, sugar and carob powder. Mix in walnuts and egg whites. Spread the dough into baking pan evenly.
- Bake for half an hour. Allow to cool for 10-15 minutes in pan; cut.

Nutrition Information

- Calories: 195 calories;
- Total Carbohydrate: 25.7 g
- Cholesterol: 10 mg
- Total Fat: 10.3 g
- Protein: 2.9 g
- Sodium: 87 mg

363. Walnut Oat Brownies

"These fudgy brownies are nutritious with wheat germ and oatmeal. TIP: If you don't have 6 semisweet chocolate squares, you can use 1 cup plus 2 tbsps. of semisweet chocolate chips as a substitute."
Serving: 1 dozen. | Prep: 15m | Ready in: 40m

Ingredients

- 6 oz. semisweet chocolate
- 1/4 cup butter
- 1/2 cup egg substitute
- 1/4 cup packed brown sugar
- 2 tbsps. sugar
- 1 tsp. vanilla extract
- 1/3 cup quick-cooking oats
- 1/3 cup nonfat dry milk powder
- 1/4 cup toasted wheat germ
- 1/2 tsp. baking powder
- 1/4 tsp. salt
- 1/4 cup chopped walnuts
- Confectioners' sugar, optional

Direction

- Melt butter and chocolate in a microwave and whisk it until smooth. Cool briefly. Whisk sugars and egg substitute together in a large bowl. Mix in the chocolate mixture and vanilla. Mix the dry ingredients and slowly add the mixture to the chocolate mixture. Mix in walnuts.
- Add the mixture to the cooking spray-coated 8-inch square baking dish. Bake it at 350° until the toothpick will come out clean once you insert it into the center, about 25-30 minutes. Put on a wire rack to cool. If you want, dust confectioners' sugar over. Slice into bars.

Nutrition Information

- Calories: 180 calories
- Total Carbohydrate: 19 g
- Cholesterol: 11 mg
- Total Fat: 10 g
- Fiber: 2 g
- Protein: 5 g
- Sodium: 145 mg

364. Warm Apple Topping

"To the astonishment of our company, my spouse and I adore cooking complete meals with the grill. This dessert was made for my mum, who can't consume majority of things that has grain. She was thoroughly delighted with it!"
Serving: 3 cups. | Prep: 10m | Ready in: 30m

Ingredients

- 3 medium tart apples, peeled
- 1/3 cup raisins
- 1 tbsp. lemon juice
- 1/3 cup packed brown sugar
- 1/4 tsp. ground cinnamon
- 1/4 tsp. ground cloves
- 1/8 tsp. salt
- 1/8 tsp. ground nutmeg
- 2 tbsps. cold butter
- 1/3 cup finely chopped walnuts
- Vanilla ice cream

Direction

- Slice every apple up in 16 wedges. On a durable foil around 18 square inches, put the sliced up apples atop. Scatter raisins then trickle lemon juice over the top. Mix nutmeg, salt, cloves, cinnamon and brown sugar in a bowl. After cutting in the butter until it turns crumbly, mix in the walnuts. Scatter it over the raisins and apples. Seal it up firmly by folding the foil around the apple mixture. At an indirect moderate heat, grill it until the apples turn tender. Cook for about 18 to 22 minutes. Before serving, put together with ice cream.

365. Whole Wheat Strawberry Shortcakes

"Fresh strawberry shortcake that's great for spring."
Serving: 6 servings. | Prep: 45m | Ready in: 60m

Ingredients

- 2-1/2 cups fresh strawberries, hulled, divided
- 1 to 2 tbsps. maple syrup
- SHORTCAKES:
- 2 cups whole wheat flour
- 2-1/2 tsps. baking powder
- 1/2 tsp. salt
- 1/4 tsp. baking soda
- 1/2 cup cold butter, cubed
- 1 large egg
- 1/2 cup 2% milk
- 1/4 cup honey
- Whipped cream

Direction

- Mash 3/4 cup of strawberries thoroughly in bowl; mix syrup in. Cut leftover strawberries to 1/4-inch slices. Add into crushed strawberries; toss till coated. Refrigerate for 1 hour, covered.
- Meanwhile, preheat an oven to 400°. Whisk baking soda, salt, baking powder and flour in a big bowl. Cut butter in till it looks like coarse crumbs. Whisk honey, milk and egg till blended in a small bowl. Mix into flour mixture till just moist.
- Turn on a lightly floured surface then gently knead 8-10 times. Roll/pat dough to 3/4-inch thick. Use a floured 2 1/2-inch biscuit cutter to cut; put on parchment paper-lined baking sheets, 2-inches apart. Bake till light brown for 12-15 minutes. Transfer to wire racks; slightly cool.
- Serving: Split shortcakes to half. Use whipped cream and strawberry mixture to fill. Top with extra whipped cream.

Nutrition Information

- Calories: 362 calories
- Total Carbohydrate: 49 g
- Cholesterol: 77 mg
- Total Fat: 17 g
- Fiber: 6 g
- Protein: 8 g
- Sodium: 549 mg

Index

P

Paprika, 13, 16, 42, 52–53, 60, 88, 108–110, 113, 122, 130, 132, 144

Parfait, 192

Parmesan, 5, 12, 22–23, 25–28, 30, 34, 44, 56, 58, 61, 71, 76, 83, 88–89, 107, 109, 113,

134

Parsley, 19–21, 25–26, 30, 34, 37, 52, 56, 66, 69–70, 75–76, 81, 84–86, 99–100, 102, 104,

109, 115, 124, 126, 130, 148, 152

Pasta, 4, 46, 51, 58, 71, 112

Pastry, 156, 163, 173, 178, 183, 189, 191

Peach, 5–7, 19, 118, 131, 163, 177–178

Peanut butter, 6–7, 38, 158, 160, 166–167, 175–176, 180–181, 185–187

Peanuts, 161–162, 169, 185–187

Peas, 4–5, 46, 48, 76, 88, 90, 111, 117

Pecan, 6–7, 32, 37, 48, 56, 99, 154, 159–160, 162– 164, 167–168, 173–174, 179, 181,

187–188

Peel, 53, 65–66, 68, 75, 86, 88–91, 95, 99, 102–104, 109, 124, 137, 150, 155, 168, 179

Penne, 4, 71

Pepper, 3–6, 11, 13, 15–18, 21–30, 32–57, 59–81, 83–87, 89–128, 130–132, 134–135,

137–153

Peppercorn, 6, 146

Pesto, 3, 34, 44

Pickle, 52–55, 60, 77

Pie, 6–7, 27, 29–30, 35, 108, 164, 173, 175, 178–179,

186, 189

Pine nut, 57

Pineapple, 4–6, 42, 57, 72, 83, 96, 118, 131, 136– 137, 141–142, 149–151, 155–156,

162–163, 172, 183

Pineapple juice, 42, 72, 83, 131, 137, 142, 172

Pinto beans, 138

Pistachio, 50

Pizza, 3, 6–8, 14, 25–26, 39–40, 169, 185–186

Plum, 26, 36, 56–57, 59, 66–67

Pomegranate, 90

Pork, 3–6, 13, 23, 43, 72, 88, 116, 118, 121–125, 127, 129–133, 136, 139–140, 142–143, 145,

149, 151–153

Pork chop, 5–6, 88, 116, 124–125, 131, 136, 142– 143, 152

Pork loin, 88, 116, 124, 136, 142–143, 152

Pork sausages, 132

Port, 6, 171

Portobello mushrooms, 39, 106

Potato, 4–5, 49, 52–54, 59–61, 65, 68–69, 75, 77, 81–82, 84–85, 88, 94, 96–100, 106–107,

113–114, 141

Potato wedges, 5, 98–99

Poultry, 116, 148

Preserves, 12, 14–15, 72–73, 131, 142, 154

Prosciutto, 39–40

Prune, 172

T

V

Conclusion

Thank you again for downloading this book!

I hope you enjoyed reading about my book!

If you enjoyed this book, please take the time to share your thoughts and post a review on Amazon. It'd be greatly appreciated!

Write me an honest review about the book – I truly value your opinion and thoughts and I will incorporate them into my next book, which is already underway.

Thank you!

If you have any questions, **feel free to contact at:** _mrholiday@mrandmscooking.com_

Mr. Holiday

www.MrandMsCooking.com

Printed in Great Britain
by Amazon